SCOTS PRIVATE LAW

AUSTRALIA
Law Book Co.
Sydney

CANADA and USA
Carswell
Toronto

HONG KONG
Sweet & Maxwell Asia

NEW ZEALAND
Brookers
Wellington

SINGAPORE and MALAYSIA
Sweet & Maxwell Asia
Singapore and Kuala Lumpur

SCOTS PRIVATE LAW

Joe Thomson

Scottish Law Commissioner and
Visiting Professor at Glasgow Caledonian University

THOMSON
™
W. GREEN

Published in 2006 by
W. Green & Son Ltd
21 Alva Street
Edinburgh EH2 4PS

www.wgreen.thomson.com

Typeset by LBJ Typesetting Ltd, Kingsclere

Printed and bound in Great Britain by
MPG Books, Victoria Square, Bodmin, Cornwall PL31 1EG

No natural forests were destroyed to make this product;
only farmed timber was used and replanted

A CIP catalogue record for this book is available from
the British Library.

ISBN–10 0–414–01656–4
ISBN–13 9–780–414–01656–9

For
Annie Thomson

PREFACE

In this book, I have attempted to give a comprehensive account of Scots private law. In particular, I have tried to show how the principles interlink in order to provide sophisticated solutions to difficult problems. In attempting to map out the sphere of Scots private law, like many others I have been greatly influenced by the work of the late Professor Peter Birks. While I am sure that Peter would have approved my motives for writing this book, it is more doubtful whether he would have been uncritical of my efforts. Nevertheless, I feel strongly that it is essential that we should try to see private law as a whole, integrated system of principles and rules and I hope that this book will help us to do so.

This book could not have been written 30 years ago. It owes an immense debt to those scholars whose work has transformed our understanding of Scots private law. The flourishing of the literature on Scots private law has been a source of great pleasure—as well as insight—to me during the 20 or so years when I had the privilege to teach the subject. I am, however, particularly grateful to my erstwhile colleague, Professor K G C Reid. The abolition of the feudal system—for which Kenneth was at least partially responsible—greatly eased my task but, more importantly, he read the chapters on property and saved me from some embarrassing errors. The errors which remain are, of course, my responsibility.

This book has had a long gestation period. Much of the material in chapter one formed the basis of my Wilson Memorial Lecture which I delivered in the University of Edinburgh five years ago. But the book's arguments have been developed over many years, often stimulated by heated discussions with colleagues and students.

I would like to thank the staff at Greens for their splendid efforts in the production of this book. Mrs Jill Hyslop, in particular, gave me great encouragement. I continue to receive excellent administrative support from Mrs Heather Ryan. But the book would have remained a daydream of a middle-aged academic, if my wife, Annie, had not nagged me for a new book dedicated to her. It was only with her support and love that I felt able to embark upon, let alone complete, this ambitious project. Whether it was sensible to do so is for others to judge.

Edinburgh,
April 1, 2006.

CONTENTS

CONTENTS

INTRODUCTION

The present author has taught Scots private law for more than 20 years. Over that period, it has become clear that while students may acquire a good working knowledge of the rules of Scots private law, they fail to obtain an overview of the system and how one area of the law relates to another. This arises for several reasons. First, the traditional exegesis of Scots private law has become unfashionable. Instead of treating the subject as a whole, we have separate courses on contract, conveyancing, delict, property, trusts, succession and unjustified enrichment. This reflects not only the increasing complexity of the rules but also the increasing specialisation of teachers (or learning facilitators!). Secondly, there has been a tendency to teach subjects contextually where the emphasis has been on the functions that the rules serve rather than their relationship with other rules and principles of private law: thus, for example, we have commercial law (including company law), family law, labour law and medical law. Thirdly, vast tracts of private law are now the province of statute rather than the common law. The judicial function is therefore to construe the language of the legislation rather than to develop the common law incrementally in accordance with legal principle. Unlike common law developments, legislation can give legal effect to rules which do not have to be consistent with pre-existing legal principle. Indeed, the purpose of a statute may be to abolish the common law rules and replace them with a new statutory regime based on totally different principles. Finally, there is no doubt that both common law rules and statutory provisions are complex. It is extremely difficult merely to understand what the law on a particular subject is, let alone how it relates to other germane rules and principles. Put another way, students become so bogged down in attempting to understand the minutiae of the law that they fail to comprehend the legal system as a whole. That they are often encouraged to do so is a serious indictment against contemporary legal education.

The purpose of this book is to attempt to redress this balance. Its subject is Scots private law. However, it is not concerned to give a detailed account of the current rules which make up that subject. Instead, it provides an analysis of how the concepts which make up Scots private law interrelate with each other. Inevitably, the discourse takes place at a level of abstraction not generally found in legal textbooks. Indeed, one of the features of the book is that I have eschewed the great tradition of teaching legal rules and

principles through the discussion of decided cases. This is because I
hope that this work will be read by a student before she embarks
on the study of a particular area of private law such as contract,
delict or property. I want the reader to approach the study of the
detailed rules of private law with some understanding of how the
concepts which make up that subject relate to each other. To do so,
I believe that it is important that the student is untrammelled by
the names and facts (and dates!) of cases: that, alas, can come
later. The student may also be relieved that there are no references
to "taxonomy" or the "ius commune", either in its medieval or
modern form(s)! However, given the crucial significance of legislation in modern private law, I have decided to discuss statutory
provisions where appropriate. The sooner a student begins to enjoy
the intellectual challenge involved in construing and understanding
statutory language the better. After all, fundamentally a lawyer is
only a person who can read and write in the sense of understanding
often difficult language and being able effectively to communicate
its meaning.

In one sense, this is an elementary book which a student should
read at the outset of his or her study of law. In so doing, he or she
will have to take much of the text on trust as I have kept citation of
authority to a minimum. However, I hope that as the student
progresses in her course and hopefully develops as a lawyer, he or
she will turn to these pages with a more critical eye and scrutinise
my analysis of the fundamental concepts of Scots private law in the
light of what she has learned from her detailed study of the subject.

CHAPTER 1

WHAT IS SCOTS PRIVATE LAW?

Throughout the world there exist coherent systems of rules and **1–01** principles called law which have their own internal methods of argumentation (or reasoning or logic) and which are capable of being enforced. There is a Scottish legal system which consists of those legal principles and rules which are valid and enforceable in a geographical area of the United Kingdom called Scotland. An important part of the contemporary Scottish legal system is Scots private law. But what do we mean by private law?

At one level, there is no distinction between public and private law. All legal rules and principles—sometimes called norms—are concerned about the conditions under which the state may legitimately, i.e. lawfully impose sanctions upon its subjects. But to analyse the law in this reductionist way is to distort how law is perceived in reality. Public law is concerned with the relationship between the citizen and the state. It identifies those institutions which are the sources of our law. These include the Scottish and the Westminster Parliaments which create law by passing statutes, Acts of Parliament. Acts or statutes are known as legislation. Other sources of law are the judges who by deciding cases in the courts develop rules and principles of what is known as the common, i.e. judge-made law. Under our constitution, both Parliaments can abolish or change the common law, usually setting up a statutory regime in its place. Thus, for example, the common law rules concerned with the contract for the sale of goods were largely abolished and replaced by a statutory regime in 1893 which in turn was repealed and replaced by the Sale of Goods Act 1979. However, provisions of statutes have to be interpreted and ultimately this will be done by the judges. By construing the statutory language the courts will be able to determine the scope of the legislation.

As well as identifying the sources of law, public law attempts to **1–02** control how political power should be exercised. Public law regulates the powers of state agencies and the relationships between them and the citizen. In particular, state agencies must not act in ways which are contrary to the rights and freedoms enjoyed by persons under the European Convention of Human Rights. For this purpose, a state agency includes courts; their decisions have therefore to be consistent with Convention Rights, i.e. Convention compatible. Legislation must also be interpreted so as to be Convention compatible. Where this is not possible an Act of the Scottish Parliament can not be enforced: an Act of the Westminster Parliament remains enforceable but the courts can issue a declaration of incompatibility, with the expectation that the legislation will be amended by the Parliament. Moreover, in areas within its competency, the law of the European Union is supreme and must be followed rather than an inconsistent common law rule or statutory provision.

The area of public law with which the layperson is most familiar is criminal law. Criminal law sets the standards of personal behaviour which must be followed in Scotland. It does so by treating certain actions as criminal and punishing the perpetrator by imprisonment or a fine or community service. A unique feature of Scots criminal law is that many crimes have been developed and remain governed by the common, i.e. judge-made law. These include murder, culpable homicide, rape, assault and theft. Statutory offences include sexual offences (other than rape), misuse of drugs and road traffic offences—the latter two being matters which are reserved to the Westminster Parliament. There is a separate system of criminal courts and prosecutions are brought by the Crown. Apart from very exceptional situations, whether or not to prosecute in a particular case is ultimately a question for the Lord Advocate who, as a member of the Scottish Executive, is responsible to the Scottish Parliament for his decision. This emphasises the public nature of criminal law and the system of criminal justice in Scotland.

1–03   Among other things, public law is concerned with the relationship between the citizen and state agencies; for example, local authorities, planning authorities, government departments and the Scottish Executive. The cases are usually concerned with an exercise of administrative discretion which a citizen regards as unfair: this could range from the refusal of a pension or other social security benefit to the granting of planning permission in spite of objections from members of the public.

Public law often allows appeals from such decisions to inquiries or tribunals. The courts have also got the power of judicial review to determine whether the decision was outwith the state agency's powers or involved a procedural irregularity or was reached without considering a relevant matter (or by considering a matter which was irrelevant) or was so unreasonable that it was a decision which no properly informed person could reach. Nevertheless the paradigmatic example of public law is the criminal law which tells the citizen what she may not do and punishes criminal behaviour by a state enforced sanction.

1–04   Like other Western liberal democracies, in Scotland there is a predilection towards a free market economy. As a consequence, members of society are at liberty to pursue their own, i.e. private personal and economic objectives. Much of private law provides legal rules and principles which empower men and women and other legal persons, for example, partnerships and companies, to achieve these objectives. There are laws on how legitimately to acquire and dispose of wealth. These include rules in relation to the ownership of property, the transfer of property while the owner is alive or on his death, agreements to deliver property or provide services by means of exchange (contracts), and reparation, i.e. compensation when persons or property are wrongfully harmed (delict). The legal rules and principles which govern these relationships constitute the core of private law.

The hallmark of a system of private law is that it gives persons legal rights. Once a person has such a right there arises a corresponding duty in others to respect that right. For instance, if a person owns property there is a corresponding duty on all other persons not to interfere with the owner's use and enjoyment of the property. Moreover, if A's property is damaged by B's wrongful conduct, A has the right to seek compensation from B who is under a corresponding duty or obligation to make reparation for the harm she has wrongfully caused. Where A enters into a contract with B, A has a right to call on B to perform and B is under a corresponding obligation or duty to do so. The correlative nature of these rights and duties is an essential feature of private law. Thus the function of private law is to provide the rules for the creation and transfer of legal rights and the principles upon which liability will be incurred if validly constituted legal rights are wrongfully infringed.

The law of property and the law of obligations are the pillars on **1–05** which private law is built. There are, of course, other important sources of legal rights in private law, for example, the law of trusts and the law of succession: but as we shall see they build upon the law of property and the law of obligations. In modern times, statute is also a source of legal rights and this is particularly true of contemporary Scottish family law and commercial law, both traditionally seen as parts of private law.

Private law therefore governs these—primarily economic—relationships. Where disputes arise as to whether a right has been validly created or wrongfully infringed, an answer should be found by the application of the relevant rule or principle of Scots private law. In relation to property and succession, it is particularly important that the law should be able to provide an answer which is clear and unambiguous, so that litigation can be avoided. Indeed, in this context, sometimes certainty of title to property overrides concepts of fairness. But certainty is also important in the law of obligations. Millions of transactions take place each day on the understanding that parties will perform the contractual obligations they have voluntarily undertaken and that if a dispute should arise the law will provide a clear answer so that the matter can be settled without recourse to the courts. And this is true—albeit to a lesser extent—for the law of delict, where large numbers of claims for compensation are settled because liability can be established by the application of the relevant rules. Thus in the vast majority of cases, the application of the relevant legal rules and principles to the *agreed facts* should provide an answer which is "correct" in the sense that it is the inevitable result of the procedures and processes accepted as legitimate legal reasoning in the Scottish legal system. This is known as rule-bound decision making. Of course, where there is a dispute about the facts of a case rather than the law to be applied, litigation may be inevitable.

A vitally important point is that in a system of private law, the rights recognised by the law should not be able to be trumped by an appeal to some form of utilitarianism or public policy considerations. If, for example, after applying the legal rules, it is clear that a person has a right to damages, compensation cannot be denied on the basis that in the circumstances it would be unfair to do so. This might arise if the payee—the person entitled to the damages—was rich while the payer—the person obliged to pay the damages—was poor. Again, when a person dies without a will, the application of the rules on intestate succession (i.e. dying without a will) can lead to harsh seeming results. If A dies survived by his mother, father and brother, half his estate goes to his brother, a quarter to his father and a quarter to his mother. It does not matter that the father abandoned A and his mother when A was an infant or that A's brother is his father's child by the woman for whom he left A and his mother. That there can be harsh results does not allow us to abandon rule-bound decision making. The sense of injustice inherent in the last example could have been avoided if A had made a will in which he made his mother the sole beneficiary of his estate.

1–06　　This is not to deny that from time to time it is recognised that the values being furthered by common law or statutory rules are out of step with contemporary notions of justice or fairness: in a democratic society, the common law or statutory rules can then be changed by legislation. These statutory changes will rarely, if ever, have retrospective effect on any rights which have already vested in persons under the unaltered law. After the new legislation has been promulgated, i.e. brought into force, it will in its turn become part of the corpus of private law and can then be used to provide rule-bound decisions. But it cannot be overemphasised that a fundamental purpose of a system of private law is that legal rights—and their correlative obligations—should not be able to be overturned or, indeed, be created, by an appeal to the evident justice or utility or fairness of so doing. Huge tracts of our economic and social lives are ordered on the assumption that the legal rights and obligations created by private law will be respected: that they cannot be set aside on the ground that to enforce the law in the particular circumstances will give results which appear to be unjust or unfair or economically or ethically unsound. This presupposes that a lawyer knows where to find the law, can isolate the key issues in factual situations, can assess the truth of the alleged facts from the evidence and can apply the relevant legal rules and principles to reach a result which can be justified by an appeal to the reasoning processes recognised as legitimate within the legal system. These are, of course, the skills which have been traditionally honed by the study of private law.

It has been argued that in determining the legal rights and obligations of persons and the correlative relationships between them, a system of private law applies a set of rules and principles which when applied in a particular situation will, in the vast majority of cases, yield a result which is justified by an appeal to legal reasoning—broadly defined—rather than what is thought to be expedient in accordance with social or economic policy. To that extent, the rules and principles of substantive law prevail because the non-legal implications of the result—its fairness, its economic value, its utility for society as a whole—are irrelevant. While this may from time to time spawn a harsh result, that is the price that has to be paid for the certainty inherent in rule-bound decision making.

That said, there are areas of private law where policy considerations do arise. They include the so-called "hard" cases where because of its novelty the law has been uncertain, or because of the open texture of the principles involved the court has a choice whether or not to extend liability. In the former category, we could place much of the law on unjustified enrichment which remains undeveloped. There is little doubt that when, as here, the law is unclear, a court will choose the rule which it considers gives the fairest result. In the latter, we could place decisions in the law of delict where the courts are sometimes asked to extend the frontiers of liability by imposing on the defender a duty of care to prevent harm in a novel situation if it is fair, just and reasonable to do so. It should be emphasised that these situations are exceptional and that in the vast majority of cases a solution can be found simply by applying the relevant rules. **1–07**

The view of private law which I have espoused presupposes a minimum of judicial discretion built into the system. In my view, private law should create rights, the substantive contents of which are well established and which therefore can be exercised and enforced with certainty. Yet a significant feature of law reform legislation in the twentieth and twenty-first centuries has been to give judges discretion to determine the existence of legal rights and whether or not they should be enforced. This judicial discretion is often to be exercised within prescribed statutory criteria but these can be very open-ended: for example, what is reasonable in all the circumstances of the case. The point is that the existence of such degrees of judicial discretion precludes the certainty inherent in rule-bound decision making. As we shall see, much of family law now involves judicial discretion, but it can be found throughout private law. In the present writer's view any further increase in judicial discretionary powers should be resisted. The extent of the discretion is such that, in deciding whether a statutory right exists or whether or not a statutory right should be exercised, a judge will—almost inevitably—be influenced by what she perceives to be socio-economically desirable. Thus non-legal factors will sometimes be crucial in determining both the existence and extent of a person's legal rights. Put another way, utilitarian considerations may prevent a person obtaining a right as well as determining how a right should or should not be exercised. Yet it can be argued that a legal right recognised by a system of private law should not be able to be trumped because a judge considers that its exercise would be unfair or unjust or socio-economically unfortunate or inconsistent with the government's or the Executive's policy in the circumstances of a particular case. Put shortly, any increase in judicial discretion can only undermine private legal rights and their correlative duties, i.e. the concept of private law itself!

1–08 We have said that the law of property and the law of obligations are the two pillars upon which the edifice of private law is built. In the following chapters we shall consider the law of property and the law of obligations respectively.

Further Reading

Gloag and Henderson, *The Law of Scotland* (11th ed., 2001)
Fundamentals of Scots Law (W. Green, 2003)

CHAPTER 2

THE LAW OF PROPERTY I

Introduction

Private ownership of property is a salient feature of Western **2–01**
liberal democracies. In this chapter we shall consider the fundamental principles of the Scots law of property. The law of property
is concerned with rights in things. These are known as real rights or
rights *in rem*. They are rights which a person holds directly in the
property itself. They are good against the whole world in the sense
that everyone is obliged to respect a real right so that any
interference with the right holder's use of the property is a wrong.
For example, if A owns a painting and B steals it, A is entitled to
recover the picture not only from B but from anyone who
subsequently acquires the painting even if he bought the picture in
good faith, i.e. a bona fide transferee for value. The owner's right
to demand restitution of his property is known as the right to
vindicate and the person who has possession of the property is
under a correlative duty to deliver the property to the owner. The
right to vindicate is good against all subsequent acquirers because
ownership is a real right *in* the thing owned and is good against the
whole world and not just the original wrongdoer, B (though the
right to vindicate from a bona fide acquirer will come to an end
after 20 years as a result of the long negative prescription).

Real rights have to be contrasted with personal rights or rights *in* **2–02**
personam. A personal right is a right which is enforceable against a
particular person (or persons) and which that person (or persons)
is under a correlative duty to perform. Personal rights are the
province of the law of obligations. For example, A enters a contract
with B in which she agrees to buy B's house. A has a personal right
against B that B will convey the title, i.e. the ownership of the
house to A and B is under a correlative duty to do so: conversely, B
has a personal right against A to be paid the price and A is under a
correlative duty to do so. If B changes her mind and refuses to sell
the property, B is in breach of contract and A will be entitled to a
decree of specific implement to compel her to perform. If A
changes her mind and refuses to pay the price, she is in breach of
contract and B can sue her for the money, an action in debt. The
contractual rights which A enjoys are only enforceable in respect of
B (and vice versa): unlike real rights they are not good against the

whole world. The person who has the right is known as the obligee: the person who is under the correlative duty or obligation is known as the obligor.

2–03   If the reason that B refused to transfer the ownership of the house to A was that B had received a better offer from C, then if B sells the house to C, B is in breach of her contract with A. As the house has been sold to C, A can claim damages from B for breach of contract.[1] If C knew about B's contract with A, then as an alternative to A's contractual remedy against B, A can sue C in delict for the wrong of inducing a breach of contract between B and A. A has a right to receive reparation, i.e. damages from C for the wrong she has suffered. But again A has only a personal right against C as only C was the wrongdoer. It is also possible for A to have B's conveyance of the property to C set aside (reduced) as a consequence of the "off side goals" rule.

Before we consider the real rights in things in Scots law, it is necessary to spend a little time on how property is classified for legal purposes.

The Classification of Property

2–04   All property is either heritable or moveable. Put simply, heritable property (heritage) is land and moveable property is all property other than land. Land includes property which is attached to the land, for example a house or a forest.
All property is also either corporeal or incorporeal. Corporeal property consists of things which have a "body", i.e. are tangible, like land or a motor car or a book. Incorporeal property consists of rights which have no physical presence, like shares in a company or the right to payment of a debt or to obtain performance of a contract. Thus we have four potential classifications of property in Scots law:

(a) corporeal heritable property—i.e. land; for example fields, forests, houses and flats. When we buy a house we purchase the land (*solum*) on which the house is built.
(b) incorporeal heritable property—i.e. rights in relation to land; for example, the lease of a house or a standard security over a house. A standard security is used where a person who has lent money to the owner of heritage "secures" the debt by having the right to sell the debtor's

---

[1] These might include the increased price A might have to pay to buy a similar house or, more controversially, the gain B made by selling the house to C rather than A, if the price B obtained from C was in fact the value of the house on the open market.

heritable property in the event of the debt not being paid. A standard security is sometimes called a mortgage. It is possible to have a standard security over other incorporeal heritable property such as a lease. The right to obtain the transfer of the ownership of land as a consequence of a contract for the sale of land (missives of sale) is also an incorporeal heritable right.

(c) corporeal moveable property—for example, motor cars, furniture, animals.

(d) incorporeal moveable property—rights to shares in companies, intellectual property such as copyright, claims for breach of contract or compensation for wrongs (delict), the right to obtain performance of a contract (other than a contract relating to the sale of heritage) or the payment of a debt.

Two points should be noticed. First, there is a natural distinction **2–05** between land and moveable property. Land, and in particular the family home, is probably the most important—and often the most valuable—asset people acquire. It is therefore perhaps not surprising that different rules and different principles sometimes apply when we are concerned with heritable as opposed to moveable property.

Second, the most common type of property, namely money, is also one of the most complex. Coins are corporeal moveable property. When they are circulating as legal tender, it will usually be impossible to identify specific coins as having belonged to a particular person, for example a person from whom they have been stolen. But money can also take the form of incorporeal moveable property. When we say that we "own" money deposited in a bank, what do we own? When A deposits £500 in an account, A is *lending* the money to the bank. It is a term of the contract between the bank and A that the bank will repay the money to A. Thus when we say that A owns the £500 he deposited in the bank, what he in fact owns is the right under the contract with the bank to have the £500 repaid, usually with interest. Moreover, the right that A owns is only a personal right. This means that if the bank should fail, A will be an unsecured creditor and when the bank is wound up in insolvency proceedings A is unlikely to obtain much—if any—of the debt that he is owed. So while we may say that A owns the money in his bank account, A has no real right in respect of the money as such but only "owns" the contractual—personal—right to payment of the debt he is owed by the bank.

A lot of money circulates as banknotes. A banknote is a written promise by a bank to pay the bearer of the note a sum of money, £5, £10, £20, £50 or £100 on presentation of the note. The bearer of the note therefore "owns" the incorporeal moveable right to demand the appropriate sum from the bank. Once again this is only a personal right and the note would be worthless should the bank fail. In practice, few people go to a bank and demand that the bank fulfil its promise by paying them in legal tender the sum promised in the note. Instead, the note is treated as money and circulates as a means of exchange. When a note is exchanged between A and B, A is in effect assigning his rights against the bank to B. However, as the bank's promise is to pay the bearer, there is no need for B to intimate the assignation to the bank before he can enforce the promise and become the "owner" of the note. Where a bank note is in circulation, it will be very difficult to establish that a particular note previously belonged to a particular person from whom it was lost or stolen. Moreover, in order to protect commercial transactions, contrary to general principle, the owner of stolen banknotes or coins cannot vindicate them from the persons who possess them. In these circumstances, the victim's remedy lies in the law of obligations—delict or unjustified enrichment—rather than the law of property.

Real Rights

2–06   For present purposes, we need only consider the following real rights:

(a) Ownership or dominium

Ownership is the right to use and dispose of property as our own. Importantly, it includes the right to possess the property. In many situations the law protects the possession of property as opposed to the ownership of property. In practice an owner's right of use is restricted by the law of nuisance and statutory regimes to protect the rural and urban environment. Ownership has traditionally been regarded as the most important real right: for this reason, the other real rights are often referred to as subordinate real rights.

A person can own all the kinds of property classified in the previous section. In particular, it should be noticed that an obligee owns the incorporeal, moveable right to enforce an obligation against the obligor: for example, the right to recover a debt or obtain specific implement of a contract or claim reparation for a wrong. Moreover, the obligee can transfer these rights to a third party—often for value: the transferee can then enforce the rights against the obligor. The transfer of these rights is known as assignation.

All the property which a person owns constitutes her private patrimony[2]: for example, her house, jewellery, sports car, bank

---

[2] However a person can sometimes own property which does not form part of his personal patrimony. This is the case when a person acts as a trustee: see paras beyond.

deposits and other investments. But in assessing the net value of her private patrimony, account must be taken of the obligations she has incurred: for example, the loan she has taken out to purchase the house,[3] money owed on credit cards and other debts, or reparation to be paid to a person whose property was damaged as a result of her negligence. A person's private patrimony is therefore usually in a state of flux. While new property enters the patrimony, other assets leave when they are transferred to someone else and the net value of the patrimony is reduced when new obligations are incurred.

(b) Rights in Security

If A lends money to B, A may wish to obtain security for the **2–07** debt. This can be done by B creating a right in security in favour of A over property owned by B. A's right in security is a subordinate real right *in* B's property, which A can realise if B fails to pay the debt. Where the security is taken over land, for example a house, it is known as a heritable security. The standard security is now the only kind of heritable security which can be used in Scots law. When a standard security is registered in the Land Register, it gives the creditor a real right in the debtor's property. Where the security is taken over corporeal moveable property, the creditor obtains a real right only when he obtains possession of the property; this is known as a pledge. Where security is taken over incorporeal moveable property, for example debts that are owed to B by C, the security is created when B assigns the debt to his creditor, A; A's right becomes real when A intimates the assignation of the debt to C.

The importance of security rights being real arises when B is unable to pay the debt and is insolvent. A can take the property that is the subject of the security out of B's private patrimony in order to satisfy the debt, i.e. the property is not available to B's trustee in bankruptcy to satisfy B's general unsecured creditors until A's debt has been paid in full. A's right to obtain repayment of the loan from B is only a personal right and if A had not obtained a real right in security over some of B's property, he would have ranked as a general unsecured creditor and A would have been fortunate to have recovered anything in the bankruptcy proceedings.

(c) Leases

(i) Leases of Land. A lease is a right to exclusive possession of **2–08** land in return for a payment known as rent. The owner of the land enters into a contract under which the tenant is entitled to occupy

---

[3] The loan will usually be secured by a standard security over the house in favour of the lender.

the property for a set period, for example a week, a month, six months, a year, 10 years or 20 years. Where the lease is for more than a year the contract of lease must be constituted in writing.[4] There must also be a specific continuing rent and an ish, i.e. a specified date on which the lease is to expire. If these conditions are satisfied, the tenant's right under the contract of lease changes from a personal to a real right when the tenant enters into possession of the property. This means that the tenant's right to have exclusive possession of the property for the duration of the lease is good against the whole world including the owner of the property, i.e. the landlord and his successors. Although a lease creates a real right in land, it will be noticed that it is the tenant's possession, not registration of the lease in the Land Register, which makes the right real. However, if the lease is for more than 20 years (a long lease), the only way to obtain a real right is by registration in the Land Register. In such a lease, there is no need for the tenant to occupy the property to obtain a real right. But it is a condition of all long leases that no part of the leased property is used as a dwelling house.

2–09 **(ii) Leases of Moveables.** A lease of moveable property, for example a car, creates a personal right only. If A, the hirer or lessee, hires a car from its owner B, the lessor, he has only a personal right against B to have possession of the property during the period of the hire or lease. This means that if B became insolvent, his trustee in bankruptcy would be entitled to recover possession of the car and A would have to rank with general unsecured creditors in respect of any claim for damages against B for breach of contract in failing to provide the car for the duration of the lease. For the same reason, if B sold the car to C during the hire period, A could not prevent C, the new owner, from exercising his right to vindicate and obtain possession of the car. A would be left with his personal right to sue B for breach of contract.

2–10 **(iii) Termination of Leases of Land.** Before a lease can be terminated, a landlord must give the tenant notice to quit at the date when it was agreed that the lease would expire: conversely, a tenant must give the landlord notice that he intends to remove at that date. The periods of notice will usually be stipulated in the lease but there are statutory minimum periods. If no notice is given, the lease is continued by what is known as tacit relocation for the period of the original lease if it was less than a year and for a period of a year if the original duration was for a year or more. Tacit relocation can continue to operate indefinitely but its oper-

---

[4] Requirements of Writing (Scotland) Act 1995, s.1(2)(b).

ation can be expressly excluded in the original lease. Under statutes, some types of tenant, for example agricultural tenants, crofters and tenants of certain dwelling houses, enjoy enhanced security of tenure. All residential tenants have statutory protection against harassment and even when the lease has expired after a notice to quit has been served, a tenant cannot be made to quit the premises without a court order.[5] Where a tenant remains in possession after a lease has been terminated by a notice to quit, he is treated as an intruder of the owner's property and can be liable to pay the owner what is known as violent profits, i.e. the highest profits that the owner could have made had he been in possession of the property.

Where the tenant has been in breach of the terms of a lease, the landlord may be able to bring the lease to an end prematurely: this is known as irritating the lease.

(iv) Assignation. A tenant may be able to transfer the lease to 2–11 another person. This is done by the tenant A (the cedent) assigning the lease to B (the assignee). On intimation of the assignation to the landlord, any rights between the landlord and A become enforceable between the landlord and B. When B takes possession of the property—or in the case of a long lease, registers the assignation—A is divested of the lease and B obtains a real right of lease against the landlord. The assignee as the tenant of the property now has possession for the remainder of the original lease. The result of the assignation is that the assignee is in effect substituted for the cedent, i.e. the original tenant, who disappears from the picture. It is therefore not surprising that in practice a lease will usually have an express provision that the tenant cannot assign the lease without the landlord's permission, though it is usually stipulated that the landlord's agreement should not be unreasonably withheld. Even without this, it will be implied that a lease cannot be assigned if there is a sufficient degree of *delectus personae*, i.e. that the identity of the tenant was important to the landlord when he granted the original lease.

The assignee acquires a subordinate real right on taking possession or by registration. So for example if A assigns the lease to B and then assigns the same lease to C, C will take priority over B if C takes possession of the property before B. It does not matter that B had intimated the assignation to the landlord before C did so. If the lease is a registered long lease, the assignation will create a real right on registration of the assignation and there is no need for the assignee to take possession of the property. A tenant may also be able to assign a lease to a creditor in security of a debt but

---

[5] In practice, most tenants leave quietly after the notice to quit has expired.

the creditor assignee will not have a real right *vis-à-vis* third parties until he takes possession of the property. This means that the debtor tenant will have to leave the property. Where the lease is a registered long lease, assignation in security is not permitted but the tenant can grant a standard security over the lease. On registration in the Land Register, the standard security becomes a real right and there is no need for the creditor to take possession or the tenant to vacate the premises.

Unless it is expressly or, through *delectus personae*, impliedly prohibited, a tenant, A, may sub-lease the property to a sub-tenant, B. The period of the sub-lease cannot exceed the period of A's lease with the original landlord: the original lease is known as a head lease. If the landlord terminates the head lease with A, A's sub-lease to B will automatically fall.

(d) Servitudes

2–12 A servitude is a right which a person in his capacity as the owner of a particular piece of land (the benefited property) has over another piece of land (the burdened property) which is owned by another person. The servitude right is a real right in the sense that it is a right which the owner of the benefited property has *in* the burdened property. So for example, the owner of the benefited property may have the right to use the burdened property as a right of way over that land: this is known as a positive servitude. A servitude is an attribute of the benefited property and can only be exercised for the benefit of that property. It can be created in writing; by express grant or reservation; by implied or inferred grant or reservation; and by possession or use for 20 years, i.e. positive prescription. If a servitude is to be expressly created, it *must* be registered in the Land Register against both the benefited and burdened properties before it becomes a real right. Where a servitude has been acquired by prescription, there is still no need for registration in the Land Register before it is constituted as a real right.[6]

Ranking of Priorities

2–13 More than one real right may exist in relation to the same piece of property at the same time. For example:

A is the owner of a house. He grants a lease to B for five years. A then grants a standard security over the house to C as security for a loan which C has made to him. There are therefore three real rights in respect of the property namely C's standard security, B's

---

[6] Title Conditions (Scotland) Act 2003, Part 7, ss.75–81. It is no longer competent to create a negative servitude, for example a right to light: existing negative servitudes have been converted into real burdens.

lease and A's ownership. It should be noticed that A has voluntarily agreed to fetter the enjoyment of his right of ownership by granting B and C real rights in his land. Accordingly A must respect the rights he has created namely B's right to have exclusive possession for the duration of the lease and C's right to call up the security and if necessary have the house sold should A default in payment of the debt. But even though he must recognise the real rights that B and C enjoy in his land, nevertheless A remains the owner: he will be able to have possession of the house after the lease has come to an end and he can have the standard security discharged by paying the debt.

What happens if the rights come into conflict? Problems are resolved by what is known as ranking, under which certain rights take priority over the others. As a general rule, priority is determined by the date of creation of the real right. So if in our example, A defaults in paying back the loan, C can call up the standard security, but he takes the land subject to B's lease. Even if the land is sold to pay off the debt, the purchaser of the house will take the property subject to B's lease which is a real right in the property and is therefore binding on A's successors until the lease comes to an end.

Priority is determined by the date when the real right is constituted. Consider the following examples:

(a) A is owed money by B. A assigns the debt to C who does not intimate the assignation to B. A later assigns the same debt to D who does intimate the assignation to B. On intimation to B, D becomes the holder of a real right. Even though the assignation to C was earlier, as it was not intimated to B, C did not obtain a real right. All that C has is a personal right against A for breach of the [contract of] assignation. If A becomes insolvent, A's right to seek payment from B is no longer part of A's private patrimony and is not an asset available to A's general unsecured creditors such as C: instead, the right to seek payment from B has become part of D's private patrimony.

(b) A grants a standard security over his house to B. B does not register it. Later A grants another standard security over his house to C. C registers it. B then registers the first standard security. As priority is determined by the date when the conflicting rights became real, C's standard security will rank over B's since C's security was registered before B's even though B's deed was executed before C's.

(c) A enters into a contract with B in which he agrees to sell his house to B. A then sells his house to C and conveys the title to C by disposition. C registers the disposition in the Land Register. By registration, C obtains the real right of ownership in the property in spite of the fact that A had earlier agreed to sell the house to B. B is left to his personal right against A to sue him for breach of the contract of sale.

2–14 A person's real right in property may be reduced, i.e. set aside, if it has been obtained in bad faith. This is known as the rule against "offside goals". This arises when the person who is seeking to obtain a real right in the property, C, knows that A, the granter of the right, has already entered into an obligation with a third party, B, which will be broken should he grant the right to C. In this case, B can seek to have the grant to C set aside, i.e. reduced—even if it has been recorded in the Land Register. The title will then revert back to A who can then be compelled to fulfil his (personal) obligation to transfer title to B which can then be registered to give B a real right in the property. So if in example (c) above, C knew of A's pre-existing contract with B, C's title to the property, while a real right because it has been registered, is nevertheless annullable (voidable): this means it can be set aside by a court in an action of reduction. It will be noticed that after reduction, the title reverts back to A and B has only a personal right to compel A to perform the contract. The remedy of reduction is therefore of little value to B if A has become insolvent, as on reduction the property will become part of A's private patrimony for the benefit of all his creditors. Thus, as an alternative to reduction, it appears B can seek an order from the court calling upon C to fulfil A's obligations to B and to transfer the title directly to B.

Moreover, if C persuaded A to break his contract with B by, for example giving him a higher price for the house, B could choose to sue C in delict. To induce a breach of a pre-existing contract is a wrong which is reparable under the law of delict as an alternative to suing the party who is in breach of contract.

For the offside goals rule to apply, the grantee must know about the granter's pre-existing obligations to the third party. Sometimes the grantee will be deemed to know about these obligations even if he has no actual knowledge. This will arise when the agreement between the granter and the third party has been registered in the Land Register. For example:

A grants a standard security over his house in favour of B. It is a term of the standard security that A cannot lease the house without the permission of the heritable creditor, B. The standard security is registered in the Land Register giving B a subordinate real right in the house. In breach of the standard security, A leases the house to C. Because the standard security was registered, C is deemed to have knowledge of its terms. C takes possession and thereby transforms the lease into a real right. But this real right, while good against the whole world including the granter, A, is voidable in that it can be set aside in an action of reduction brought by B. This might happen if A defaults in payment of the loan which is secured by the standard security. B could seek to have the lease reduced and could then enforce the security against the house untrammelled by the lease. Contrast this with the situation where A enters into a lease with C *before* A grants a standard security to B. If C has taken possession thereby obtaining a real right in the lease, then B takes the standard security over the house subject to the lease. If B enforces the security by selling the house to D, B's lease continues as it is a real right which is not only good against A but also his successors. Thus C will retain exclusive possession of the house until the lease expires.

Common Property

Although more than one real right may exist in the same piece **2–15** of property at the same time, it is an axiomatic principle of Scots law that there cannot be more than one real right of ownership in the same piece of property at any one time. If A has the real right of ownership in her flat, no one else can be the owner of that flat even though it might be subject to other real rights such as a standard security or a lease. This is true of moveable as well as heritable property. If a man gives his fiancé an engagement ring on condition that she will return the ring to him if she should break off the engagement, she is nevertheless the owner of the ring and could, for example, sell it to a third party who would acquire a good title from her. If she then broke off the engagement, her former boyfriend cannot claim that he is the owner since she did not transfer the ownership of the ring back to him before she sold it to the third party. The boyfriend cannot vindicate the ring from the purchaser: instead, he is left to his personal right against her for breach of her implied promise to return the ring to him if she broke off the engagement.

But Scots law does recognise common ownership. This is where a single piece of property is held by two or more people as an undivided whole, i.e. each is entitled to enjoy all the property as owner and her rights of occupation are not restricted to a particular physical part of the property. This is *pro indiviso* ownership, i.e. ownership of undivided or whole property. So if for example A and B own a house *pro indiviso* in common, each has the right to possess the whole house and is not restricted only to particular rooms. Each of the common owners has a separate share of the *pro indiviso* whole of the property. Where property is owned in common by two persons, for example husband and wife, in the usual case each has a one half *pro indiviso* share. But there is no reason why co-owners should always have equal shares. A man may gift a house to his daughter and her husband stipulating that his daughter should have a ninety per cent *pro indiviso* share and her husband a 10 per cent *pro indiviso* share. But because he has a *pro indiviso* share, the husband is entitled to occupy the whole of the house along with his wife: he is not restricted to a tenth of the space in the house! The common owners' *pro indiviso* shares in the property are legal—not physical—constructs.

2–16 Common ownership of heritable property arises when title is taken in the names of more than one person, for example, to A and B. It is still common to find a survivorship clause, for example, to A and B and the survivor. Such a clause is a type of special destination. This means that if A predeceases B, A's *pro indiviso* share passes automatically to the survivor, B.

Moveable property can also be owned in common. For example, a group of persons may have *pro indiviso* shares in the ownership of a racehorse. Indeed, by virtue of s.25(1) of the Family Law (Scotland) Act 1985, there is a presumption of common ownership by spouses or civil partners of household goods obtained in prospect or during their marriage. Household goods are any goods kept or used during the marriage or partnership in the matrimonial of family home for the couple's joint domestic purposes. It may therefore surprise a married couple or partnership to know that, for example, they are presumed to have one half *pro indiviso* shares in their pots and pans, refrigerator, settee and bed but not the wife's golf clubs or the husband's jewellery.

2–17 Since each co-owner has a separate *pro indiviso* share, she may do what she wishes with it. Thus, a co-owner may sell her share to a third-party who then becomes entitled as a co-owner to occupy the whole of the property with the existing co-owners. Again, a co-owner is free to grant a standard security over his share or give it away as a gift during his lifetime (an *inter vivos* donation). In none of these juristic acts is there any need to obtain the consent of the other co-proprietors. Thus a husband can sell his one half share of the matrimonial bed without the consent of the other co-owner, his wife: the purchaser will then have the right as co-owner to occupy the whole of the bed!

A co-owner can also bequeath her share by will. It is here that a survivorship clause may cause difficulties, i.e. where the title is taken in the names of A and B and the survivor. It is settled that such a clause cannot prevent A or B disposing of their shares during their lifetime. But where both parties have contributed to the purchase of the property, the courts will readily infer that there is a contractual agreement between the parties that neither can revoke the arrangement by testamentary deed (a will). Where only one of the parties has purchased the property, this principle does not apply to the party who bought the property and she is free to dispose of her own *pro indiviso* share by will. The other party (the donee) is treated as having received his share as a gift from the purchasing co-owner (the donor) and the court will readily infer that he took the gift under the condition that the donor should obtain his share if the donor survives him. Consequently the donee cannot dispose of his share by will; but even in such circumstances he is free to dispose of his share during his lifetime.

Where a co-owner disposes of his *pro indiviso* share, it is axiomatic that the disponee as a new co-proprietor can occupy the whole of the property along with the pre-existing co-owners. Where the property is used as the co-owners' home, this can create practical difficulties, especially when it is remembered that the consent of all the co-owners is *not* required before a share is sold or otherwise transferred to a third party. However, where spouses or civil partners are co-owners of the matrimonial or family home, if a spouse or civil partner disposes of his share to a third party, the new co-owner is not allowed to occupy any part of the house while the other co-owning spouse or civil partner continues to reside there.[7] This statutory protection only applies where the co-owners are married or are civil partners: it does not apply if, for example, the co-owners were unmarried heterosexual or homosexual cohabitants.

It is a hall-mark of common ownership that each co-owner is **2–18** entitled to realise the value of his share of the property. Where this cannot be agreed, any co-owner is entitled to apply to court for an action of division and sale. The court has no discretion to refuse such an application. The court will then decide whether the physical division of the property between the co-owners is practical. If it is not, as is usually the case, the court *must* order a sale and each co-owner is entitled to his proportionate share of the proceeds. At one time this principle applied even where the co-owners were spouses and the property was the matrimonial home. So for example a husband could insist on an action of division and sale even though his wife, the other co-owner, wished to continue to live in the house with their children. To alleviate this problem, legislation now provides that where a matrimonial or family home is owned in common by a married couple or civil partners, if one of the spouses or civil partners brings an action of division and sale of the property, the court has a discretion, having regard to all the circumstances of the case, to refuse or postpone granting decree where the continued occupation of the house by the other spouse or civil partner is in their interests or in the interests of the family.[8]

Joint Ownership

As we have seen, where property is owned in common, each co- **2–19** proprietor has a separate *pro indiviso* share of the whole of the property and is free to use his share as he chooses. Exceptionally, property may be owned by more than one person under an

---

[7] Matrimonial Homes (Family Protection) Act 1981, s.9 (spouses); Civil Partnership Act 2004, s.109 (civil partners).
[8] Matrimonial Homes (Family Protection) Act 1981, s.19 (spouses); Civil Partnership Act 2004, s.110 (civil partners).

arrangement where the owners do not have separate *pro indiviso* shares: instead there is one, single title which is owned jointly by the co-proprietors. The most important form of joint property in Scots law is that of trustees, who jointly own the property which makes up the trust fund. The assets of an unincorporated association, such as a club, are also owned jointly by the members. The property belongs to the persons who are from time to time trustees or, in the case of an unincorporated association, members. If for example a trustee dies, the title to the property remains with the surviving trustees. Because joint owners do not have any separate share of the property, the individual trustee has no property interest which he can dispone or transfer and he has no right to seek an action of division and sale. The trust deed or rules of the association will lay down rules for the administration of the fund or property, usually allowing decisions to be made by a majority of trustees or members.

Further Reading

Gordon, *Scottish Land Law* (2nd ed., 1999)
Reid, *Abolition of Feudal Tenure in Scotland* (2003)
Rennie, *Land Tenure Reform* (2004)
Rennie, *Land Tenure and Tenement Legislation* (2nd ed., 2005)
Stair Memorial Encyclopedia, Vol. 18 (Property)
Thomson, *Family Law Reform* (2006)

CHAPTER 3

THE LAW OF PROPERTY II

Acquisition of Ownership

Ownership is the most important of the real rights in property **3–01** recognised by Scots law. The other real rights, such as rights in security, leases of land and servitude rights are subordinate real rights compared with ownership itself. Indeed, only an owner of property can create certain subordinate real rights in his property such as a lease of land or a standard security (except, of course, a standard security granted by a tenant over a long lease—but even here we say that the tenant "owns" the lease). Because of its fundamental significance, in this and the next chapters we shall examine in some detail how ownership of property is acquired. There are two situations which must be considered:

    (a) original acquisition. This arises when property becomes the subject of ownership for the first time or a previous owner's title is extinguished so that a new title can be acquired in respect of the property; and

    (b) derivative acquisition. This arises when owner A transfers title to B who then becomes the new owner of the property. In this situation the new owner *derives* his title from a previous owner. The previous owner is divested of his title which is invested in the new owner.

Original Acquisition

(a) Occupation (Occupatio)

Ownership of corporeal moveable property which has never **3–02** previously been owned can be acquired by what is called occupation (*occupatio*) or seizure. Occupation occurs when a thing has been appropriated by a person, i.e. he has taken possession and control of the object. The most common case when a person becomes an owner by occupation is when he captures or kills a wild animal such as a rabbit or fish. In practice, many animals are protected by game and wild life conservation legislation. Landowners do not own the wild animals which live on their land or swim in their rivers: instead, they have the right to hunt or fish. Thus even though a poacher is unlawfully on land, she will be the owner of any wild animals that she fishes or shoots even though the property she has acquired by occupation may be confiscated under the criminal law should she be caught!

Occupation is only possible if the thing seized has never been owned. Lost property continues to belong to the owner who lost it. If, however, an owner abandons property the Crown, i.e. the State becomes the owner. There is therefore no room for the operation of occupation in respect of abandoned property such as buried treasure: this belongs to the Crown and not the person who discovers it. There is an exception to this rule where a wild animal which has been captured escapes from its owner: it appears that it can again be the subject of occupation. Under the Civic Government (Scotland) Act 1982 if the bona fide finder of lost or abandoned property surrenders it to the police, the police may return it to the finder if it has not been claimed by its owner within two months of being found.

(b) Accession (Accessio)

3–03   Accession occurs when two pieces of property become joined together in such a way that one piece, the accessory, has been subsumed into the other, the principal. The doctrine only operates in respect of corporeal property.

Two pieces of property must have become joined together, one of the pieces must be subordinate to the other, and the attachment must be permanent. If these criteria are satisfied, the owner of the principal becomes the owner of the accessory because the accessory is deemed to have lost its identity and merged with the principal. Thus if an engine is installed in a motor car it will accede to the vehicle and will be owned by the owner of the car (moveable to moveable): if frescoes are painted on the walls of a house they will accede to the house and will be owned by the owner of the house (moveable to heritable): when land is reclaimed by the retreat of tidal waters, it accedes to the adjacent dry land (heritable to heritable). Of these the most important in practice is the accession of moveable property to heritage. This is traditionally known as the law on fixtures. The classic situation is when a house is built on land: as it is being built, the moveable property, bricks, wood etc, attach to the land so that as a consequence of accession the house becomes the property of the owner of the land. On occasions it can be difficult to determine whether the attachment is sufficiently permanent for the doctrine to operate; where, for example, heavy machinery is fixed to the floor of a factory.

The criteria are applied objectively and the intentions of the parties are irrelevant. For example if central heating is installed in a house, the doctrine applies and the owner of the house will own the central heating: a subsequent sale of the house will automatically include the central heating which has become part of the house. However, if the house is heated by electric and gas fires, the doctrine does not apply as the attachment of the moveable property to the house is not sufficiently permanent. Therefore a subsequent sale of the house will not automatically include the fires as they have not become part of the house. It is for this reason that the purchaser of a house will often contract to buy moveable property which has not acceded such as carpets, curtains and fires.

Where accession has occurred, the accessory becomes part of the **3–04** principal. If the accessory was moveable property and the principal was heritage the moveable property becomes heritable. And most importantly, since the accessory no longer exists as soon as it has become part of the principal the ownership of the accessory is automatically terminated. As the ownership of the property which has acceded does not depend on the title of the previous owner but on the operation of the doctrine of accession, this is a form of original as opposed to derivative acquisition.

It follows that accession can have drastic consequences for the owner of the accessory property. If the doctrine operates, his real right of ownership is terminated because legally his property—the accessory—ceases to exist. So, for example, if A builds a house on land which belongs to B, the house will be owned by B as a consequence of accession even though A believed that he, A, owned the land. Nor does it matter that the owner of the principal acted in bad faith. For instance, if B steals wood from A which B uses to line the walls of the library in his house, the wood will be owned by B as a consequence of accession: because the wood no longer exists as separate property, A cannot vindicate it and demand its return from B. The law of property requires certainty of title above considerations of fairness.

In both these examples, A is not without a remedy but it lies in **3–05** the law of obligations rather than the law of property. In the first, where B was enriched at the expense of A as a consequence of A's error, B may be obliged to make recompense to A under the law of unjustified enrichment. Normally, B would have to pay to A the difference in value between the land with, and the land without, the house. In the second, B has committed a wrong when he stole the wood, and A can sue B for compensation under the law of delict. Alternatively, A can seek recompense from B if B's gain from the wrong was greater than A's loss, i.e. if the wood was worth more being part of a library than lying in A's yard. It must be stressed that these are personal rights and would be of little value to A if B was insolvent. And unlike the right to vindicate, A would have no right at all against a bona fide transferee for value of the principal property after accession had taken place.

After accession, the property becomes that of the owner of the principal. This means that if the principal and accessory are subsequently separated, the owner of the principal retains the ownership of the accessory, now separate property, *i.e.* the ownership of the accessory does not revert to the previous owner. Thus if in the second example, B stripped the wood from the walls of the library, he retains the ownership of the wood which does not revert to the ownership of A. Once again we can see the importance that the law of property gives to certainty of title.

Where the principal actually produces the accessory, the owner of the principal owns the accessory as a consequence of accession. This is known as accession by fruits. Accordingly, the owner of a cow owns its unborn calf, the owner of a raspberry bush owns the unpicked raspberries, the owner of the soil, the trees or crops growing there. After severance—the young animal is born, the raspberries are picked, trees are hewn and the crops are harvested—the owner of the principal retains ownership of the accessory which has now become separate property. This is an application of the general rule that where there has been accession, the owner of the principal retains ownership of the accessory should it subsequently become separated.

(c) Specification (Specificatio)

3–06   Specification is concerned with the situation where material owned by A is made into a new thing by B: for example, cream owned by A is churned into butter by B. If the new thing cannot be restored to its original materials, the new thing belongs to the maker. Thus in our example, since the butter cannot be turned back into cream, the butter is owned by B and not A.

It has been argued that specification should operate only when the maker of the new property has acted in good faith. It is difficult to see why good faith should be necessary. As we have seen, there is no need for good faith on the part of the owner of the principal property before accession operates to extinguish an owner's title to the accessory property. As in accession, we should only be concerned with the physical state of the property in order to determine whether the doctrine of specification should operate. If good faith was a requirement before specification could operate, it would make a purchaser of the new property vulnerable to a claim for restitution of the property by the owner of the materials: for if the maker had been in bad faith, the owner of the materials would be the owner of the new property and could then vindicate it from any person who had possession of the new property including a bona fide transferee for value. To avoid this consequence it is thought that good faith on the part of the maker should not be necessary before specification operates. The owner of the materials will have a claim against the maker of the new property in unjustified enrichment for recompense or in delict for reparation: but, unlike vindication, these are only personal rights and will be of little value if the maker of the new property is insolvent.

(d) Commixtion (Commixitio) and Confusion (Confusio)

Here we are concerned with the situation where a thing owned **3–07** by A is mixed with a thing owned by B and the mixture cannot be separated into its original components. The classic Scottish example is blending whiskies together. In such circumstances, there will be common ownership of the mixture between the owners of its components. The size of their *pro indiviso* shares will reflect the proportions that each co-owner contributed to the mixture. Consequently, each co-owner can demand division and sale of the mixture. If the mixture is sold by one co-owner without the agreement of the others, he can only transfer title to his own share to a third party, who becomes a co-owner with the other co-owners who can demand a division and sale. Where the third party believed that he was purchasing the outright—as opposed to *pro indiviso*—ownership, he will be left to his personal rights against the seller in contract or delict.

Where the mixture creates a new thing, specification operates instead of commixtion: or if one component can be treated as the principal property, the rules of accession will apply. If the components can be separated, the mixing has no effect at all on the ownership of the components.

(e) Prescription

In certain circumstances, a person can acquire a real right in **3–08** property as a result of possessing it for a period of time. This is known as positive prescription. We shall consider positive prescription and other effects of possession in this section.

One of the most important attributes of ownership is that the owner is entitled to possession of her property. It is therefore not surprising that there is a presumption that, where a person has possession of corporeal moveable property, he is the owner of the property. This presumption can be rebutted if it can be shown that the property is in fact owned by another person: this could arise, for example, if it could be proved that the possessor had stolen the property from its owner. If two or more persons have possession of such property there will be a presumption of common ownership: again this presumption can be rebutted.

Nevertheless, in relation to corporeal moveable property, it appears that possession over a period of years does not of itself enable the possessor to obtain ownership of the property. In other words, there is no positive prescription in respect of corporeal moveable property. However, under s.8 of the Prescription and Limitation (Scotland) Act 1973 (the 1973 Act) the ownership of corporeal moveable property is subject to the long negative prescription of 20 years. This means that if an owner does not exercise the right of ownership for 20 years, his right to do so comes to an end. For example, if A lends a book to B but does not

seek its return then after 20 years A loses ownership. But because
there is no positive prescription of corporeal moveable property, B
does not become the owner when A ceases to be owner. The
property will be regarded as abandoned, i.e. a *res nullius*. Since the
book has been owned by A, B cannot acquire ownership by
occupation and instead it will belong to the Crown. If, however,
corporeal moveable property has been stolen, the owner's right to
recover property from the thief is imprescriptible, i.e. it does not
prescribe after 20 years.[1] But it is only the right to recover from the
thief—or a person privy to the theft—that does not prescribe. Thus
if the thief has sold the property to a bona fide purchaser, the
owner's right to vindicate the property vis-à-vis the purchaser
prescribes after 20 years: but even then the purchaser has not
become the owner and the property, in theory at least, will be
owned by the Crown!

3–09   As we said earlier, land is often treated differently from other
forms of property. It has long been the law of Scotland that a
person can acquire real rights in land as a consequence of
possession, i.e. by positive prescription. For example, a positive
servitude can be acquired merely by exercise, apparently as a
matter of right, for a continuous period of 20 years.[2] In other cases
there must be a constituent deed known as a foundation writ. This
deed must be *ex facie* valid: for example, it must be signed by the
granter. It must not be a forgery. Then, if founding on the deed,
the grantee (or his successors) possesses the land continuously,
openly, peaceably and without judicial interruption for a period of
10 years, the grantee becomes the holder of the real right which
the deed purported to convey.[3] Thus, for example, if A disponed a
house to B which in fact was owned by C, if B possessed the house
for 10 years, then he would become the owner by positive
prescription. In other words, C's title would be extinguished and B
would acquire a new title to the land. Indeed, positive prescription
can operate when the foundation writ has been granted *a non
domino* (i.e. by a non-owner). What this means is that B could ask
A to grant him a disposition of land that both knew that A does
not own: if B possesses that land for 10 years, he acquires
ownership by positive prescription. As so often in property law, in
so far as establishing title is concerned, the good faith of the
grantee is not a relevant issue. Before positive prescription can
operate in these cases, the foundation writ has to have been
recorded in the Register of Sasines, the old Register of Deeds. But,
most land in Scotland is now subject to the system of registration
of title in the Land Register of Scotland under which the scope of

---

[1] 1973 Act, para.(g) of Sch.3.
[2] *ibid.*, s.3(2).
[3] *ibid.*, s.1(1).

acquisition of land by positive prescription is much reduced. This can only be understood after registration of title has been explained.

It should be noticed that, in contrast to the ownership of corporeal moveable property, the ownership of land is imprescriptible, i.e. it is not subject to the long negative prescription of 20 years.[4] So for example, if A squats on B's land for 30 years, A can still seek to have B ejected from the property. But if B was possessing A's land in reliance on a foundation writ, then positive prescription could operate after 10 years. In this case, A's ownership is extinguished when B becomes the owner of the land by positive prescription. Because he is no longer the owner of the property, A cannot then seek to eject B. But this arises as a consequence of the operation of positive as opposed to negative prescription.

(f) Registration of a Real Right in Land in the Land Register

Ownership of land—as well as other real rights in land—is **3–10** obtained by registering the deed which grants the right in the Land Register of Scotland set up by the Land Registration (Scotland) Act 1979. Registration gives the grantee a statutory title to the real right in question. Thus if A dispones a house to B which is in fact owned by C, then as soon as the disposition is registered, B becomes the owner of the property. Put another way, as soon as the deed is registered, C's ownership is extinguished and B becomes the owner of the house. There is no need for B to possess the land for 10 years. Moreover, so far as title is concerned, good faith on the part of A or B is not necessary.[5]

It may be open to C to seek rectification of the Register on the ground that, according to the ordinary rules of property law,[6] the wrong person appears on the Register as the owner and that the Register is therefore inaccurate. In our example, if the Keeper accepted that the deed was not granted by the owner, he could rectify the Register and substitute C's name for B's whereby B's title is extinguished and C obtains the ownership of the property. But if the registered owner, B, is in possession of the property, rectification will not be allowed unless the inaccuracy was B's fault, i.e. it arose as a consequence of B's fraud or carelessness. Where rectification is refused for this reason, C would normally have a claim for indemnity (i.e. compensation) against the Keeper.

It will be clear that the acquisition of the ownership of land **3–11** involves two systems of law. First, the legal system laid down by the

---

[4] *ibid.*, para.(a) of Sch.3.
[5] In practice, such cases are rare as the Keeper will not usually accept a deed he considers to have been granted *a non domino*.
[6] i.e. the pre-registration of title law of property.

1979 Act which provides that the person who is registered as owner *is* the owner as a matter of law (positive system). Secondly, the pre-1979 Act principles of ordinary pre-registration property law which are used to determine whether the person registered as owner would be owner under that (i.e. pre-1979 Act) system: if not, the Register is inaccurate and can be rectified[7] (negative system). As it involves two systems of law, Scots land law is now "bijural".

The Keeper may only have been prepared to register a title on the basis that indemnity is excluded. Where indemnity has been excluded, rectification is possible even when the proprietor is in possession and not at fault. If, as usually will be the case, the Keeper has excluded indemnity in respect of a deed granted by a non-owner, then the former owner can seek rectification and, if successful, will obtain a new statutory title. Since the right to seek rectification is only lost when the long negative prescription has expired, the registered owner's title remains vulnerable to rectification for 20 years. However, where indemnity has been excluded, it is provided by s.1(1)(b) of the Prescription and Limitation (Scotland) Act 1973 that, if the owner possesses the property described in the title sheet for 10 years, his title becomes exempt from challenge: consequently, the former owner cannot seek rectification even though his right to do so has not prescribed under the long negative prescription. Thus when dealing with registered title, positive prescription only operates where indemnity has been excluded and its function is not to enable the registered proprietor to acquire ownership of the land but rather to prevent his statutory title from being set aside as a consequence of rectification. Traditionally, positive prescription operated to confer ownership after 10 years' possession and thereby extinguish the title of the previous owner.

The reason for this is that registration of a disposition in the Land Register is always original—as opposed to derivative— acquisition of the ownership of land. When A, the owner, dispones land to B, on registration of the disposition A's title is extinguished and B acquires a new—statutory—title to the property. This may be subject to rectification but until the register is rectified B is the owner. For example:

(i) A dispones land to C. A then dispones the same land to B. C registers the disposition in the Land Register thereby acquiring a statutory title to the property. If B is then able to persuade the Keeper to register his disposition, B will become the owner of the property and C's title is extinguished. Under the ordinary rules of property law,

---

[7] Or an indemnity paid by the Keeper.

because he registered before B, C's real right should have had priority over B's. The Register is therefore inaccurate. C can seek rectification and if successful would obtain a new statutory title and B's title would be extinguished. If C failed, he would usually obtain payment of indemnity from the Keeper. Alternatively, C could sue A for breach of contract in granting a disposition to B of the land he had already sold to C, i.e. C has also a personal right against A to sue him for breach of contract.

(ii) A enters into a contract with C for the sale of A's land. B persuades A to break his contract with C and sell the land to B. A dispones the land to B. B registers the disposition in the Land Register thereby acquiring a statutory title to the property. Under the ordinary rules of property law, C could seek reduction of the disposition and compel A to grant a disposition to him on the ground that B's real right was an "offside goal". The Register is therefore inaccurate. C can seek rectification and if successful could eventually[8] obtain a new statutory title and B's title would be extinguished. Alternatively, C could sue A for breach of contract in granting a disposition to B of land that he had already agreed to sell to C or C could sue B in delict for inducing A to break his contract with C, i.e. C has a personal right against A for breach of contract and a personal right in delict against B for reparation.

While registration of a deed in the Land Register is a form of original acquisition of ownership of land, nevertheless we have to use the ordinary rules of property to determine whether the Register is inaccurate thus triggering the possibility of rectification. This involves issues which are the same as arise in relation to derivative acquisition, in particular the principle that no one can transfer a title which he does not have, *nemo dat quod non habet*. And as we have seen, the registered owner's title may be annullable, i.e. can be reduced because of, for example, the "offside goals" rule. These issues will be discussed in detail in the next chapter.

(g) *Incorporeal Moveable Property*

In the case of intellectual property such as copyright or a design **3–12** right, the first owner is the author or the designer, respectively. A person who has been granted a patent is obliged to register it in

---

[8] (i) C would have to have B's disposition reduced; (ii) the Keeper would enter A as owner in the Register; (iii) A would grant a disposition to C and (iv) the Keeper would register C's disposition by entering C as owner.

the register of patents. Shares in a company are owned by the shareholder and share certificates are evidence of a shareholder's title to the shares.

It has been argued that a person can be said to "own" personal rights. For example, if A lends money to B, A has a personal right against B to have the loan repaid. In other words, A "owns" B's debt. This is important because A is entitled to assign the debt to a third party, C ,who may pay A for the assignation. C's payment to A will usually be less than the sum B owes, but A will avoid the difficulties of enforcing payment and the risk that B will become insolvent before the debt is paid. If C intimates the assignation to B, he will have a real right and his assignation will have priority if A should later assign the same debt to another person, D. If C delays in intimating the assignation and D intimates her assignation before C, D's assignation will have priority. After intimation, B must pay the debt to the assignee and not the original creditor, A (the cedent).

3–13   Because of the possibility of assignation, it is useful to regard A, the obligee or creditor, as the "owner" of the debt even though what is owned is only a personal right and could prove of little value if B, the obligor or debtor, should become insolvent before the debt is paid.

An obligee or creditor will become the owner of a personal right when the legal criteria for the formation of the obligation are satisfied. These criteria will be discussed in detail in later chapters. It should be remembered that in the case of bank notes, the bank promises to pay the *bearer* the sum stipulated in the note. It therefore follows that the person who has the possession of the note is the obligee and can call on the bank to perform. In practice, the note is simply transferred as a means of exchange, i.e. as currency from one person to another and there is no need of intimation of the assignation to the obligor, i.e. the bank.

Further reading

Carey Miller and Irvine, *Corporeal Moveables in Scots Law* (2nd ed., 2005)

Gretton and Reid, *Conveyancing* (3rd ed., 2005)

Halliday's Conveyancing Law and Practice in Scotland, Vol. 1 (2nd ed., 1996)

Halliday's Conveyancing Law and Practice in Scotland, Vol. 2 (2nd ed., 1997)

Johnston, *Prescription and Limitation* (1999)

CHAPTER 4

THE LAW OF PROPERTY III

Derivative Acquisition of Ownership

Introduction

Derivative acquisition arises when A, the owner of property, **4–01** transfers the ownership of the property to B who becomes the owner in turn: as a consequence of the transfer, A is divested of the ownership of the property and B is invested with ownership. B's title to the property *derives* from A's. The validity of B's title is, inter alia, dependent on the validity of A's title as well as whether or not the transfer has been executed properly. Traditionally in Scots law, the transfer of the ownership of property is known as the conveyance of the property.

Transfer of ownership is either voluntary or involuntary. In the former, the owner wishes to transfer his property to the transferee: in the latter, he does not wish to do so. This would arise when an owner becomes insolvent and his property is transferred to his trustee in bankruptcy: or when he dies and his property is transferred to his executor to be distributed in accordance with the provisions of his will or the rules of intestate succession (when the deceased dies without a will or his will does not dispose of all his property). We shall consider the law of succession in Chapter 11. In both voluntary and involuntary transfer the transferee has to consent to the transfer. No one can be compelled to accept the ownership of property unless he has agreed to do so: thus we can avoid having a white elephant thrust upon us.

The *nemo dat* principle

Before A can transfer ownership to B, A must be the owner of **4–02** the property. If A is not the owner he cannot transfer the ownership of the property to B, as a person cannot transfer what he does not have: *nemo dat quod non habet*—the *nemo dat* principle.

Thus if A steals C's horse and purports to transfer the ownership to B, B cannot obtain a valid title to the horse as it is stolen property. The ownership of the horse remains with C even though A has possession and therefore the benefit of the presumption of ownership. Even if B is a bona fide transferee for value of the horse, A cannot transfer what he does not have and therefore B does not become the owner of the horse. Therefore C can vindicate the horse and demand that B give him, the animal's owner, possession of the horse. If B bought the horse from A, B has a personal right to sue A for breach of the term implied in every contract of sale of goods that the seller has the right to sell the goods: s.12 of the Sale of Goods Act 1979.

There might be other reasons why A does not have title to transfer to B. If A had acquired the horse from C, the purported transfer of ownership between C and A could have been defective with the result that A acquires no title at all or his title is vulnerable to being set aside, i.e. to be reduced. For example, if C had transferred the horse to A believing that he was D, this error could be so fundamental that the conveyance is null and ownership does not pass from C to A and therefore A has no title to convey to B. In these circumstances it is said that A's title is null or void.

4–03   Usually, however, the transfer between C and A is not so fundamentally flawed as to be a nullity. Instead, the conveyance may be liable to be reduced, i.e. A's title can be set aside. In these circumstances, A's title is said to be annullable or voidable. For example, if C was old and vulnerable, i.e. facile, and transferred the ownership of the horse to A because A had threatened to put C in a nursing home, the conveyance could be set aside on the ground of facility and circumvention, i.e. the conveyance had been obtained when the transferor was facile and vulnerable to pressure from the transferee. But until it is set aside, the conveyance is effective to transfer the ownership of the horse to A so that A has a good title to pass to B at any time before the transfer from C to A is reduced. If A has transferred ownership to B *before the conveyance from C to A has been reduced*, the right to reduce the conveyance is lost. Therefore B will obtain a good title which cannot be challenged by C.

Thus, in applying the *nemo dat* principle, it is necessary to determine whether or not the transferor A is the owner of the property. In turn, this may involve consideration of how the transferor A obtained title. As in the mistaken identity example above, there can be occasions when the conveyance by C to the transferor A is null. However, these are exceptional cases. Defects of consent such as facility and circumvention, duress and error induced by misrepresentation will generally only render the conveyance annullable. Until set aside, the transferor A will therefore have a good title to transfer to B, a bona fide transferee of the property, and the transfer to B will bar the right of C, the previous owner, to seek reduction of the earlier conveyance. In effect, the title of the bona fide acquirer will be protected except in cases where the property has been stolen.[1]

Where a previous owner, C, has lost the right to have a **4-04** conveyance reduced because his transferee, A, has conveyed the property to a bona fide transferee, B, what remedy does C have against A? The answer lies in the law of obligations. If the defect in the conveyance was caused by a wrong (delict), for example if C was induced to transfer the property to A as a result of A's fraudulent misrepresentation, then C could seek reparation from A for the value of the property. Even if the defective title did not arise from a wrong, for example if C was induced to transfer the property as a result of A's innocent misrepresentation, C may be able to obtain recompense from A to the extent that A remains enriched as a consequence of the transfer.

For example, C is induced to gift property to A as a result of A's innocent misrepresentation. A sells the property to B. If the price is still in A's private patrimony, its retention is without cause, it has no legal basis as C could have had the conveyance of the property to A reduced on the ground of A's innocent misrepresentation. The enrichment is therefore unjustified and prima facie A should transfer the price he received from B for the property to C. If C had *sold* the property to A, he can only obtain recompense from A to the extent that the price A obtained from B was greater than the price A paid to C. In both cases, C's rights against A are personal rights and will be of little value if A was insolvent.

The *nemo dat* principle applies to all kinds of property, heritable as well as moveable. But as we have seen, in relation to land a grantee acquires an original statutory title as soon as the disposition is registered in the Land Register. The *nemo dat* principle becomes important if the title is challenged on the ground that the Register is inaccurate because the granter of the disposition had no title to dispone. In principle the Register can be rectified by extinguishing the grantee's statutory title and creating a new statutory title in favour of the person entitled to be the owner in accordance with the ordinary rules of property law.

There are exceptional situations where the *nemo dat* principle does not apply and a non-owner can confer ownership of property on another. These will be discussed at the end of this chapter.

The Transfer of Ownership—the Conveyance

What is required to transfer the ownership of property from A to **4-05** B depends on the nature of the property. A conveyance is a juristic act, i.e. "an act in the law". But often conveyances are preceded by

---

[1] If B is in bad faith, i.e. knows that A's title is voidable, B will still obtain a valid title. The "offside goals" rule will apply so that A's conveyance to B remains liable to be reduced by C. However, until reduction, B has a valid—if voidable— title which he can, in turn, transfer to another person any time before reduction.

other kinds of juristic acts, in particular a contract between the granter and grantee of the conveyance. Here the transfer of ownership amounts to the *performance* of the obligations created by the preceding juristic act. Accordingly, what amounts to a valid transfer of property may sometimes depend on the nature of the preceding juristic act as well as the nature of the property. Indeed, there are situations when the conveyance and the preceding juristic act appear to coincide. Nevertheless, it is important for accurate legal analysis to remember that even if intimately connected, the preceding juristic act is always a separate "act in the law" from the conveyance.

The following are common examples of conveyances of property:

(a) Sale of heritable property

4–06   A agrees to sell his house to B. Once the terms are agreed and the agreement put into writing, there will be a contract for the sale of the land: the contract is known as missives of sale. Under Scots law a contract for the transfer of a real right in land is not constituted unless it is in writing and signed by the parties: s.1(2)(a)(i) of the Requirements of Writing (Scotland) Act 1995. Because no contract is formed until the written formalities are satisfied, as a general principle either party is free to withdraw from the agreement before it is put in writing. Once the contract is formed, A has an obligation to transfer the title to B and B has an obligation to pay the price. As the property concerned is land, i.e. heritage, in order to perform his contractual obligation to transfer the title A grants a disposition transferring the ownership of the property to B. A must deliver the disposition to B who is then entitled to register the deed in the Land Register. In executing and delivering the disposition, A fulfils his contractual obligation to transfer the ownership of the property. But, of course, B does not obtain a real right in the land until he registers the disposition in the Land Register: only by doing so does B obtain ownership of the house and A's title is extinguished.

It will be noticed that A retains the ownership of the land until B registers the disposition. His ownership of the property is not affected by delivering the disposition although he would be in breach of his contractual obligations if he attempted to prevent B from registering the disposition. This is important if A becomes insolvent. If this occurs before A has delivered the disposition and before B has paid the price, B can withhold payment as A is no longer able to provide B with a good title and is not able to fulfil his contractual obligations. But once the disposition has been delivered to B, A has fulfilled his contractual obligations even though A's ownership of the property has not been extinguished. Therefore if A becomes insolvent after he has delivered the disposition to B but before the disposition has been registered, the house is still A's property; it is still part of A's private patrimony. It will fall to A's trustee in bankruptcy for the benefit of his creditors, if the trustee registers his act and warrant before B registers the disposition. Moreover, as A has fulfilled his contractual obligations, the trustee in bankruptcy can retain the price if it has been paid or, indeed, demand payment if B has not yet done so!

There is an exception to this rule where A is a company and has granted to a creditor a security known as a floating charge over "property . . . comprised in its [i.e. the company's] property and undertaking": s.462(1) of the Companies Act 1985; s.53(7) of the Insolvency Act 1986. It has been held that the company's "property and undertaking" does not include land of which the company was the registered owner but which had been purchased by a third party who had paid the price and to whom a disposition had been delivered but which had not yet been registered before the company became insolvent. Accordingly, the land was not subject to the security when the floating charge crystallised on the company's insolvency.

Although A remains the owner of the land until B registers the disposition, it is well settled that the risk of damage to or destruction of the property passes to the purchaser as soon as the contract, i.e. the missives of sale, has been formed. So for example, the purchaser of a house takes the risk that the house that he has bought will burn down between the date that missives are concluded, i.e. when the contract is formed and the date of entry when he takes possession of the property. This means that the purchaser should take out insurance in respect of risks to property he does not possess and over which he has no control. This makes little sense. And so in practice a purchaser's solicitor will often negotiate an express term in the missives of sale that the risk is not to pass to the purchaser until the date of entry. It is by utilising the law of contract that persons can expressly stipulate the rules that are to apply in their situation and thereby change the rules which would have otherwise applied in the absence of their contract. Rules which would have applied in the absence of different express contractual provisions are known as a default regime.

(b) Gift

A promises B that he will make B a gift. Under Scots law, a **4–07** gratuitous unilateral obligation, i.e. a promise, is not constituted unless it is in writing and signed by the promisor: s.1(2)(a)(ii) of the Requirements of Writing (Scotland) Act 1995. (Few people are aware of, let alone fulfil, these formalities when they promise to give someone a present: and so, as a general rule, a promisor incurs no liability if he changes his mind and decides not to give a present to the promisee, i.e. the person to whom the promise is made). On the assumption that A's promise is put in writing and signed by him, A will be under a gratuitous unilateral obligation to transfer the ownership of the property which is the subject of the gift to B. Where this is corporeal moveable property such as a watch or a horse, ownership is transferred by physical delivery (*traditio*), i.e. when the horse or watch is delivered by A into the possession of B. If before delivery, A changes his mind, he will be in breach of his gratuitous unilateral obligation and B can seek specific implement to compel him to perform or alternatively, damages for breach. If A had promised to give heritable property to B, on the assumption that all the formalities are satisfied, A will be obliged to deliver a disposition to B which B can register in the Land Register thereby obtaining ownership of the property and extinguishing A's title to the land. In these circumstances, the disposition will often stipulate that the property is being conveyed to the grantee "for love, favour and affection".

In practice it is rare for A to promise B that A will give a gift to B. It is rarer still for such a promise to be put into writing so that it can become enforceable as a gratuitous unilateral obligation. Instead, A will often decide to give B a present without telling B of his intention to do so. The mere intention to make B a gift is not a juristic act and is unenforceable by the intended donee, B, who will often have no idea of A's intention. For this reason, A is able to change her mind and decide not to donate any property to B. However, if A wishes to fulfil his intention to gift the property to B, A must transfer the ownership of the property to B with the consent of B. Again, the conveyance of the title will depend on the nature of the property. Thus, for example, corporeal moveable property must be delivered to the donee; there must be a disposition of heritage to the donee which can be registered in the Land Register; bank notes must be delivered to the donee who will then become the bearer to whom the bank's obligation is owed; other incorporeal property will have to be assigned to the donee and intimated to the obligor.

It is an axiomatic principle that in the ordinary case of gift, a donor can change her mind at any time before ownership of the property has been transferred to the donee. But it is possible for the donor to become personally barred from changing her mind. This would occur if, for example, the donor had informed the donee that he was to receive a gift and then encourages the donee to expend monies or otherwise act to his detriment in the expectation of receipt of the gift. But it is also an axiomatic principle that once ownership has passed to the donee, the donor can no longer change her mind and demand the return of the property. For example, if with the intention of giving her a present, A gives his mistress a chinchilla wrap worth £10k or conveys a house to her "for love, favour and affection", then she becomes the owner of the wrap as soon as it is delivered to her and the owner of the house as soon as the disposition is registered in the Land

Register. Once she has become its owner, A cannot demand that the property be returned. This can have devastating effects for donors. If for example parents make a gift of money or land to their children, they have no right to have the property returned if they fall on hard times: and under Scots law children have no obligation to aliment, i.e. maintain their parents!

It may be for this reason that there is a presumption against donation. What this means is that if B has possession of property that formerly was owned by A there is a presumption that A did not intend to gift the property to B when it was transferred to B. The onus lies on B to rebut the presumption by establishing that A intended B to have the property as a gift. This could be done if, for example B could show that A transferred the property to B at Christmas or on B's birthday. For this reason it is sensible to ask a donor expressly to stipulate that the transfer of a large sum of money or very valuable property was indeed intended as a gift. Ironically, perhaps in the light of the example given in the previous paragraph, there is no presumption against donation when the transfer of ownership is from parent to child: but the presumption against donation does apply in relation to transfers between spouses, civil partners and cohabitants.

(c) Sale of Goods

The most common juristic act which precedes the transfer of **4–08** ownership of property is a contract for the sale of goods. A contract for the sale of goods is a contract for the transfer of the ownership of corporeal moveable property in return for money, i.e. the price of the goods. Unlike a contract for the sale of land, no formalities are required: s.1(1) of the Requirements of Writing (Scotland) Act 1995. It is therefore enough that the parties are agreed that goods should be sold. The agreement can be written or oral or by conduct, for example when A picks up a newspaper in a shop and pays for it at the check-out. Where the parties have not expressly agreed the terms of their bargain, certain terms will automatically be implied into the contract by virtue of the provisions of the Sale of Goods Act 1979 (the 1979 Act) which provides a statutory codification of the law on the sale of goods. Indeed, the only matter upon which the parties must expressly be agreed is the goods to be bought and sold, as it is settled that a buyer must pay a reasonable price if the parties have not agreed a price in the contract: s.8(2) of the 1979 Act.

When the contract of sale is formed, the seller is obliged to transfer the ownership of the goods to the buyer and it is an implied term of the contract that the seller has a right to sell the goods: s.12(1) of the 1979 Act. The buyer is under a corresponding contractual obligation to pay the price of the goods. Goods are corporeal moveable property. As we have seen, in the case of gift, title to corporeal moveable property is transferred when the property is delivered to the donee. At common law this was also the case when the conveyance was preceded by a contract for the sale of goods. Thus ownership was transferred from the seller to the buyer when the seller delivered the goods to the purchaser. But as in contracts for the sale of land, the risk of damage to or destruction of the property passed to the buyer as soon as the contract was formed. However, the traditional rules on the conveyance of the ownership of goods when they are sold has been altered radically by statute and the law is now to be found in Part 3 of the 1979 Act.

4–09 As a general principle, ownership of property cannot be transferred while the goods are unascertained, i.e. are unidentified, such as generic goods: s.16. When the goods are ascertained, i.e. identified for a particular contract, or are specific, i.e. were intended to be the subject matter of a particular sale at the time the contract was made, then ownership can be transferred between seller and buyer. But instead of delivery being the way in which ownership is transferred, the 1979 Act provides a different method of conveying the ownership of the goods which are being sold. Under s.17(1) of the 1979 Act, "Where there is a contract for the sale of specific or ascertained goods the property in them is transferred to the buyer at such time as the parties to the contract intend it to be transferred". The "property" in the goods means the ownership of the goods. Thus the transfer of the ownership of the goods no longer turns on the delivery of the goods to the buyer, a juristic act which is separate from the preceding contract of sale: instead, it turns on when the parties *intended* the ownership of the goods to be transferred. Nevertheless, the transfer of ownership is still a separate juristic act from the formation of the contract of sale even though the existence of both now turns on the intention of the parties.

There is no difficulty if the parties expressly stipulate when they wish the ownership of the goods to pass. But in the vast majority of sales the parties do not do so. Thus it is necessary to infer the intention of the parties from the terms of the contract, their conduct and all the circumstances of the case: s.17(2) of the 1979 Act. Because of the difficulty of establishing the parties' intentions, s.18 of the 1979 Act has rules for ascertaining the intention of the parties on when the ownership of the goods should pass: the presumptive intention of the parties laid down by the rules will operate unless it is clear that they had a different intention. These are the rules:

4–10 Rule 1—Where there is an unconditional contract for the sale of specific goods in a deliverable state, it is presumed that the property in the goods passes to the buyer when the contract is made. It does not matter whether the time of payment or the time of delivery is later.

The effect of this provision may seem to telescope together the contract of sale and the conveyance of the ownership of the goods. Nevertheless, they are still two separate juristic acts. The reason why the ownership of the goods is conveyed from seller to the buyer is because the parties intend title to pass. The rule is that in the absence of evidence to the contrary, there is a presumption that it was the intention of the parties that ownership should pass at the time the contract is formed. So for example, A agrees to sell a particular puppy from a litter to B. As the contract is for the sale of specific goods, unless there is evidence to the contrary it is presumed that the parties intended that B should become the owner of the dog at the time the contract was formed. It does not matter that the parties have agreed that B does not have to pay the price until the date when the puppy will actually be delivered or that the date of delivery is not to take place until the puppy is eight weeks old. Therefore B becomes the owner of the puppy as soon as the contract is formed.

Rule 2—Where there is a sale of specific goods and the seller has to do something to the goods to put them into a deliverable state, it is presumed that the property does not pass until the thing is done and the buyer has been informed. So for example, if A and B had agreed that the puppy should not be delivered until its tail had been cut, then there is a presumption that the parties intended that ownership should not pass to B until he had been informed by A that the dog's tail had been cut.

Rule 3—Where there is a sale of specific goods in a deliverable **4–11** state and the seller has to do something to the goods to ascertain the price, for example, weigh or measure them, it is presumed that the property does not pass until the thing has been done and the buyer informed.

Rule 4—Where goods are sold on approval or a sale or return basis, it is presumed that ownership passes to the buyer when he signifies his approval or acceptance to the seller or fails to return the goods within the contractually stipulated period or a reasonable time.

Rule 5—Where there is a contract for unascertained goods or future goods, there is a presumption that the ownership will pass to the buyer when goods of that description and in a deliverable state are unconditionally appropriated for that contract. In this context "appropriated" means that the goods have been earmarked as the subjects of the sale. So if in our example, A agreed to sell B a puppy from his bitch's litter, then this is a sale of unascertained goods as the particular puppy to be sold has not been identified at the time the contract is formed: if the bitch had not had her puppies at the time the contract was formed, it would be a contract for future goods. But once the seller has appropriated a particular puppy for the purpose of the sale or the buyer has chosen a particular puppy, then it is presumed that title then passes to the buyer. The appropriation must have the respective approval of the seller or the buyer, but such approval can be given in advance of the appropriation. So for example, B could agree that A should choose the puppy to be sold to him once the puppies are born.

4–12　　These rules are technical and artificial. For instance, if B agrees with A to buy all the puppies in the litter, that is a contract for specific goods and the ownership of the puppies passes from A to B at the time the contract is made: but if B agrees to buy one puppy from the litter, that is a contract for unascertained goods and it is only when a puppy has been appropriated by A as the subject of the sale that ownership passes to B.

Nevertheless, the position is relatively clear. Ownership of the goods being sold passes when the parties intend it to pass. Where the goods are unascertained at the time the contract is formed, ownership cannot pass until goods have been identified and appropriated as the subject of the contract: it is presumed that the parties intended the ownership to pass when the goods were so earmarked. Where the goods are specific and in a deliverable state at the time the contract is formed, it is presumed that the parties intended the ownership of the goods to pass at the time the contract is formed. The Rules in s.18 only apply where there is no contrary intention. It is therefore open to the parties expressly to stipulate when ownership of the goods is to pass. It is their intention that will ultimately determine whether or not ownership of the goods has been conveyed from the seller to the buyer.

This has several important repercussions. If A sells goods to B, the parties can agree that the ownership of the goods is not to pass to B until B has paid for the goods or paid any other sums which are outstanding between them. In these circumstances, A will retain the ownership of the goods even if B has possession of them. This is known as a retention of title clause. For example, A sells goods to B but reserves title until B pays for the goods. If B becomes insolvent before he has paid for the goods, then A can vindicate the property, i.e. exercise his real right as owner in the goods, and is not restricted to his personal right to sue for the price which may be of little value owing to B's insolvency.

4–13　　To be able to vindicate, A must still be the owner of the goods. If his right of ownership has been extinguished while the goods have been in B's possession, A will no longer be able to vindicate and will be left to his personal remedies against B. This might happen if A sold raw materials to B. Even though A reserves title until payment of the price, if B uses the raw materials to manufacture a product, A may cease to be the owner as a result of specification: then it is B and not A who is the owner of the product manufactured from the raw materials. A is therefore restricted to his personal right to sue for the price or alternatively a personal right under the law of unjustified enrichment to seek the value of the manufactured goods. But both these claims are only personal rights and will be of limited value if B is insolvent.

The rule that transfer of title depends on the intention of the parties rather than delivery of the goods might appear to threaten the principle that a security right over corporeal moveables can only be created if the debtor transfers possession to the creditor. For example, A lends B £5k. If A wishes security over B's watch for his loan, B must transfer the possession of the watch to A. This is known as pledge. However, why should B not "sell" the watch to A for £5k and the parties agree that the ownership of the watch should pass to A while B should continue to have possession of the property? Indeed, as the watch constitutes specific goods in a deliverable state, rule 1 would apply and it would be presumed that it was the parties' intention that the ownership of the watch would pass to A as soon as the contract was formed. A would undertake to "sell" the watch back to B on the payment of £5k plus a sum that would amount to interest on the "loan". This arrangement would circumvent the need for the creditor to have possession of the property before there is a valid security. Because of this possibility, s.62(4) of the 1979 Act provides that the statute's provisions about contracts for the sale of goods do not apply to a transaction in the form of a contract of sale which is intended to operate by way of pledge or other security. Accordingly, the principle that property passes when the parties intend it to pass and the presumption in rule 1 that ownership of specific goods will pass when the contract is formed, do not apply to sales operating by way of pledge. Thus in the example, A does not become the owner of the watch in spite of the apparent sale between A and B and therefore has no real right in the watch which would give him an advantage over B's unsecured creditors should B become insolvent. To obtain such a security the ordinary rules for the constitution of a pledge must be followed and the possession of the watch transferred to A.

It should be noticed that s.62(4) of the 1979 Act does not affect **4–14** the validity of a reservation of title by the seller until the price or all sums owed have been paid by the buyer. In a reservation of title situation, the goods are owned by the seller (creditor) until the buyer (debtor) pays the price or the other debts. Because he has retained title, the seller continues to have a real right of ownership in the property which can be exercised should the buyer become insolvent. While this will give the seller an advantage over unsecured creditors of the buyer, this is because the seller remains owner of the property not because he has a security right over property which is or has been owned by the buyer: A security transaction involves a right over property owned by someone else: because B owned the watch in the example the apparent sale was by way of a security. Where there is a retention of title clause, the buyer-debtor does not become the owner of the property until the price or other debts are paid. If he became insolvent before the price or other debts were paid, he will not have become the owner of the goods. As the goods were never owned by the debtor they cannot be the subject of a security transaction. Therefore the sale with the reservation of title clause cannot fall foul of s.64(4) of the 1979 Act as it is not a sale by way of pledge or other security. It is irrelevant that the practical effect of a reservation of title is to give the seller-creditor priority over unsecured creditors if the debtor becomes insolvent because the seller has always had a real right of ownership in the goods.

Under s.20(1) of the 1979 Act it is stipulated that risk of damage to or destruction of the goods remains with the seller until the property in them is transferred to the buyer. It therefore follows that where the ownership of the goods *has* been transferred to the buyer, the risk passes to him whether or not the goods have been delivered. For example, if A sells a painting to B, Rule 1 of the 1979 Act applies and it is presumed that the parties intended that the ownership of the painting should pass to B at the time the contract was formed. This means that B takes the risk of damage to or destruction of the picture before it has been delivered to him and while he has no control over it. If delivery of the goods is delayed through the fault of either seller or buyer, they are at the risk of the party at fault but only in respect of losses which would not have arisen but for the default: s.20(2) of the 1979 Act.

4–15   It was always open to the parties to alter these rules by making alternative provision in their contract. As there was little merit in the rule where the purchaser was buying specific goods from a retailer for domestic use or consumption, it became quite common in practice for the seller to agree that risk was not to pass to the buyer until the goods were delivered. The law has been amended better to reflect social realities and s.20(4) of the 1979 Act now provides that where there is a consumer contract in which the buyer is a consumer, the goods remain at the seller's risk until they are delivered to the consumer. This provision is only concerned with the passing of risk in consumer contracts of sale, i.e. where the purchaser is buying the goods for private use or consumption and the seller sells them in the course of his business. It does not affect the passing of risk in other contracts of sale of goods, i.e. business to business, private person to private person or consumer seller to business buyer. Nor does it affect the principle that in all contracts of sale, property in the goods passes when the parties intend it to pass and that their intentions can be presumed from the rules in s.18 of the 1979 Act unless it is clear that the parties have a different intention.

The ownership of the property passes from the seller to the buyer when the parties intend it to pass. As previously mentioned, this is a separate juristic act from the contract of sale of goods which precedes or accompanies it. This remains true even if there is a presumption in the case of specific goods in a deliverable state that the parties intend the title to pass as soon as the contract is formed as opposed to, for example, the time when the goods are delivered to the buyer. Given the close temporal proximity of the formation of the contract and the passing of title, the question arises how, if at all, the conveyance of the ownership of the goods is affected by any defects in the contract of sale.

As in the case of contracts for the sale of heritage, the parties may have contracted under such defects of consent that both the contract and the subsequent conveyance are null. Such cases are extremely rare but could arise if the seller contracted under an error as to the identity of the buyer so that the sale and the transfer of ownership were to the wrong person. In such circumstances, title has never been transferred to the buyer who has no title to pass to a third party. But usually a defect of consent only renders a contract and conveyance annullable (voidable). Until the conveyance and the contract have been reduced, the buyer has a valid, if vulnerable, title to the goods. He therefore has a title which he can pass to a third party. If the third party transferee is in good faith not only does she obtain the ownership of the goods but the original seller loses his right to have the defective conveyance and contract reduced. Where the third party acquirer has purchased the goods, s.23 of the 1979 Act provides[2] that, when the seller of goods has a voidable title to them, but his title has not been avoided at the time of the sale, the buyer acquires a good title to the goods provided he buys them in good faith and without notice of the seller's defect in title.

For example, A is induced by B's misrepresentation to sell his **4–16** watch to B. Assume the contract and the conveyance can be annulled as a consequence of B's misrepresentation. The contract is for the sale of specific goods in a deliverable state. Under rule 1 it is presumed that the ownership of the watch passes to B as soon as the contract is formed. Before he has been paid, A delivers the watch to B. Without paying A, B then sells the watch to C, a bona fide purchaser. Because of B's misrepresentation, the conveyance and the contract can be set aside in an action of reduction but until then B has a good, if vulnerable, title to the property. As B has sold on the watch to a bona fide purchaser before the conveyance and sale have been set aside, by s.23 of the 1979 Act C acquires a good derivative title to the ownership of the watch and A loses his right to seek reduction. A is left to his right to sue in debt for the price or in delict for the value of the watch if the misrepresentation was fraudulent or negligent. If the misrepresentation was innocent A could sue under the law of unjustified enrichment for any difference between the agreed price and the price B obtained from C. But these are only personal rights and could be of little value if

---

[2] Section 23 is a statutory statement of a well established principle of the law of property.

B was insolvent. On the other hand, if this was an exceptional case where the conveyance and the contract were null because of the fundamental nature of the error induced by B's misrepresentation, then no title would be transferred to B and B would have no title to pass to C even though he is a bona fide purchaser. Section 23 of the 1979 Act would not apply as B's title was void and not merely voidable. A would remain the owner of the watch and could vindicate it from C. C would be left to sue B for breach of the term implied in every contract for the sale of goods that the seller has the right to sell the goods: s.12 of the 1979 Act.

The preceding contract of sale may be unenforceable because it is illegal. This could occur if, for example, the seller sold goods when he did not have the appropriate licence to do so or the goods were sold using the wrong measures, for example imperial rather than metrical. The contract is unenforceable in the sense that the buyer cannot obtain specific implement to compel performance; the seller cannot sue in debt for the price; and neither buyer nor seller can sue for damages for breach of contract. But the illegality will not necessarily taint the transfer of ownership of the goods. Where the parties intend that the ownership should pass to the buyer when the contract is formed, the buyer's title is not vulnerable once the goods are delivered.[3] Consequently he has a good title to pass to a bona fide transferee of the goods. If the seller has retained possession of the goods, even though the buyer is the owner he will not be able to compel the seller to deliver the goods to him as he has to rely directly on the illegal contract to establish that he is the owner.

4–17 Where the buyer has become the owner and the goods have been delivered to him, he cannot be sued for the price if the contract is unenforceable because of illegality. Nevertheless, the goods were transferred to him on the understanding that the seller would be paid. Because the contract is illegal and the seller cannot sue for the price, the legal basis for the buyer having the goods has gone. Therefore the seller will have a claim under the law of unjustified enrichment for restitution of the goods or their value. However, the buyer may be able to establish that it would be inequitable for him to have to restore the goods or pay their value if, for example, he could show that the seller was more morally reprehensible than him in entering an illegal contract.

Section 21(1) of the 1979 Act stipulates that in general the *nemo dat* principle applies to the sale of goods. This means that a buyer will not acquire title to the goods unless the seller was the owner or sold them as the agent of the owner. But the Act then provides two

---

[3] The 1979 Act does not apply to illegal contracts, but the common law does. Accordingly, ownership of specific goods passes on delivery, not when the contract is formed.

important exceptions to the principle. The first is where the seller retains possession of the goods. A sells goods to B. The ownership of the goods has passed to B but A retains possession. A then sells and delivers the goods to C. Section 24 provides that A should be deemed to be authorised by B to sell the goods to C provided C received them in good faith and without notice of A's transaction with B. Therefore C becomes the owner of the goods and B is left with a personal right to sue A for breach of their contract of sale in being unable to convey the ownership of the goods. It should be noticed that s.24 is only triggered if A has delivered the goods to C. If A sells the goods to C but does not deliver the goods to him, the *nemo dat* principle applies. B will remain the owner and it will be C who will be left with the personal right to sue A for breach of the implied term that a seller has the right to sell the goods.

The second is where the buyer is in possession of the goods. A **4–18** sells goods to B. The ownership of the goods has not been transferred to B (typically because there is a retention of title clause) but A has delivered the goods to him. B then sells the goods to C and delivers them to him. Section 25 provides that B should be deemed to be authorised by A to sell the goods to C provided C received them in good faith and without notice of any rights A might have over the goods, for example a reservation of title. Therefore C becomes owner and A is left with a personal right to sue B for the price of the goods. It should be noticed that as in section 24, this provision is not triggered unless the goods are delivered to C. If they are not, the *nemo dat* principle applies and C will be left with a personal right to sue B for breach of the implied term that a seller has the right to sell the goods. In addition, C must receive the goods in good faith and without notice of any rights A may have over the goods. This means that a reservation of title by A would not be effective to prevent C obtaining the ownership of the goods provided C did not know of the existence of the reservation in A's contract with B. This is a reason why in practice reservation of title clauses are of restricted utility where the seller agrees to part with the possession of the goods.

There is another important statutory exception to the *nemo dat* principle. This is concerned with motor cars which are being bought on hire purchase. A wants to buy a car on hire purchase. He chooses a car from a dealer. The dealer receives the price of the car from a finance company that is prepared to lend the money to A. The finance company becomes the owner of the car. The finance company (the lessor) then enters into a contract of hire with A (the lessee or hirer) under which A agrees to hire the car for a fixed period. During that period A undertakes to pay regular instalments which will repay the principal of the loan and interest. It is a term of the contract of hire that after the instalments have been paid the finance company will sell the car to A for a nominal sum. During the period of the hire, while A has possession of the car, the finance company is its owner. If A purports to sell the car to B during that period, he will be in breach of the hire contract which will usually provide that the lessee is not to part with possession of the car without the agreement of the lessor. Moreover, applying the *nemo dat* principle, A has no title to transfer to B. The finance company remains the owner of the car and will be able to vindicate it from B. B is left with a personal right to sue A for breach of the implied term that he has a right to sell the car. This would usually be of little value to B as A will often be insolvent as that is usually the reason he could no longer pay the instalments and had to "sell" the car to B in the first place.

4–19　　It is to alleviate this mischief that ss.27–29 of the Hire Purchase Act 1964 (the 1964 Act) provide a further exception to the *nemo dat* principle. Where B is a private purchaser and is in good faith and has no knowledge of A's contract with the finance company, then A will be deemed to have been vested with the ownership of the car at the time of the sale to B. Accordingly, A will have a good title to transfer to B. It will therefore be the finance company that will be left to its personal right to sue A for breach of the contract of hire in selling the car to B. B will also obtain a good title if A had sold the car to a motor dealer and B had bought the car through the dealer. (The dealer may be liable to the finance company in unjustified enrichment for the profit that it made on the sale to B.)

To be a private purchaser it is enough that B is not a car dealer or a finance company. Therefore the 1964 Act applies if B buys the car for business as well as for domestic use, so the concept of private purchaser is considerably wider than that of consumer in a consumer contract. However, before B obtains the statutory protection there has to be a valid contract of hire purchase between A and the finance company. If, for example, A lied about his identity (as opposed to his creditworthiness), the error is so fundamental that it prevents a contract arising between A and the finance company, i.e. the purported contract of hire purchase between the finance company and A is null or void. As there is no contract of hire purchase at all, then the provisions of the 1964 Act are inapplicable. B will not obtain a good title and the finance company will be able to vindicate the car from him. B will be left to pursue his personal right against A for breach of the implied term under s.12(1) of the 1979 Act that the seller has a right to sell the goods.

(d) Incorporeal Property

4–20　　It is common for people who hold incorporeal heritable property, such as a lease or standard security, to regard themselves as owners. Moreover, it has been contended that it can be useful to talk of owning personal rights such as contractual obligations. This is because personal rights can be sold in the same way as corporeal moveable property. For example, if B owes A £5k, A can sell C this right to recover £5k from B. Often C will pay A less than £5k, but A will have immediate finance and will, of course, be saved from having to pursue B for the money.

The way in which the ownership of such rights is transferred is by assignation. In the example above, A will sign a document transferring to C his rights against B. This is known as an assignation. A is known as the cedent and C is the assignee. C must then intimate the assignation to B, the debtor in the original obligation. It is only when the assignation is intimated that the right to the debt passes from A's private patrimony to C's private patrimony. It is for this reason too that priority of assignations is determined by the date of intimation to the original debtor rather than the date of the assignation. Therefore, if, after having assigned the debt to C, A then assigned the same debt to D, D will have priority if D intimates the assignation to B before C does so. C will not be able to sue B for the original debt since that right belongs to D but will be able to sue A for assigning the same debt to D in breach of the contract of sale of the debt.

Where the right being assigned is a real right such as a lease of **4–21** land, the transfer is complete only when the assignee takes possession or registers the assignation in the Land Register.[4] Intimation is only required if personal rights are also being transferred. This would happen if A lent money to B and had a standard security over B's house in respect of the debt. If A assigned the debt and the standard security to C, C must intimate the transfer of the debt to B and register the assignation of the standard security in the Land Register.

Some real rights cannot be assigned because they benefit a particular piece of land. For example, a servitude cannot be assigned on its own as it benefits the benefited property and is only enforceable by the owner or tenant of that property. This is also the case with real burdens, for example, restrictions on the use of property, which can only be enforced by the owner or tenant of the benefited property.

The Extinction of Real Rights

If a real right in property is not exercised for a continuous period **4–22** of 20 years, it will be extinguished by the long negative prescription: s.8(1) of the Prescription and Limitation (Scotland) Act 1973

---

[4] These are not alternatives. An assignation must be completed in the same ways as the original real right. So, for example, the assignation of a standard security requires registration in the Land Register: possession of the deed will not suffice.

("the 1973 Act"). The right of ownership in land or the rights of a tenant under a registered long lease do not however prescribe: s.8(2) and Sch.3(a) and (b) to the 1973 Act. While the ownership of moveable property does prescribe and the right to vindicate the property is therefore lost after 20 years, prescription does not operate against a thief or a person privy to the theft. Thus if A lends B his book, A loses the right to vindicate the book if for 20 years he has not attempted to obtain possession. If B stole the book, A's right to vindicate the book from B never prescribes. But if after five years B sold the book to C, a bona fide transferee, A's right to vindicate the book against C would prescribe 20 years later as C is not a person who was privy to the theft.

As two rights of ownership cannot exist in the same property at the same time, the ownership of land is extinguished when a person registers a disposition of the same property in the Land Register thereby acquiring a new statutory title to the land. This is, of course, subject to the right of the previous owner to seek rectification of the Land Register and thereby gain a new statutory title when the Register is corrected. This right to seek rectification is subject to the long negative prescription.

4–23   Where the real right is for a fixed term, the right will come to an end when the period expires. Thus a lease of land for 20 years will be extinguished when that period expires, subject to tacit reloca-tion. Moreover, a person can always discharge his rights; for example, a creditor will discharge a standard security over the debtor's land when the loan is repaid. The ownership of corporeal moveable property is lost if the property is physically abandoned with the intention to abandon it. It will then automatically be owned by the Crown. Subsequent ownership of the property must derive from the Crown, i.e. abandoned corporeal moveable prop-erty cannot be the subject of subsequent original acquisition.

Ownership ceases when the property is destroyed. This is why a person ceases to be the owner of the accessory property when it is subsumed in the principal property and the doctrine of accession applies. Similarly, if a person's property is used in the manufacture of a new product, she loses the ownership of that property by operation of the doctrine of specification. For example, B uses A's steel to build a motor car. When the car is made, B becomes the owner of the vehicle and A ceases to be the owner of the steel. A is therefore unable to vindicate the steel from B as in law it has ceased to exist. Moreover it is thought that it would not matter if B had stolen the steel: A would still cease to be the owner. However, although he no longer has ownership, A is not without a remedy. Where, as in the case of theft, he has been the victim of a wrong, A can claim damages in delict for the value of the steel and compel B to disgorge all the profits he has made from the sale: if, however, the steel was transferred to B by mistake, A can claim recompense for its value under the law of unjustified enrichment and, if the car has been sold on, this would include a share of the profits proportionate to the amount of steel that was used to build the car. Even so, these are only personal rights which will be of limited value if B was insolvent and was faced by claims from other creditors.

A subordinate real right over incorporeal property will come to an end when the incorporeal property is extinguished by law. For example, a standard security over a registered lease will be extinguished when the term of the lease expires.

When money is deposited in a bank, the bank (debtor) has a **4–24** duty to repay the sum to the depositor (creditor), usually with interest. The depositor has a right to be paid. This is a contractual right and thus a personal right. This is not problematic unless the bank becomes insolvent—which can happen!

There are innumerable ways in which a man or woman can be parted from the ownership of their money. Consider the following examples:

(a) A person enters into a contract for the sale of unascertained goods, for example furniture, and pays in advance of delivery. While the buyer has transferred the ownership of the money to the seller, she has only a personal right against the seller that the ownership of the goods will be transferred to her when the goods are ascertained. If the seller becomes insolvent before the goods are ascertained, the buyer may sue the seller either for damages for breach of contract—when she can recover compensation for any profits she would have made on re-selling the goods—or for restitution of the price. But these are only personal rights against the seller and could be of little value in the circumstances. This is because the buyer lost the ownership of her money when she paid it to the seller before the goods were ascertained. If the goods had been ascertained when the contract was formed or when the price was paid, ownership of the goods would have passed to the buyer and the goods would not form part of the seller's patrimony for the benefit of his creditors.

(b) A is induced by the fraudulent misrepresentation of B to transfer £10k to B. A is no longer the owner of the £10k and has no real right in the money. However, a fraudulent misrepresentation is a wrong and under the law of delict A can sue B for damages to compensate A for his loss. But this is a personal right and will be of little value if B is insolvent. If B has successfully speculated with the £10k and it is now worth £50k, there are rules under which A can "trace" the £10k through the transactions which increased its value to £50. Rather than seeking reparation for the loss of the £10k, A can argue that the wrong, i.e. the fraudulent

misrepresentation, generates a right to have B disgorge all
the profits that he made from the fraud. Again this is only a
personal right and may be of little value if B is being sued
by other victims of his fraudulent behaviour. Because A is
not the owner of the £10k he transferred to B, i.e. A no
longer has a real right in the money, even if the fund can be
traced A cannot demand payment of £10k ahead of the
claims of B's other creditors. It should also be remembered
that, when money is stolen and is put into circulation, the
"owner" of the stolen money cannot vindicate it but will
have a personal right against the thief or any *mala fide*
transferees for restitution of the value of the money and
any profits that they made from it.

It will be clear from these examples that, where there has been a
wrongful interference with property rights, the law of obligations
may be able to provide a remedy even though the victim is no
longer the owner of the property. Equally, where the victim
remains the owner, the law of obligations provides him with a wide
range of potential remedies when wrongful behaviour has had or
may have a deleterious affect on his property. It is to the law of
obligations that we now turn.

Further reading

Davidson and Macgregor, *Commercial Law in Scotland* (2003)
Ervine, *Consumer Law in Scotland* (3rd ed., 2004)

CHAPTER 5

VOLUNTARY OBLIGATIONS I

Introduction

In the last chapter we saw how the transfer of the ownership of **5–01**
property is often preceded by a juristic act. Of these the most
common is a contract. A contract is an agreement between two or
more parties in which they undertake to perform (or refrain from
performing) a particular act. The reason why each party is legally
obliged to perform is simply because they have voluntarily agreed
to do so. Their voluntary agreement is the source of the parties'
contractual obligations. In a contract of sale, for example, the seller
agrees to transfer the ownership of property to the buyer: in return,
the buyer agrees to pay the seller the price of the land or goods. It
is an example of a voluntary obligation in that the seller and buyer
voluntarily agree to convey the ownership of the property and to
pay the price. However, once the agreement has been reached the
parties are obliged to perform what they have voluntarily agreed to
do. Each party has a personal right to compel the other to perform.
Failure to perform is a breach of contract which gives rise to a
claim for damages as an alternative to a decree ordering specific
implement, i.e. performance of the contract.

Sale is a paradigm of a contract in Scots law. However, any
agreement between two (or more) parties is prima facie a contract
if the parties intend their agreement to be legally binding. Thus as
well as contracts for the sale of land and goods, parties can enter
into a wide variety of contracts. These include:

(a) a contract of hire of moveables under which the owner
agrees to transfer the possession of moveable property to
the hirer and the hirer agrees to pay a rental or a hire
charge;

(b) a lease of heritage is a contract under which the landlord
agrees to give a tenant possession of the property and the
tenant agrees to pay rent: the tenant will obtain a real right
in the property when the tenant takes possession or registers a long lease;

(c) a contract of loan under which A agrees to lend money to
B which B agrees to repay with interest over or after a
period of time: if B fails to repay the loan and any accrued

interest, A can recover the money loaned and interest in an action for debt;

(d) a contract of employment under which the employee agrees to provide services to the employer and the employer agrees to pay the employee a wage or salary;

(e) a contract for services under which an independent contractor such as a builder or plumber or accountant or solicitor agrees to provide services and the client agrees to pay a fee.

5–02 In short, contract is one of the most important legal devices ever invented as it enables persons to engage in commerce and to regulate their—largely economic—relationships by binding agreements. But it is important to remember that a contractual obligation only gives rise to a personal right, i.e. a personal right to demand performance from the other party to the contract or damages for breach. Other juristic acts such as conveyance of title or possession of property or registration are necessary before a party to a contract can obtain a real right in any property which is the subject matter of the contract.

The contracts we have been discussing are onerous agreements in the sense that both parties undertake reciprocal obligations. Thus in a contract of sale, for example, the seller undertakes to transfer the ownership of the goods or land and the seller undertakes to pay the price. But Scots law also recognises gratuitous contracts in which both parties agree that one of them should act for the benefit of the other without receiving any reciprocal obligation in return. For example, A and B can agree that B can give £100 to A. The source of B's obligation arises from B's agreement with A. Such contracts are very rare.

More common is a promise or unilateral obligation under which the promisor, A, undertakes an obligation to perform or refrain from performing a particular act for the benefit of the promisee, B. The obligation arises as soon as A promises B that he will perform (or refrain from performing) such conduct. There is no need for an agreement between A and B before A's obligation arises: but it is always open to B to refuse A's largesse thereby preventing A thrusting a white elephant upon her. A's promise will often be gratuitous in the sense that B does nothing in return for the performance of the promise; for example, if A promises to give B a present or leave her a legacy in his will. But there can be nongratuitous, i.e. onerous promises where, while A is under an obligation to perform as soon as the promise is made, B cannot compel A to perform until B has fulfilled a (purified) condition. For example, if A promises a reward to B if B finds A's lost dog, B must find the dog before she can demand the reward; although A has been under an obligation to pay her from the moment the promise was made, the promise cannot be enforced until B purifies the condition by finding the dog. In both onerous and gratuitous unilateral obligations, the reason why A is obliged to perform is because he voluntarily promised B that he would do so: but the distinction is important because in Scots law a gratuitous promise is not *constituted*—and is therefore unenforceable by the promisee—unless and until the promise is made in writing and subscribed by the promisor.

Formation and Performance

It is important to distinguish between the formation of a **5–03** voluntary obligation and the performance of the obligation. In this section we shall restrict the discussion to contract but the principles are also applicable to unilateral obligations.

A contract is formed when A and B reach an agreement to perform or refrain from performing a particular act. They must intend that the agreement is to be legally binding. Once such an agreement is reached the parties are obliged to perform the acts which they have undertaken to perform in the contract. For example, A and B agree that A will sell a commodity to B for £X. It is a term of the contract that delivery will be six months from the date of the formation of the contract and that the price will be paid on delivery. This means that, from the date of the formation of the contract, A is obliged to deliver the commodity in six months time and B is obliged to accept delivery and pay £X. If the market value of the commodity rises to £X + Y during the six months period, A is still obliged to deliver the commodity to B for £X, the price agreed in the contract. Conversely, if the market value of the commodity falls to £X − Y during the six months period, B is still obliged to accept delivery of the commodity and pay £X, the price agreed in the contract. Neither party can escape from her contractual obligations merely because she has made a bad bargain. Because each party knows that she can hold the other to the contract, they are able to plan their business with the expectation that their contracts will be performed in accordance with the terms which have been agreed.

Where there is a period between the date on which the contract is formed and the date on which the obligations are to be performed, the contract is known as an executory contract. But in the vast majority of contracts, there is no—or only a very small—gap between formation and performance of the contract; for example, the purchase of a newspaper. Where formation and performance of the contract coincide, the contract is known as an executed contract. But if the performance of an executed contract is defective, there will still have been a breach of contract and the innocent party will be entitled to sue for breach.

Nevertheless, it is an executory contract which best illustrates the **5–04** nature of the obligations generated by agreement. As soon as the contract is formed the parties are obliged to perform what they have agreed to do, even though the performance is not due until some date in the future. This means that if one party changes her mind after a contract is formed and intimates that she will not perform her obligations when the date for performance falls due, the other party can treat her repudiation as a breach of contract and sue for damages. When a contract is formed, both parties have the expectation that the obligations thereby created will be performed. It is that expectation interest which the law of contract serves to protect. Put another way, the law of contract looks forward. It enables persons to manage their lives on the assumption and expectation that the obligations undertaken by persons with whom they have contracted will be performed and that they themselves will have to perform their own side of the bargain.

As a general rule, a contract is formed when the parties have reached an agreement which they intend to be legally binding. Whether the parties have reached an agreement is ascertained objectively in the light of what they have said and done. In the vast majority of cases, it will be relatively easy to determine whether an agreement has been reached: but where a contract has to be inferred from conduct, for example flagging a taxi or selecting goods in a super market, it may be difficult to determine precisely when agreement was reached. A contract may be made on one of the parties' standard terms. This often happens when one of the parties is a consumer, i.e. she is not contracting in the course of a business while the other party is contracting in the course of business; for example, when a person books a holiday with a travel agent or buys a car from a second hand car dealer. Where there have been prolonged negotiations between the parties, there are intricate rules on offer and acceptance to help determine whether or not agreement has been reached.

Particularly where the exchange is valuable, the agreement may be in writing. While this is useful in providing evidence of the agreement and its terms, as a general rule there is no need for writing before a contract is formed under Scots law: s.1(1) of the Requirements of Writing (Scotland) Act 1995 (the 1995 Act). There are exceptions to this rule, for example consumer credit agreements. But perhaps the most important exception are contracts relating to real rights in land. Section 1(2)(a)(i) of the 1995 Act provides that a written document subscribed by the parties is necessary to constitute "a contract or unilateral obligation for the creation, transfer, variation or extinction of a real right in land".

---

[1] Where the parties have made the agreement in a commercial context, it is presumed that they intended it to be legally binding: conversely, where the agreement is made in a family or social context, it is presumed that they did not intend it to be legally binding. Both presumptions are rebuttable.

For example, a contract for the sale of a house is not formed until there is a written agreement (missives of sale) subscribed by the seller and purchaser (or their agents, for example solicitors). Even though there may have been an oral agreement of sale, both parties are free to change their minds before the agreement is put into writing as only then is a contract formed and the sale is binding on both parties. Similarly, a disposition will not be effective to transfer title until it is drawn up in writing and subscribed by the granter: though, of course, ownership of the property does not pass to the grantee until the grantee has registered the disposition in the Land Register.

However, a person who is a party to an oral agreement to sell **5–05** land may be personally barred from denying the existence of a contract because of the absence of writing, if the provisions of ss.1(3) and 1(4) of the 1995 Act are satisfied. These provisions are complex:

> "(3) Where a contract . . . is not constituted in a written document . . . but one of the parties to the contract ('the first person') has acted or refrained from acting in reliance on the contract with the knowledge and the acquiescence of the other party to the contract ('the second person')—
>
>> (a) the second person shall not be entitled to withdraw from the contract . . . and
>>
>> (b) the contract . . . shall not be regarded as invalid, on the ground that it is not so constituted, if the condition set out in subsection (4) below is satisfied.
>
> (4) The condition referred to in subsection (3) above is that the position of the first person—
>
>> (a) as a result of acting or refraining from acting as mentioned in that subsection has been affected to a material extent; and
>>
>> (b) as a result of such a withdrawal as is mentioned in that subsection would be adversely affected to a material extent."[2]

The idea is relatively simple. If the provisions can be triggered, a **5–06** party who could have denied the existence of the contract on the ground that it had not been constituted in writing becomes personally barred from doing so and the agreement is no longer treated as invalid because of the absence of writing. In this way informal agreements which are prima facie unenforceable because

---

[2] The phrases omitted in the sub-sections relate to gratuitous unilateral obligations and trusts. These are discussed later in para.5–08.

of the absence of writing are transformed into valid, enforceable contracts relating to real rights in land.

When will the provisions be triggered? Let us assume that A and B have an oral agreement under which A will purchase B's house for £200k. As it is an agreement to sell a real right in land, i.e. the ownership of the property, no contract is formed unless and until it is constituted in writing. Therefore B is prima facie entitled to withdraw from his agreement with A for any reason, for example that another person is prepared to purchase the house for £250k. However, B will be personally barred from doing so if A can rely on ss.1(3) and 1(4) of the 1995 Act. A is "the first person" as he is the person who wishes to continue with the agreement: B is "the second person" as he is the person who does not wish to continue with the agreement. A must show that in reliance on the agreement he has acted—or refrained from acting—with *the knowledge and acquiescence* of B. Therefore if B does not know of A's conduct, A's attempt to rely on ss.1(3) and 1(4) must fail. And so if A had raised a loan with C in order to pay for the house, the fact that he had done so would only be relevant if B knew that A was approaching C for a loan. Assuming B did know about the loan, A must then establish that he has been affected to a material extent by that conduct (i.e. the conduct that is known to and acquiesced in by B). It is thought that taking out a loan is not a trivial matter and that the material extent criterion is satisfied. A must then go on to show that he would be adversely affected if B withdrew from the agreement. This would be satisfied if for example A could not cancel the loan without incurring substantial penalties.[3]

5–07 It is important to note that we are only concerned with the actings of the first person which were known to and acquiesced in by the second person. The conduct of the second person on its own cannot trigger the statutory bar. Thus a second person remains free to deny the existence of a contract on the ground of defect in form even though he had previously acknowledged or even attempted to enforce the informal agreement.

---

[3] In the example, A has suffered as a result of a combination of (i) his conduct in reliance of the agreement which was known to B, i.e. the loan from C and (ii) B's withdrawal which would lead A to incur penalties if he cancelled the loan. In other words, the adverse effects of the withdrawal (s.1(4)(b)) arise from A's conduct which satisfies both ss.1(3) and 1(4)(a). However, read literally, there is no need for the first party to be *adversely* affected as a consequence of conduct that satisfies ss.1(3) and 1(4)(a): it is enough that he was adversely affected by the withdrawal. If, in our example, ss.1(3) and 1(4)(a) are satisfied because B knew about the loan but the loan can be renegotiated so that A did not suffer any financial hardship, A could still plead the provisions provided the withdrawal adversely affected him even if this was a consequence of conduct that was not known to B and could not therefore satisfy ss.1(3) and 1(4)(a); for example, if after the agreement A had given notice to terminate his lease and was therefore rendered homeless when B withdrew from the agreement.

We have spent a little time on these provisions because they are difficult to understand. They are also a statutory example of an important doctrine in private law known as personal bar. If A allows B to act in reliance on A's conduct, A will be personally barred from denying his conduct if it would be detrimental to B to do so. Moreover, ss.1(3) and 1(4) of the 1995 Act are also relevant to the constitution of unilateral obligations and trusts.

Unilateral Obligations

In Scots law a promise as well as agreement can be the source of **5–08** a voluntary obligation. Where A, the promisor, makes a promise to B, the promisee, A undertakes a unilateral obligation which prima facie is enforceable by B. A's obligation is created by the declaration of his will when he made the promise and his intention that the promise should be legally binding. Thus for example, if in the course of his business, A promises to give B a 10 per cent discount off the price of any goods she subsequently bought from him, that is a unilateral obligation which is enforceable by B: accordingly, if B buys goods from A and A refuses to give her the discounted price, B can sue A for breach of A's promise to do so. Because B must order goods from A before A's promise is enforceable, this is an onerous unilateral obligation.

However, where the unilateral obligation is gratuitous and has not been made in the course of a business, it is not enforceable unless it has been constituted in writing: s.1(2)(a)(ii) of the Requirements of Writing (Scotland) Act 1995. For example:

A promises to give B a gift of £10k. As B does not have to do anything for A before B would be entitled to seek performance of the promise, it is a gratuitous unilateral obligation. But such an obligation is not created—and is therefore unenforceable—unless it is constituted in writing and subscribed by the promisor, A. Even if B anticipates A's performance of the promise and borrows £5k to buy an engagement ring, the unilateral obligation nevertheless remains unenforceable unless and until it is constituted in writing. But if A knew that B was going to borrow the money from the bank, then ss.1(3) and 1(4) of the 1995 Act may be satisfied and the promise would no longer be invalid because it was not constituted in writing. It should also be noted that a unilateral obligation relating to a real right in land has to be constituted in writing whether or not it is gratuitous: this is because all voluntary obligations relating to real rights in land have to be constituted in writing.[4]

---

[4] 1995 Act, s.1(2)(a)(i).

The Terms of a Contract

5–09   The parties must be agreed on the material terms of their contract. In practice, it is unusual for the parties to negotiate each term of their agreement. Often a contract will proceed on the basis of one of the parties' standard terms. These will be incorporated into the contract either by express agreement usually in the form of a written contract signed by the parties or by reference in a contractual document signed or brought to the attention of the parties at the time the contract is formed. If they negotiate at all, it will be about core issues such as the cost or date of delivery of the goods and services. In addition, certain terms will be implied into particular contracts either by statute or the common law. In a contract for the sale of goods, for example, the Sale of Goods Act 1979 provides that there is an implied term that the seller has a right to sell the goods[5]; that if the goods are sold by description, the goods will conform to description[6]; and that where the seller sells goods in the course of a business, the goods supplied will be of satisfactory quality.[7] Indeed, s.8(2) provides that where the parties have not agreed a price in the contract (or the manner in which a price can be fixed) then the buyer must pay a reasonable price.

It is axiomatic that the parties are free to agree terms which vary or exclude the terms that would otherwise be implied by the law. Therefore, for example, the parties can agree a price which is not reasonable in the sense that the price is too expensive from the buyer's point of view or too cheap from the point of view of the seller. Similarly, a seller could expressly exclude the obligation that the goods are of reasonable quality. Moreover the contract can make provision on what is to happen in the event of defective performance. It could provide that if the particular goods were not available, the seller should be able to substitute similar goods: in that event, there would be no breach of contract as the seller has excluded the obligation that the goods should conform to description. Or the contract could provide that any damages for breach should be restricted to a sum which was much less than the amount that would be payable under the ordinary law of damages; for example, that the amount to be paid as damages should be limited to the price of the goods. Conversely, the contract might provide for penalties to be paid in the event that performance did not take place by a particular date or if a debt was paid earlier than anticipated and the lender would therefore receive less interest than he thought he would earn at the time the loan was agreed. The parties can make express provision changing the time when

---

[5] Sale of Goods Act 1979, s.12.
[6] *ibid.*, s.13.
[7] *ibid.*, s.14.

the risk of damage to property should pass from seller to buyer in contracts for the sale of heritable and moveable property. Again the parties can contract that ownership of corporeal moveable property should not pass until the price of the goods—and indeed any other debts owing to the seller—are paid by the purchaser. In short, prima facie the parties are free to alter the terms of the contract and, perhaps even more importantly, the legal consequences of subsequent events on the rights and duties of the parties to the contract. This is the essence of the doctrine of freedom of contract.

It will be obvious that this freedom can be abused particularly **5–10** where one party is in a stronger economic position than the other. For example, the supplier of goods to a retailer could stipulate that the retailer should indemnify the supplier for any damages that the supplier had to pay to a person who was injured by a defective product that the supplier had manufactured and the retailer had sold. This means that the retailer rather than the supplier-manufacturer takes the economic risk of the goods being defective: and this would be particularly unfair if the supplier-manufacturer was not only in a stronger economic position than the retailer, but the retailer was also unable to obtain the product from another source. In consumer contracts, exemption clauses under which the non-consumer excludes or limits liability for breach of contract can be extremely unfair. So too are clauses hidden away in the small print of the non-consumer's standard form terms which might, for example, provide a "penalty" if the consumer exercises a contractual right to withdraw prematurely from the contract. Statute now provides that some of these terms, particularly when they occur in consumer contracts, are unenforceable or can only be enforced if they can be shown to be fair and reasonable in all the circumstances of the case.[8]

Defective Contracts

An agreement which appears to be a contract may be defective. **5–11** As a consequence, it may be unenforceable. Moreover, other juristic acts which have taken place on the basis that the contract was valid may also be affected. For example, if A conveys property to B on the assumption that there is a valid contract of sale between A and B, the conveyance may be liable to be set aside and the ownership of the property transferred back to A if the contract of sale was defective. Moreover, it may also be necessary to unravel the economic consequences of the parties' performance of a contract which turns out to be defective: often resort has to be

---

[8] Unfair Contracts Terms Act 1977; Unfair Terms in Consumer Contracts Regulations 1999.

made to principles of the law of delict and unjustified enrichment
to enable this to be done. It is because defective contracts raise
important theoretical issues that they will be treated in some depth
even though the questions—fortunately—do not arise frequently in
practice.

Null "Contracts"   *Void*

5–12   An apparent contract may be so defective that it is treated as
never having arisen, i.e. as null. This occurs when one or both of
the parties did not have the capacity to enter into such a contract:
for example, one (or both) of the parties had not reached the age
of legal capacity to contract or in the case of an artificial legal
person such as a company, was acting beyond its legal powers in
entering the particular contract (acting ultra vires). It can also arise
when the parties to the contract did not in fact reach agreement.
As the question of whether the parties reached agreement is
determined objectively, i.e. whether a reasonable person, looking at
the actings of the parties, would infer that they had reached
agreement, such cases are rare. They have arisen very occasionally
when the parties have been in error as to:

(a) the subject matter of the contract (as opposed to the
     quality of the subject matter of the contract);
(b) the identity of the parties to the contract (as opposed to the
     creditworthiness of the parties): in effect, this is restricted
     to cases of impersonation; and
(c) the kind of contract that they are purporting to enter.

When an apparent contract is null, it has never existed and there
is no need to have a court order rescinding or reducing the
agreement: though the parties can seek a declarator that there
never was a valid contract viz. that the contract is and always has
been null. Where a contract for the sale of goods is null, it will
usually follow that the conveyance of the ownership of the property
is also null and that the purchaser is not and never has been the
owner of the property. In the case of the sale of land, where the
contract is null any subsequent disposition will be subject to
reduction and the Land Register may be rectified. Where one of
the parties has performed his side of the apparent agreement, he
has no right to demand reciprocal performance since the contract
does not exist. For the same reason he cannot obtain damages for
breach of contract. Instead, he must look to the law on unjustified
enrichment for relief. Consider the following examples:

(a) A agrees to buy goods from B for £5k. A pays the price at
     the time the agreement is made. Before delivery, it is
     discovered that the contract is null. Because the contract

does not exist, B is not under a contractual duty to deliver the goods and A has no right to obtain specific implement or damages for breach of contract. But the £5k was transferred to B as the price of goods he was obliged to deliver to A under a valid contract of sale. Since the contract of sale is null, B's retention of the money is without cause and B is regarded as being unjustifiably enriched at A's expense. B is therefore under an *ex lege* obligation to return the money to A in order to reverse the unjustified enrichment. This is known as restitution.[9]

(b) A enters into a contract with B to sell B's goods on an agreed commission. After A has sold the goods, it is discovered that the contract is null. Because the contract does not exist, A has no contractual right to the commission and cannot sue for breach of contract. However, A performed the services in the belief that he was contractually obliged to do so and that he would be paid a commission. A did not intend to donate his services to B. In these circumstances, if B was to retain the benefit of A's services without payment, B would be unjustifiably enriched. B is therefore under an *ex lege* obligation to recompense A for A's services: this will be payment at the market rate for the services rendered by A which will be similar to, but not necessarily the same as, the commission that A and B agreed in their purported contract.

It will be noted in these examples that B received a benefit after the parties had entered into the apparent contract. If A has incurred expenditure during contractual negotiations or with a view to fulfilling his obligations under the contract, prima facie it is not recoverable from B. It is only when B has received a benefit from A's performance of his purported obligations under the null contract that B is obliged to make restitution or recompense under the law of unjustified enrichment.

Annullable Contracts *Voidable*

The right to rescind

In the vast majority of situations where a contract is defective, **5–13** the contract is valid but is vulnerable in that it can be set aside and treated as though it was null. Such contracts are annullable as opposed to null. Setting aside or annulling the contract is known as rescission. A contract can be rescinded by one of the parties simply intimating to the other that the contract has been set aside. If the

---

[9] In Scots law, a claim for restitution of money is known as repetition.

other party disputes the annulment, it will be necessary to go to court for a declarator that the contract has been rescinded. Where the contract is in writing and takes the form of a deed, it is necessary to obtain a court order setting the contract aside: this is known as an action of reduction. In an action for specific implement or damages for breach of contract, any ground for reduction of the contract can be pleaded as a defence (*ope exceptionis*).[10]

Although it is annullable, until it is rescinded the contract subsists and is prima facie enforceable. Any conveyance of property following on from such a contract will operate to transfer title, albeit that the conveyance might also be vulnerable to be set aside. Until rescission takes place, the transferee will have a valid title to the property which she in turn can transfer to a bona fide transferee for value and the latter's title is no longer vulnerable to rescission/reduction. For example:

A agrees to sell a painting to B for £5k. The ownership of the painting is transferred to B. The contract is annullable. A can rescind the contract: B must transfer the ownership of the painting back to A and A must return £5k to B. But if before the contract has been rescinded, B sells the painting to C, a bona fide transferee for value, because the contract is only annullable, B has a good title which is transferred to C. C's title to the painting will therefore be valid and is not vulnerable to rescission by A. Moreover, since C paid B for the painting, C has not been enriched: therefore A has no claim against him on the basis of unjustified enrichment.[11]

The right to have a contract rescinded can be lost if there has been unnecessary delay in pursuing the remedy or the party entitled to rescind has affirmed the validity of the contract. The latter is known as homologation and before it can operate the party must know about the defect which renders the contract annullable: it is another aspect of the general doctrine of personal bar. The right will also be lost if *restitutio in integrum* is not possible at the time the contract is to be set aside. It is a precondition of rescission that the contract can be unravelled and *both* parties returned to the position in which they would have been if the contract had not been made. If this is not possible, the contract cannot be rescinded. For example:

(a) A buys a car from B for £5k. The contract is annullable by A. If before the contract has been rescinded, the car is involved in an accident and is badly damaged, A loses the

---

[10] An action of reduction must be brought in the Court of Session but reduction can be pled *ope exceptionis* in the sheriff court as well as the Court of Session.

[11] If C was in bad faith, A's remedy would be to seek rescission of C's contract with B on the basis of the "off-side goals" rule: It cannot be a claim in unjustified enrichment as C is not enriched as he paid B for the picture.

right to rescind as A cannot restore the car to B in the condition in which he bought it.

(b) A buys a car from B for £5k. The contract is annullable by B. If before the contract has been rescinded, A sells the car to C, a bona fide transferee for value, B loses the right to rescind because A cannot restore the car to him as the property rights of a bona fide third party, C, have intervened.

The rule that *restitutio in integrum* is a pre-condition of rescission appears out-dated. While it can perhaps be justified where the property interests of third parties have intervened before the contract has been rescinded, in other cases any economic imbalances arising when the contract has been set aside can be adjusted by the law of unjustified enrichment. In the first example above, on rescission A would be entitled to recover the price but B would be entitled to recompense for the use of the car which A enjoyed while the contract subsisted. Moreover, A could assign to B any rights he had under the law of delict to obtain reparation for the damage done to the car in the accident and/or any rights to compensation in respect of the car under a policy of insurance.

Improperly obtained consent

When does a right to rescind arise? The answer is when the **5–14** consent of one of the parties has been improperly obtained or one[12] of the parties has contracted under error. Objectively there is agreement between the parties—otherwise the contract would be null. However, as one of the parties' consent is defective, the law allows that party to have the contract set aside. Examples include the following:

(a) Where the party's consent has been obtained as a consequence of duress, i.e. force and fear. This can include economic duress caused by threatening unlawful conduct such as breach of an existing contract or inducing a breach of an existing contract which the victim has with a third party.

(b) Where the party's consent has been obtained by undue influence. This arises when one party has assumed a position of dominant influence over the other and has abused this position by entering into a contract with the subservient party to her serious detriment. Such a relationship will be readily inferred where the parties are husband and wife, parent and child or solicitor and client. In the

---

[12] Very occasionally both parties may be under error but where this is so the contract will usually be null because objectively there is no agreement.

case of a husband and wife, it has been held that if the
husband induces his wife to enter into a disadvantageous
contract with a third party, for example to provide security
to a bank for her husband's business debts, the contract
with the third party can be set aside if the third party has
not acted in good faith towards the wife by ensuring that
she had independent legal advice before entering the
agreement.
(c) Where a person is insane, he lacks capacity to contract and
any purported contract will be null. However, as a result of
age, physical infirmity or mental health, a person can
become facile, i.e. weak minded in the sense of being liable
to be influenced by persuasion or intimidation to act
against her own interests. The element of persuasion or
intimidation is known as circumvention. Where a party's
consent was obtained when she was facile as a consequence
of the other party's circumvention, then the contract can be
set aside.

Uninduced Error

5–15   A contract can also be rescinded when a party's consent to
contract has been made under error. Where the error has not been
induced, the scope of the doctrine of error as a ground of
annulment is kept within the narrowest of limits. The error must go
to the root of the contract and be related to express or implied
provisions of the contract, i.e. it must be an error in transaction
rather than an error in motive. Thus for example, a contract of sale
can be set aside if at the time the contract was made, unknown to
the parties, the goods had perished. This is because the parties
entered into the contract under error that the implied condition
that the goods existed was purified when in fact it was not. This is
an error in transaction: and in the case of the non-existence of the
goods the error clearly goes to the root of the contract.[13] However,
the parties can expressly contract out of the doctrine of error. In
our example they could have expressly agreed that the seller should
take the risk of the goods being destroyed at the date of formation
of the contract and if this happens the seller should find substitute
goods. In these circumstances, there is no room for the doctrine of
error as the parties have anticipated what should occur if the goods
do not exist at the time the contract is formed thus displacing the
implied condition that the goods must exist at the time the contract
is made. There is therefore no error in relation to the transaction.
    This is an illustration of how parties are free to make specific
provisions in their contract which displace the rules which would
otherwise apply.

---

[13] This principle has now been put on a statutory basis: s.6 of the Sale of Goods Act
   1979.

Induced Error

Where the error has been induced by a misrepresentation, **5–16** however, the contract can be rescinded even though the error is in motive and does not go to the root of the contract. For example:

A purchases a picture of a clown from B under the uninduced error that it is a painting by Picasso. In fact it is a painting by Braque. This is not an error in transaction nor does it go to the root of the contract. A bought a painting that he thought was by Picasso but which the seller did not stipulate was by Picasso or indeed any other artist. The subject matter was a portrait of a clown and that is what A has received. But if before the contract was made, B told A that the painting of the clown was by Picasso then when it is discovered after the sale that it is not by Picasso, A can have the contract rescinded on the ground that he entered into the contract under an error induced by B's misrepresentation. It does not matter (a) whether or not the error is in transaction or (b) whether or not the error so induced goes to the root of the contract.

Put another way, we could say that where an error has been induced by an operative misrepresentation, it will be deemed to go to the root of the contract. Accordingly, the scope of error as a ground of rescission is greatly extended when it can be shown that the error was induced by an operative misrepresentation.

It is important to be clear when a misrepresentation is operative. The following criteria must be satisfied:

(a) the misrepresentation must have been made by one party to the contract, the misrepresentor, to the other party to the contract, the misrepresentee;

(b) the misrepresentation must be a false statement of fact. A statement of pure opinion is not therefore a misrepresentation unless (a) the misrepresentor is lying, in which case he is misrepresenting the state of his mind or (b) the misrepresentor is in a better position than the misrepresentee to have access to the facts on which the opinion is based and he can be taken to have misrepresented those facts.[14] For the same reason a statement of future intention is not a misrepresentation unless the misrepresentor is lying at the time the statement is made when, again, he is misrepresenting the state of his mind.

---

[14] Thus if as in our example, B states that the painting is by Picasso, that is a misrepresentation as it is a false statement of fact. If B states that in his opinion the painting is by Picasso, that is not a misrepresentation. But such a statement would be a misrepresentation if B was lying and he knew that it was not a Picasso as he is misrepresenting the state of his mind or if B was an expert on Picasso and A was not, so that B could be taken as misrepresenting the facts on which his opinion was based.

(c) The misrepresentation must take the form of a statement or some other positive misleading act made *before* the contract was formed. Therefore silence does not amount to a misrepresentation unless there is a duty to disclose. This could arise if there was a fiduciary or quasi fiduciary relationship between the parties, for example trustee and beneficiary or solicitor and client. There are also contracts of the utmost good faith (*uberrimae fidei*) where disclosure of material facts must be made, for example to disclose any serious illnesses when entering a contract of life insurance. These instances aside, the law allows a person to make a good bargain when contracting with another at arms' length: he can say nothing while the other contracts under error as to the value of property being bought or sold.[15]

(d) The misrepresentation must have in fact induced the misrepresentee to enter into the contract, i.e. there must be a causative link between the misrepresentation and the misrepresentee entering into the contract.

(e) The misrepresentation must be material in the sense that the matter misrepresented was sufficiently important that it would have induced a reasonable person to enter into the contract. This is the reason that advertisements which puff up the qualities of a product do not amount to a misrepresentation, i.e. that a reasonable person would not be induced to enter into a contract as a result of such an advertisement!

5–17 If a misrepresentee can establish that she entered into a contract under an error induced by an operative misrepresentation, then she will be entitled to rescind the contract. But rescission is not the only potential remedy generated by a misrepresentation. If the accuracy of the statement which amounts to a misrepresentation has become a term of the contract, the misrepresentee can elect to sue for breach of contract. If the misrepresentation was made by a person who knew that his statement was false, he will have committed fraud and will be liable under the law of delict to make reparation. Similarly, there could be a delictual obligation to make reparation if the misrepresentor owed a duty of care to the misrepresentee which was broken by making a statement without reasonable care, i.e. liability in negligence. In other words, an operative misrepresentation may entitle the misrepresentee to a

---

[15] Thus provided he says nothing, A can buy a painting from B for £5 knowing that it is worth £50k and that B clearly has no idea of its value. But if before the contract was formed, A stated that the picture was a fake which was only worth £5, B could have the contract rescinded on the basis of error induced by misrepresentation.

number of rights from the whole spectrum of the law of obligations. Consider the following examples:

(a) A purchases a painting from B for £10k. He was induced to do so by B's statement that the painting had once belonged to Queen Victoria. This is not true. A is entitled to rescind the contract provided *restitutio in integrum* is possible. A returns the painting. B is obliged to return the price since there is no longer a legal basis for its retention and under the law of unjustified enrichment, A is entitled to restitution (repetition) of the money.

(b) A purchases a painting from B for £10k. He was induced to do so by B's statement that the painting had once belonged to Queen Victoria. This is not true. If it had belonged to Queen Victoria it would have been worth £15k. Without the Royal connection, it is only worth £1k. If A can show that it was a term of the contract that the painting had been owned by Queen Victoria, A can sue for damages for breach of contract and recover his expectation interest. This will be the difference between what the painting is worth (£1k) and what it would have been worth if the contract had been performed properly (£15k), i.e. £15k–£1k = £14k. This is £4k more than A would obtain by rescinding and recovering the price. Moreover, if he sues for breach, A does not have to give the painting back to B: *restitutio in integrum* is not required.

(c) On the other hand, assume that A had made a bad bargain and even with the Royal connection the painting would only have been worth £5k. If A sues for damages for breach of contract, in this scenario his expectation interest is the difference between what the painting is worth (£1k) and what it would have been worth if the contract had been performed properly (£5k), i.e. £5k − £1k = £4k. Here A should elect to rescind the contract on the ground of misrepresentation and thus recover the price (£10k): but he will of course have to return the painting to B as *restitutio in integrum* is a precondition of rescission.

(d) A purchases a painting from B for £10k. He was induced to do so by B's statement that the painting had belonged to Queen Victoria. If it had belonged to Queen Victoria it would have been worth £15k. Without the Royal connection, it is worth £1k. It is not a term of the contract that the painting was owned by Queen Victoria. However, when he made the statement, B knew that it was false, i.e. he committed fraud. A could rescind the contract and recover the price but he must return the painting to B. A cannot recover his expectation interest in a claim for breach of contract as it was not a term of the contract that the painting belonged to the Queen. However, the fraudulent misrepresentation is a wrong for which A is entitled to reparation under the law of delict. A is entitled to be put in the position he would have been if the delict had not taken place, i.e. he is entitled to recover his *status quo* or reliance interest. This would be the difference between what he paid for the painting (£10k) and its current value (£1k), i.e. £10k − £1k = £9k. But if he sues in delict, A does not have to give the painting back to B, i.e. *restitutio in integrum* is not required. A similar result may follow if the statement was made carelessly as opposed to fraudulently. A duty of care arises between parties to a potential contract, if one of the parties assumes responsibility for the economic interests of the other, knowing that the other will rely on his expertise.[16] Such a duty would arise if B was an art expert and in a better position than A to know about the provenance of the painting. Again, A could recover his *status quo* interest and would not have to return the painting to B. The claim in delict would be particularly useful if in the scenario outlined above, A had made a bad bargain and the painting would only have been worth £5k with the Royal connection; in these circumstances, A would still recover £9k if he sued in delict. It should be noted that there is no liability in delict merely because B has made a misrepresentation. It has to be established that the statement was made either fraudulently or negligently. If this cannot be done and it is a case of an innocent misrepresentation, the misrepresentee's only remedy is rescission and restitution (repetition) of the price.[17]

5–18   These examples illustrate the unitary nature of the law of obligations. A particular factual situation can generate rights in contract, delict and unjustified enrichment. The pursuer can elect which of these rights he wishes to enforce but he cannot do so in a way which would be doctrinally incoherent. Thus for example, a misrepresentee cannot sue for breach of contract at the same time as seeking rescission of the contract. The effect of rescission is to annul the contract, i.e. treat it as though it had always been null. To seek damages for breach of contract involves asserting that the contract existed and is therefore incompatible with the rescission of the contract. A misrepresentee will also have to elect between

---

[16] Scots law now accepts that a duty of care to prevent economic loss as a result of negligence can arise between parties to a contract: Law Reform (Miscellaneous Provisions)(Scotland) Act 1985, s.10.

[17] If, of course, the accuracy of the misrepresentation was a term of the contract, the misrepresentee could sue for breach of contract as outlined in example b above.

suing in delict or for breach of contract. While contract damages compensates the expectation interest and the *status quo* or reliance interest is protected by delict damages, the misrepresentee will in practice choose the measure of damages which in the circumstances is larger. He cannot choose both as there will inevitably be some overlap and the law does not allow a pursuer to be compensated twice for the same loss.

Illegal Contracts

A contract can be illegal. At common law certain contracts are **5–19** treated as unlawful because they are criminal per se, for example the hire of a contract killer, or contrary to public policy, for example a contract to bribe a witness. A statute may also expressly or impliedly[18] render a contract illegal. In these cases the parties' knowledge or intention is irrelevant: as a matter of law the contracts are illegal. On the other hand, a perfectly valid contract can be rendered illegal if at the time it is formed one or both parties intended to perform it in an unlawful way, for example in breach of statutory regulations. Here the parties' intention to commit an offence in performing the contract renders the contract illegal.

The effect of illegality is that the contract is unenforceable as a contract. This means that neither party can seek specific implement nor damages for breach of contract. For example:

A transfers £5k to B, a member of a licensing committee, in order that B will ensure that A's public house licence is renewed. This is a bribe and the contract is illegal. B does not attempt to ensure that the licence is renewed. A cannot seek implement of the agreement or damages for B's breach. The loss lies where it falls, i.e. B retains the £5k: this is a quasi-sanction to discourage licensees from attempting to bribe officials.

Allowing the loss to lie where it falls may appear to be justified **5–20** in our example because A knew that it is wrong to bribe an official, i.e. to pervert the course of justice. However the merits of this doctrine are more difficult to defend when the reason the contract is illegal rests on a technical breach of a statute and does not involve any immoral conduct. The law on unjustified enrichment can, it is thought, provide more sophisticated solutions in these difficult cases. Consider the following examples:

---

[18] This is a question of construction of the statute. For example, where a statute provided that it was a criminal offence to supply goods without an invoice being given to the purchaser, it was held that a contract in which the purchaser did not receive an invoice was impliedly illegal. The courts are generally reluctant to infer that a contract is impliedly illegal merely because its performance has breached a statutory regulation, for example when a contract of carriage involves a breach of the Road Traffic legislation.

(a) A enters into a contract to sell goods to B. The contract is
illegal because the parties have sold the goods by Imperial
rather than metric measure. A conveys the ownership of
the goods to B. After they have been delivered to B and
sold on to C, B refuses to pay the price because the
contract was illegal. Because of the illegality, A cannot rely
on the contract and sue for the price. But, as a matter of
the law of property, the ownership of the goods was
transferred to B.[19] A did not intend to donate the goods to
B. In these circumstances, if B was to retain the benefit (i.e.
the price from the sale of the goods to C) without paying A
for the goods, he would be unjustifiably enriched. Therefore B is under an *ex lege* obligation to recompense A for
the value of the goods. This will be the market value of the
goods which should be similar to, though not necessarily
the same as, the contractually stipulated price. It is open to
B to argue that in the particular circumstances of the case
it would be inequitable to compel him to recompense A.
This is unlikely to succeed on the facts of this example. But
if the sale was illegal because A did not have a licence to
sell the goods and the system of licensing had been
introduced to protect purchasers like B, then such a
defence might succeed on the basis that A was more
blameworthy than B.

(b) A enters into a contract to buy goods from B. The contract
is illegal because the parties have sold the goods by
Imperial rather than metric measure. A pays the price but
B refuses to transfer the ownership of the goods to A. As
the contract is illegal, A cannot obtain specific implement
or damages for breach of contract. However, when he
refuses to transfer the ownership of the goods, B's retention of the price has no longer any legal basis and under
the law of unjustified enrichment, A has a right to restitution (repetition) of the money. This means that B is under
an *ex lege* duty to return the price to A. It is open to B to
argue that in the particular circumstances of the case it
would be inequitable to compel him to return the money to
A. This is unlikely to succeed on the facts of this example.
But if the sale was illegal because A had bought the goods
in breach of rationing regulations during war time and was
a black marketeer, then such a defence might succeed on
the basis that A was more blameworthy than B.

It is thought that the approach outlined above provides a
principled yet sufficiently flexible way to readjust any economic

---

[19] There could be exceptional cases where this might not be so: for example if, as in
the case of child pornography, the mere possession of the goods was criminal. *Sed
quaere?*

imbalances between the parties after partial performance of an illegal contract. In particular, it allows the court to take into account the extent of each party's moral turpitude in determining whether it would be inequitable to order the restitution or recompense that is prima facie due under the law of unjustified enrichment. In each case, the onus would lie on the defender to show that it would be inequitable to order him to do so. Approaching the issues in this way, once again illustrates the interlocking nature of the law of obligations. The principle of the law of contract that illegal contracts are unenforceable and any losses from partial performance of the contract must lie where they have fallen is now tempered by the principle of the law of unjustified enrichment that any gains from partial performance of the contract should prima facie be reversed unless it can be shown in the circumstances to be inequitable to do so.

Frustration

As a general rule events which occur after a contract has been **5–21** formed have no effect on the parties' obligations to perform what they have undertaken under the contract. Indeed, it is precisely for this reason that parties enter executory contracts. For example, A agrees to buy goods from B for £X. If the market falls and A could obtain the goods for £X–Y, A is still obliged to pay £X: conversely, if the market rises, and B could sell the goods for £X + Y, B is still obliged to sell the goods to A for £X. There can, however, be exceptional situations where an external event occurs which has such drastic effects that the parties' performance of the contract is or would be radically different from what had been envisaged by them. In these circumstances the law relieves the parties from their obligation to perform or engage in further performance of the contract. This is known as the doctrine of frustration

In short, a contract will be frustrated if after the formation of the contract an event occurs which goes to the root of the contract in that performance would be radically different from that originally envisaged by the parties when the contract was made. Consider the following example:

A entered into a contract with B under which B would provide a reception for A's wedding at B's hotel. After the contract was formed but before the wedding, the hotel burned down. It cannot be rebuilt before the wedding. In these circumstances, the contract is frustrated since any purported performance would be radically different from that originally anticipated by the parties. Accordingly, both parties are automatically freed (discharged) from further performance of their obligations under the contract. But if there had been a clause in the contract that if the hotel was not available because it had been damaged by fire, the reception could take place in another venue owned by B, the contract would not have been frustrated when the hotel burned down as the parties had made express contractual provision for what was to constitute performance of B's obligations in the event that the hotel was not available. In other words, as in the case of the doctrine of error, the parties are free expressly to contract out of the doctrine of frustration; such terms are known as *force majeure* clauses.

5–22 It should be emphasised that a contract is not frustrated merely because performance has become less profitable, or, indeed, unprofitable for one of the parties: economic hardship in itself does not constitute frustration. The event must render performance *radically* different from that envisaged by the parties.

The subsequent event must not have been caused by one of the parties to the contract. In the example above, if the fire at the hotel had been caused by B, the contract would not have been frustrated. Instead, B's conduct in destroying the hotel so that performance of the contract becomes impossible would amount to a material breach of contract. As the innocent party A would then be entitled to treat himself as freed from further performance of his obligations under the contract and can seek damages from B for breach of contract.

The effect of frustration is that both parties are discharged from further performance of any outstanding obligations under the contract. But what happens if there has been partial performance of the contract before the frustrating event occurs? Consider the following examples:

(a) A enters into a contract with B under which B will build a house for A for £300k. The land on which the house is to be built is owned by A. It is a term of the contract that the price is to be paid in instalments of £50k every six months. The first instalment is due when the contract is formed. A pays the first instalment. A week later war is declared and all building materials are requisitioned by the government for the duration of the hostilities. These last five years. After the war has ended, B proposes to begin building the house. It is thought that the contract was frustrated by the war. A and B were therefore automatically discharged from performance of their obligations under the contract. A is no longer obliged to allow B on to his land in order to build the house and B has no right to do so. A is also freed from performance of the obligation to pay the outstanding instalments. Moreover, the first instalment of the price was transferred to B in part payment of the house that B was to build. When the contract was frustrated, the legal reason for the transfer of the money disappeared. In other words, further retention of the payment is without legal cause and B is unjustifiably enriched. B is therefore under an *ex lege* obligation to return the £50k instalment to A, i.e. A has a right to restitution (repetition) of the money.

(b) A enters into a contract with B under which B will build a house for £300k. The land on which the house is to be built is owned by A. It is a term of the contract that the price is to be paid when the house is completed. After half the work is done, war is declared and all building materials are requisitioned by the government for the duration of hostilities. These last five years. After the war has ended, B proposes to continue building the house. For the reasons discussed in (a), it is thought that the contract has been frustrated and both parties are discharged from performance of their contractual obligations. However, by the time the contract was frustrated, A had received the benefit of the half-built house which he owns by virtue of the accession of the building materials to A's land. But B did not intend to donate the house to A. Therefore A's retention of the benefit amounts to unjustified enrichment and A is under an *ex lege* obligation to pay B for the value he has received at his expense, i.e. B has right to recompense from A to the extent of the value of the half-built house which may be similar to, but is not necessarily the same as, half the contractual price of building the house. It should be noted that before the law of unjustified enrichment is relevant, one of the parties must have been enriched at the other's expense. So for example, if B had not begun the building before the frustrating event, he cannot recover from A any outlays he might have incurred in preparing to perform the contract, for example by buying building materials.

Again parties can use *force majeure* clauses to "contract out" of the application of the law of unjustified enrichment in the post-frustration situation. Instead, the parties can agree a contractually stipulated mechanism to redress any losses that have occurred as a consequence of partial performance and, indeed, provide for the re-negotiation of the contract in the light of the altered circumstances.

Further reading

McBryde, *Law of Contract in Scotland* (2nd ed., 2002)
MacQueen and Thomson, *Contract Law in Scotland* (2000)
Woolman and Lake, *Contract* (3rd ed., 2001)

CHAPTER 6

VOLUNTARY OBLIGATIONS II

Breach

6–01 A breach of contract arises when a party to a contract fails to perform the obligations he has undertaken under the contract. These include total non-performance (repudiation), late performance, defective performance, for example delivering goods that do not conform to description or which are not of reasonable quality, failure to pay the price of goods or services and failure to pay a debt. The contract-breaker does not have to be at fault before there is liability: even though he has tried his best,[1] prima facie he has committed a breach of contract whenever he fails to perform his contractual obligations.

A breach is material when it is so serious that it goes to the root of the contract in the sense that the purported performance is radically different from what the innocent party was entitled to expect. At one extreme, a party may simply refuse to perform, i.e. repudiate the contract. If she repudiates before the date when performance is due, this is known as an anticipatory breach of contract. In these circumstances, the innocent party can elect to treat the anticipatory breach as an actual material breach of contract. Alternatively, he can wait until the date for performance arrives. He can then elect either (i) to perform his obligations and attempt to compel the other side to perform or (ii) treat the continuing repudiation as a material breach.

In the case of defective performance, the breach has to be serious before it is regarded as material. However, in certain situations even a minor breach must be treated as material. For example, in consumer contracts for the sale of goods, any breach of s.14 of the Sale of Goods Act 1979 (implied term that goods have to be of reasonable quality) is treated as material. Thus if A bought a family car and the wing mirrors are broken, there is a material breach of s.14 even if the mirrors can easily be replaced:

---

[1] Some terms stipulate that the party need only take reasonable care: if so, strict liability is displaced and there will only be a breach of that term if the party has been at fault.

if A bought a van for his business and the wing mirrors are broken, there is a breach of s.14 but it will not be material if the mirrors can be easily replaced. Moreover, it is open to the parties expressly to stipulate that *any* breach of a particular term of their contract is to be regarded as material: if so, there will be a material breach even if the effect of the breach is objectively trivial. This is another example of the parties' freedom expressly to regulate their contractual relationship: but the less serious the consequences of the breach, the clearer it must be that the parties had expressly stipulated that such breaches are to be regarded as material.

Specific Implement and Interdict

When a breach occurs, the innocent party can seek a decree of specific implement compelling the party in breach to perform his contractual obligations. Where the breach consists of the contract breaker doing something that he undertook not to do, the innocent party may seek an interdict ordering the contract breaker to desist from such conduct.

6–02

In practice, specific implement is not used as much as might be thought because of the difficulty of enforcement of the decree against a determined contract breaker; the sanctions available, fines and imprisonment, might appear draconian in most circumstances. Where specific implement is useful is in the context of the sale of a real right in land after the contract of sale has been formed, i.e. written missives have been concluded; should the seller change her mind and refuse to convey the property, the purchaser can seek a decree of specific implement and the clerk of court can sign the disposition instead of the seller if she continues to refuse to do so.

Many cases of breach of contract involve the failure to pay a sum of money. This could arise when the contract breaker fails to pay the price of goods or services or where a debtor fails to repay a loan. Here the innocent party is entitled to an order demanding that the money be paid. While, in effect, a decree of specific implement, this is known as an action for debt. Unlike a claim for damages, in seeking payment of a debt, the innocent party does not have to mitigate her loss. In a case of anticipatory breach, if the innocent party elects to perform, he may be able to sue the contract breaker for payment in respect of the unwanted goods or services when he would have had to have mitigated his loss if he had treated the anticipatory breach as an actual material breach of contract.

Rescission—Termination

6–03   When a material breach occurs, the innocent party has the right
to rescind the contract.[2] What this means is that the innocent party
is freed from performance of any contractual obligations which
were due to be performed at a date later than that of the material
breach. For example, A, a consumer, agrees to buy goods from B,
payment to be made on delivery. On arrival, the goods are not of
reasonable quality. This is a material breach under section 14 of
the Sale of Goods Act 1979. A can rescind the contract by rejecting
the goods and since the breach occurred before the date of the
purported delivery, A is free from performance of the obligation to
pay the price. The contract subsists up until the date of rescission
and A remains theoretically liable for any breach that A might
have incurred before B's material breach.[3] In other words, rescission for material breach is basically prospective: it does not involve
unwinding the contractual relationship between the parties. Unlike
rescission for defective consent, the contract is not set aside, i.e.
treated as being null and *restitutio in integrum* is not necessary
before the innocent party can regard himself as discharged from
further performance of his obligations under the contract. Because
of this, it is unfortunate that in Scots law the word "rescission" is
used to describe both these remedies. In the present writer's view,
rescission[4] should be used to describe annulment. Rescission for
material breach could be called termination since it terminates the
innocent party's duty to perform any obligations which were due to
be performed after the date of the material breach. But it must be
emphasised that it is the innocent party's obligation of *future
performance* not the contract that is terminated. The contract may
contain terms which are intended to regulate the position between
the parties after a material breach such as an arbitration clause, an
exemption clause or a penalty clause: these terms continue to be
applicable after termination. And it is because the contract is not
annulled when the innocent party exercises the right of termination, that he is entitled to sue for damages for the losses he has

---

[2] Where their obligations are interdependent, the innocent party can elect to
withhold performance of her obligations until the contract breaker performs the
obligation, non-performance or defective performance of which constitutes the
material breach. This is known as retention and arises from the principle of
mutuality of contract. Thus for example, a buyer can withhold the price of
defective goods until the seller repairs or replaces them so that they are of
reasonable quality or a tenant can withhold rent until the landlord has performed
his obligations under a lease to repair the property.

[3] This is controversial. It can be argued that since B is *ex hypothesi* in material
breach of contract, he is barred by the principle of mutuality from seeking the
counterpart performance from A.

[4] Where the contract takes the form of a deed, rescission necessitates an action of
reduction.

sustained as a consequence of the material breach and any earlier breaches of the contract.

As in the case of frustration, problems can arise when there has been partial performance of the contract before the innocent party exercises the right of termination. Consider the following examples:

(a) A, a consumer, agrees to purchase goods from B. A pays the price in advance of delivery. When the goods are delivered they are not of reasonable quality. This is a material breach of contract under s.14 of the Sale of Goods Act 1979. A elects to terminate his duty to perform any obligations which were due to be performed after the date of the material breach and therefore rejects the goods. A is entitled to sue B for damages for breach of contract. Alternatively, he is entitled to restitution (repetition) of the price. On one view, the material breach of contract is a wrong which itself generates the right to repetition of the price. In other words, restitution of the price arises from the breach of contract and is a contractual remedy. On the other hand, it has been argued that the right to repetition emanates from unjustified enrichment. A transferred the money to B on the basis that in return B would supply him with goods of reasonable quality. When B fails to do so and A exercises his right of termination, further retention of the price by B is without a legal basis and under the law of unjustified enrichment B is under an *ex lege* obligation to restore the benefit to A, i.e. A has the right to restitution (repetition) of the price. The difficulty with the unjustified enrichment analysis is that if B, acting in good faith, had changed his position by spending the money, he could claim that in the circumstances it was inequitable to compel him to restore the price to A. Such a defence would not be available if the right to repetition was treated as a contractual remedy.

It will often be to A's advantage to sue for damages so that, for example, he could recover the increased cost of purchasing alternative goods: in such cases the damages are more than the price. But this will not be so if A has made a bad bargain, i.e. if the market value of the goods has fallen so that A would have made a loss even if the goods were of reasonable quality. Here A's right to restitution of the price will be more valuable that his claim for damages for breach of contract.[5]

---

[5] This issue is controversial. It can be argued that where A has made a bad bargain, the right to restitution should be "capped" by the maximum damages he could obtain for breach of contract. This is largely of only theoretical importance. Given the market fluctuations in his favour, B has every incentive not to commit a material breach.

(b) A purchases land from B. A pays the price to B. A takes entry to the land. It transpires that B is not the owner and cannot give A a good title to the property. A exercises the right of termination. Whether under the law of contract or unjustified enrichment A is entitled to restitution (repetition) of the price. If A has occupied the property, he may be liable to pay recompense to the true owner.[6]

(c) A is the agent of B. Under the contract he is paid on commission every six months. In breach of his contract, A works for C while continuing to work for B. This is a material breach of contract and B exercises his right of termination. As the breach occurred before B was obliged to pay commission to A, on termination B is entitled to refuse to pay the contractually agreed commission to A. However, A has provided services, i.e. a benefit to B. A did not intend to donate the services. Under the law of unjustified enrichment, B is under an *ex lege* obligation to recompense A for the value of the services he has rendered. This will be similar—but not necessarily the same as—the rate of commission which they had agreed in the contract. A's remedy is clearly generated by the law of unjustified enrichment: as A is the contract breaker, the law of contract does not provide her with any remedies.

Damages for Breach of Contract—Contract Damages

6–04   The purpose of damages for breach of contract (contract damages) is to put the innocent party in the position she would have been if the contract had been properly performed; prima facie contract damages are therefore a substitute for performance of the contract. Put another way, the purpose of contract damages is to protect the innocent party's *expectation interest* that the contract will be performed: contract damages look to the future not to the past. Accordingly, the innocent party can obtain compensation for those losses which at the time the contract was made, the parties could reasonably contemplate as arising from the breach. But it is also axiomatic that the innocent party must take reasonable steps to minimise her loss and this can reduce the damages substantially.

Consider the following examples:

(a) A contracts to buy goods from B for £5k which in the ordinary course of business he will sell on to C for £5.5k. B

---

[6] Similarly, if a buyer uses goods before he rejects them and claims repetition of the price, the seller may have a claim for recompense in respect of the purchaser's use and enjoyment of the goods. This is expressly enacted in s.48C(3) of the Sale of Goods Act 1979 when a consumer rescinds under s.48C(1).

repudiates the contract. A is entitled to sue for the expectation interest of her profit from selling to C the goods she bought from B. Prima facie her contract damages are £0.5k. But A must mitigate her loss. If she can obtain substitute goods from D for £5.2k, it is reasonable to do so and her contract damages are reduced to £0.3k. If A could obtain substitute goods from D for £5k or less, her contract damages are reduced to nothing.

(b) A contracts to sell goods to B for £5k. Of the £5k, £0.5k represents profit. B wrongfully rejects the goods. A is entitled to sue for the expectation interest of her profit from the sale to B. Prima facie her contract damages are £0.5k. But A must mitigate her loss. If she can sell the goods to C for £4.7k, it is reasonable to do so and her contract damages are reduced to £0.3k. If A could sell the goods to C for £5k or more, her contract damages are reduced to nothing.

Where the breach arises from defective performance, the mea- **6–05** sure of damages is either the difference in value between the defective and non defective performance or the cost of cure of the defect. Thus for example:

A, a consumer, buys a car from B for £10k. The engine is defective. If the difference in value between A's defective car and a non-defective car is £1k and the cost of cure is £0.5k, A can elect either measure. If A has not paid for the car when the defect is discovered, she can claim damages in the form of a reduction of the price.

Where the defective performance has not led to any diminution of the value of the goods or other property,[7] the courts are not prepared to allow damages on a cost of cure basis if it would be disproportionate to do so. Instead, a modest non-compensatory award can be made in recognition that the innocent party did not have the performance he was entitled to receive: this is sometimes known as "performance damages" or "loss of amenity" consumer surplus!

If a breach of contract results in physical harm, for example a **6–06** person is injured by defective goods which he has bought, contract damages will include compensation for pain and suffering: this is known as *solatium*. But in the absence of physical harm, contract damages do not include compensation for any upset or distress caused by the breach. Nevertheless, damages can be awarded (i) for disappointment if the purpose of the contract was to provide

---

[7] For example, a swimming pool that was not built to the contractual specifications but could still be used and was as valuable as a pool conforming to the specifications.

entertainment or pleasure and (ii) for loss of amenity if the object of the contract was to assure the innocent party the amenity existed.

We have considered the situation where a breach of contract has prevented the innocent party from obtaining a profit from the contract: subject to the duty to mitigate, it is the purpose of contract damages to enable the innocent party to recover her expectation interest. But what if the innocent party has made a bad bargain? Consider the following example:

A sells goods to B for £5k. In fixing the price, A estimated that it would cost him £4.5k to manufacture the goods. Owing to market fluctuations, it costs A £5k to manufacture the goods. B wrongfully rejects the goods. The purpose of contract damages is to put the innocent party into the position she would have been if the contract had been performed properly. If B had accepted the goods, A would have expended £5k in return for a price of £5k and made no profit. Therefore A's original expectation interest of a profit of £0.5k has *in fact* been reduced to nil. Accordingly, B's breach of contract has not caused A 's loss as the loss would have occurred even if B had accepted the goods.

The cost of manufacturing the goods is known as A's reliance or *status quo* interest. The reliance or *status quo* interest is protected by the law of delict. The purpose of reparation, delict damages, is to put the victim of the delict into the position she would have been if the delict had not taken place: delict damages look to the past not to the future.[8] It is a fundamental principle of the law of obligations that a breach of contract is not in itself a wrong for the purpose of enabling the innocent party to sue for delict damages and thereby recover her reliance interest. To do so, would run a coach and four through the principle that a person is not entitled to be compensated for making a bad bargain.[9]

This must be distinguished from those situations where there is concurrent liability in contract and delict and the innocent party/ victim can elect to sue in either one or the other. The first of these is a breach of contract which results in physical/mental harm to the innocent party or physical damage to his property. Thus for example, it is a term of the contract of employment that an employer must take reasonable care for the safety of his employee while at the same time the employer is under a delictual duty to

---

[8] However, in order fully to assess economic loss deriving from physical harm, it is often necessary to make projections as to a victim's future health and earning prospects.

[9] In exceptional cases where the expectation interest is unknown, the innocent party has recovered her reliance interest, for example the cost of fitting out an expedition to salvage a non-existent ship which the contract breaker had warranted had sunk in a particular part of the ocean.

take reasonable care to prevent an employee from sustaining physical/mental harm. If an employee is injured he can therefore sue either in contract or in delict: but it is largely irrelevant which he chooses, as the standard of care expected of the employer is the same, i.e. there will be a breach of contract only if he did not take reasonable care and it is only if he did not take reasonable care that there will be a breach of the delictual duty.

The second situation is when the innocent party sustains pure **6–07** economic loss. Where A and B are parties to a contract, B can owe A a delictual duty to take reasonable care to prevent A sustaining pure economic loss if (i) B has assumed responsibility for A's economic interests and (ii) B knows that A will rely on B's expertise in the provision of advice or other services. Here we are concerned with the liability of such professions as accountants, banks, financial advisers, lawyers, surveyors and valuers. For example, A may transfer money to B to be used in a business to be run by B. It is agreed that in return for the funding, A will be entitled to a share of the profits of B's business. Owing to B's negligence, the business fails. A can sue in contract damages for loss of his share of the profits, i.e. his expectation interest or in delict damages for the amount he had transferred to B, his reliance interest.

Many of these cases are concerned with the situation where B has provided A with advice or information in respect of proposed transactions between A and a third party, C. For example, A hires B, a surveyor, to carry out a survey on C's property. Owing to his negligence, B values the property at £500k. In fact it is only worth £400k. In reliance on that survey, A lends £400k to C and takes out a standard security for that sum over the building. As a result of a general fall in property prices, the value of the property drops to £200k. C defaults on the loan. A's loss is £200k. If A sues B for contract damages, he can recover £100k, the difference between the value warranted by B and the actual value of the property at the time of the survey: the rest of his loss is due to the general fall in the value of property, i.e. because A made a bad bargain with C. Similarly, if A sues B for delict damages, he can only recover that part of his loss which was reasonably foreseeable as a consequence of the information being wrong, i.e. B's £100k negligent under-valuation of the property: the rest of his loss was due to the general fall in the value of the property. Only if B was fraudulent when he made the valuation, would B be liable for *all* A's losses arising from the transaction with C.

On the other hand, if B had advised A to lend money to C—as opposed to providing him with information on the value of C's property for the purpose of a standard security—then even if B was merely negligent, he would be liable in delict damages for all the losses arising from the transaction. This is probably also the case in relation to contract damages.

6–08   In cases of liability for pure economic loss, it is therefore not surprising that the contract will usually contain a term excluding or limiting liability for contract damages and denying that B is assuming responsibility for A so that a duty of care to prevent A sustaining pure economic loss does not arise. Such exemption clauses have no effect unless they can be shown to be fair and reasonable.[10] But provided the term is fair and reasonable, we can again see how the parties to a contract are free to displace the legal principles which would otherwise apply in the absence of such a clause. On the other hand, an exemption clause purporting to limit or exclude the liability of a business for causing death or personal injury is void.[11] Therefore a business can no longer exclude or restrict by contract term its liability for breach of a duty to take reasonable care to prevent a person sustaining physical/mental harm.

When performance is discharged by frustration or an innocent party terminates performance in response to a material breach of contract, economic imbalances resulting from part performance of the contract can be redressed by the law on unjustified enrichment.[12] However, as a general rule, a breach of contract is not in itself a wrong which generates rights to restitution or recompense. Consider the following example:

A lends B £100k to be used in B's business, X. It is a term of the contract of loan that B will retain £100k of his own capital in business, X. In breach of that term, B transfers £50k of his own capital into another business, Y. Y business flourishes. B's £50k is now worth £150k. A sues B for breach of contract. It is established that A's investment is now worth £120k but that it would not have been any more even if B had not removed the £50k from the business. A has therefore not sustained any loss from B's breach of contract and he is therefore not entitled to any contract damages. Moreover, B's breach of contract is not treated as a wrong which triggers a right to restitution. In other words, A cannot argue that B's breach of contract gives rise to an *ex lege* obligation on B to disgorge in favour of A a proportion of the profits he has made as a consequence of his breach of the loan agreement.

The situation would be different if A and B were partners in the X business. When B invested the money in the Y business, this would be a breach of the fiduciary relationship which subsists between partners. This is a wrong which creates an *ex lege*

---

[10] Unfair Contracts Terms Act 1977, ss.16(1)(b) and 24(4). This is also the case where an exemption clause purports to limit or exclude liability for physical damage to property.

[11] *ibid.*, s.16(1)(a).

[12] However, an innocent buyer's right to repetition of the price after a material breach by the seller may well be a contractual remedy *stricto sensu*.

obligation on B to disgorge the profits he has made in the Y business in favour of the partnership he has with A. This is so whenever there is a breach of a fiduciary relationship, for example trustee and beneficiary: it has also been extended to quasi-fiduciary relationships, for example the Crown and civil servants or members of the forces who abuse their positions in order to obtain monies.

In addition, where the contract consists of a negative obligation, while the innocent party's primary remedy is an interdict to prevent the breach, if the breach has occurred it has been treated as a wrong which gives rise to a claim for recompense. For example, A sells land to B. It is a term of the contract that B can build up to 5 dwelling houses on the site. In breach of that term, B builds 10. A has not sustained any loss and therefore contract damages are not available. It would appear that the breach is nevertheless a wrong which triggers a right to seek recompense. This would be calculated on the basis of what B would have had to pay A in order to obtain a release of his—negative—obligation not to build more than five dwelling houses on the land.

Title to Sue

Contracts and unilateral obligations create rights and duties **6–09** between the parties. The right to have performance of the contract or promise, is a right enjoyed by the obligee (creditor) against the obligor (debtor). If the obligor fails to perform, the obligee can seek specific implement or damages for breach of contract or unilateral obligation, i.e. promise. But these voluntarily created obligations are paradigms of personal rights which can only be enforced against the obligor. As personal rights they are of little value if the obligor becomes insolvent unless they have been underpinned by a real security in the obligee's favour over the obligor's property, for example a standard security. Moreover, because the rights created are personal rights which can only be enforced against the obligor, as a general rule only the obligee has title to sue for specific implement or damages for breach. In the case of an unilateral obligation, only the promisee has title to sue the promisor: in the case of a contract, the obligor can only be sued by another party to the contract. This is sometimes known as privity of contract.

There are two major exceptions to the doctrine of privity. First, where A, the stipulator, enters into a contract with B, the debtor, under which A and B intend that B makes a payment or other performance to a third party, C, the third party can have what is known as a *jus quaesitum tertio*. This is a right to compel the debtor to perform the obligation in C's favour even though C is not a party to the contract between A and B. Before a *jus quaesitum tertio* arises it must be clear that A and B intended not only to benefit C but also intended to give up their right to change their minds, i.e. that their intention to benefit C was also intended to be irrevocable. This is usually done by publicising the contract (to C or more generally) so that C knows that he has acquired rights under the contract.

We have argued that the rights created by voluntary obligations are often considered by the obligee to be his property, i.e. he "owns" the personal right to enforce the obligation. For example, if A lends money to B, A has a personal right against B to have the loan repaid. A "owns" B's debt. A can assign the debt to C who on intimation to B will have a real right to be paid by B and C's assignation will have priority should A have assigned the same debt to another party. C has a real right only in the sense that on intimation the right to the payment of the debt from B is no longer part of A's private patrimony should A become insolvent. But C, the assignee, only "owns" a personal right against B which would be of little value should B become insolvent. Nevertheless, the right of an assignee to sue the original obligor on a contract to which he was not the original creditor is the second major exception to the principle of privity of contract. C has no better rights than the cedent, A. The original debtor, B, can therefore plead against C any defences which he would have had against a claim by A, for example that the original contract was null or annullable.

Further reading

McBryde, *Law of Contract in Scotland* (2nd ed., 2002)
MacQueen and Thomson, *Contract Law in Scotland* (2000)
Woolman and Lake, *Contract* (3rd ed., 2001)

CHAPTER 7

OBLIGATIONS ARISING FROM WRONGS

Introduction

Ex lege obligations are obligations which are thrust upon the **7–01** obligor by operation of the law, in contrast to obligations which the obligor creates voluntarily by virtue of making a promise or entering into a contract. In many cases the obligation arises in response to a voluntary act or omission of the part of the obligor. So for example, if A damages B's car as a result of careless driving, while A's driving is a voluntary act, A's obligation to make reparation to B for the harm incurred when his car was damaged by A's negligence arises *ex lege*, i.e. regardless of A's will or intention. In this and the next chapter we shall consider obligations which arise as a consequence of the obligee having been the victim of a wrong, i.e. a delict perpetrated by the obligor. As a general principle a wrong triggers a right to obtain reparation, i.e. compensation or damages for the losses arising from the harm sustained by the victim. Sometimes, however, the victim has the right to obtain an interdict to prevent the recurrence of the delict (or to prevent harm being sustained by a threatened delict). Again, a wrong can also give rise to a right to restitution and recompense or a right to compel the obligor to disgorge any profits that he has made from the delict. We shall examine the nature of the wrongs and the remedies they trigger in the context of the interests which have been infringed.

Property Rights

We have argued that a hallmark of a system of private law is **7–02** the recognition of real rights in property. In this section we shall consider the way in which the law of obligations operates to protect property rights and provides a range of remedies when property rights are wrongfully infringed.

(a) Heritable Property

Trespass. Trespass is the wrong committed when the defender **7–03** enters onto land owned by the pursuer without the pursuer's permission.[1] The pursuer is entitled to ask the defender to leave and can use reasonable force to compel him to do so. If it appears that trespass will recur, the pursuer is entitled to an interdict ordering the defender not to enter the pursuer's land. Damages are not awarded merely because trespass has taken place: but the defender will be obliged to compensate the owner if he has in fact caused physical harm to the land.

Trespass is a temporary intrusion onto the land. If the trespasser intends to occupy the property for an indefinite period, then two further wrongs may occur. First, if the owner is not in possession at the time, the trespasser is liable for intrusion: secondly, if the owner is in possession and is wrongfully removed by the trespasser, the trespasser is liable for ejection.[2] In these circumstances, the owner can seek a court order to have the trespasser summarily removed from the property. In addition, he is entitled to what are known as violent profits. These are the greatest profits the owner could have made if he had been in possession of the land as well as compensation for any damage in fact caused by the trespasser. In the case of agricultural land, violent profits would be based on the crops that the rightful owner could have grown: in the case of houses, violent profits were customarily twice the rent the house could have obtained. It does not matter that the owner would not in fact have used the land profitably in such ways. Not only are violent profits not compensatory, but they also compel the defender to disgorge profits that he may well not have earned. In effect they act as a sanction against wrongful occupation of heritable property. But they also illustrate graphically how a wrong can generate a remedy which is not limited to reparation of the victim's losses.

7–04 Nuisance The owner of property is entitled to use it: but he must do so in such a way that he does not unduly disturb other people's enjoyment of their own property. If he does, he can be liable in nuisance. Before there can be a nuisance, the defender's actions must produce effects on the pursuer's land which go beyond what a person could reasonably tolerate: *plus quam tolerabile*. It is not enough that they cause inconvenience: the effects of the defender's conduct must be *intolerable*. Examples of nuisances include noise, smells, the emission of smoke and flooding from burst pipes.

The primary remedy is interdict, i.e. an order that the defender should stop causing the nuisance so that the pursuer can enjoy

---

[1] This, of course, is now subject to the statutory right to roam enjoyed by citizens in Scotland under the Land Reform (Scotland) Act 2003.
[2] Intrusion and ejection are possessory remedies. Technically it is the person in possession of the land (who will often be the owner) who has title to sue.

her property in peace. Interdict will be granted if the pursuer can show that the effects of the defender's conduct were *plus quam tolerabile*. There is no need to establish that the defender was at fault in causing the nuisance. However, where the nuisance has caused harm to the pursuer's property, it is necessary to show that the defender was at fault (*culpa*). In other words, that the nuisance was caused deliberately by the defender or through his negligent, i.e. careless conduct. The measure of damages is the diminution in value of the pursuer's property as a result of the harm caused by the nuisance. Where the property has been damaged, for example by a flood, this may be equated to the cost of cure. Where a business lost customers while it was affected by a nuisance, the diminution in value of the property during that period has been taken to be the loss of profits.

Where the defender uses his land deliberately to interfere with his neighbour's enjoyment of her property, he will be liable *in aemulationem vicini*. This means there can be liability even if the effects of the defender's actions on the pursuer's use of her land are not *plus quam intolerabile* and would not constitute a nuisance: on the other hand, the pursuer must show that the defender's predominant purpose in using his property as he did was to cause harm to the pursuer. This will be very difficult to prove.

Fault or *Culpa*. Land can be damaged either deliberately, for 7–05 example by throwing a stone to break a window or carelessly, for example when a bonfire gets out of control and the fire spreads to neighbouring property. The owner of the land is entitled to seek reparation for the damage to his property provided that he can establish that the harm was a result of the defender's fault or *culpa*. The principles of the general liability to make reparation for harm caused by fault or *culpa* will be discussed in the next chapter.

(b) Corporeal Moveable Property

Wrongful Interference with Moveable Property. It is generally 7–06 accepted that there is no delict of trespass to corporeal moveable property: merely to touch or hold such property without the owner's permission does not in itself give the owner a right to damages. However, the owner is entitled to an interdict if a person occupies his corporeal moveable property without his permission, for example a "sit in" on board a floating oil installation or a "break in" at his holiday caravan. Moreover, when the defender uses the property without the owner's permission, the defender will be under an *ex lege* obligation to pay recompense to the owner for wrongful use of his property: here it is the wrong and not the principle of unjustified enrichment which generates the right to recompense. So if for example B regularly rode A's horse without A's permission, the wrongful use of the horse triggers a right to seek recompense from B as well as an interdict ordering him not to ride the horse again without permission. Recompense would be based on what is a reasonable fee for the hire of a horse.[3]

Where corporeal moveable property is stolen, the owner retains the right to vindicate the property from the thief or any third party into whose hands it has come. It does not matter that the third party was a bona fide transferee for value.[4] The right to vindicate is lost if the property ceases to exist in its original form. Then the owner of the stolen property is entitled to recompense for the value of the property and any profit gained from its sale or the sale of its substitute. As against the original thief, this right to recompense is generated by the wrong, i.e. the theft of the property. In principle, it can also be brought against any subsequent transferee who acquires the property in bad faith, i.e. who knew that the property had been stolen and was therefore privy to the theft.[5] Since an owner can vindicate against a bona transferee for value of the property, it could be argued that this right to seek recompense should also be available against her. On the other hand, once the stolen property can no longer be vindicated because it has been used up or transformed, as against bona fide transferees it could be contended that the claim for recompense can only be generated by unjustified enrichment. If so, the bona fide transferee for value will not be liable because, as she gave value for the property, she has not been enriched.[6] It will be clear that wrongful interference with corporeal moveable property is

---

[3] The right to obtain recompense replaces the old action of spuilzie where the owner was entitled to violent profits as well as the return of his property if it had been wrongfully seized from him. Technically spuilzie remains a competent action.

[4] However, the owner's right to vindicate from a bona fide third party comes to an end if he has possession of the property for twenty years. But the third party never becomes the owner of the property and as the property has become a res nullius it is owned by the Crown. An owner never loses his right to vindicate against the thief or a person privy to the theft: Prescription and Limitation (Scotland) Act 1973, s.8 and para.(g) of Sch.3.

[5] The original owner cannot obtain recompense more than once for the same interest. For example, if he has obtained the value of the stolen property from the thief, he cannot obtain its value again from a subsequent transferee. However, he can receive from the subsequent transferee recompense for any profits he has made from selling on the stolen property or its substitute.

[6] A bona fide transferee without value, for example a donee, would have been enriched and, in the absence of a change of position or other defence, is obliged to make restitution.

paradigmatic of when a wrong triggers a right to restitution or recompense in Scots law.

Fault or *Culpa*. Corporeal moveable property can be destroyed 7–07 or physically damaged either deliberately or carelessly. The owner of the property is entitled to seek reparation for the damage to the property if he can establish that the harm was caused by the defender's fault or *culpa*. The principles of the general liability to make reparation for harm caused by fault or *culpa* will be discussed in the next chapter.

(c) Incorporeal Moveable Property

(i) Goodwill, intellectual property and confidential information. 7–08 The goodwill of a business can be a very valuable asset. An important element of goodwill is any marketing device whereby customers recognise the product and can distinguish it from rival products. These include names and the "get up" of the product. If a particular marketing device is part of the goodwill of A's business, the law protects A's goodwill by preventing it being undermined by any competitor, B, who "passes off" his own product as that of A by using a similar marketing device. The primary remedy is interdict but damages can also be awarded. Where intellectual property, for example patents and copyrights, is subject to a statutory regime, the statutes provide remedies for misuse of the property. In addition, the common law has developed protection for misuse of confidential information. First, the information must be such that a reasonable person would appreciate that it is confidential. This could be as a consequence of the nature of the information itself or the circumstances in which it is imparted. Secondly, the protection flies off if in fact the information is no longer confidential at the time relief is sought. Thirdly, the breach of confidence can be justified if it was in the public interest that the information should be made more generally available. The primary remedy is interdict to prevent the publication of the information. If the information has been published, damages can be awarded as reparation for any loss sustained. But breach of confidential information also triggers a right to have the defender disgorge all the profits he has gained as a result of publishing the information.

(ii) Money—Pure Economic Wealth. Money is a form of incor- 7–09 poreal moveable property. In this section we are using the term, money, as a synonym for wealth which does not take the form of land or corporeal moveable property. It includes stocks and shares and other investments as well as money in a bank or building society. More importantly perhaps, it is intended to include the wealth that arises from economic relations between persons: for example, anticipated profits from existing or future contracts. In short, we are concerned in these paragraphs with relief for pure economic loss sustained as a consequence of wrongful conduct. This should be distinguished from derivative or parasitic economic loss. This is loss which arises as a consequence of physical damage to property (for example, the cost of repairs to a car damaged in a road accident) or physical or mental injury to a person (for example, loss of wages while recovering from injuries sustained in a road accident).

Fraud

7–10 Fraud arises when a person engages in positive conduct which is intended to deceive another and cause her harm. In most cases the positive conduct takes the form of a misrepresentation (by words or conduct) and the harm is pure economic loss.[7] Consider the following examples:

   (a) A presents falsified business accounts to B. As a conse-
       quence, B buys the business from A for £X. The business
       is only worth £X—Y. If A knew that the accounts were
       false and intended to deceive B so that B would buy the
       business, A is fraudulent. A is liable for all the losses
       sustained by B which are a direct result of the fraud.
       These include not only the difference in the price paid for
       the business and its actual value but also any further
       losses sustained by B when attempting to run the
       business.[8]
   (b) A tells B that a painting was owned by Queen Victoria. As
       a consequence, B buys the painting from A for £X. The
       painting was never owned by Queen Victoria and is only
       worth £X—Y. If A knew that the painting was never
       owned by Queen Victoria and intended to deceive B, A is
       fraudulent. B can rescind the contract and obtain repeti-
       tion of the price but he must then return the painting to
       A. As an alternative, B can keep the painting and sue A in
       delict for his loss, i.e. the difference between the price he
       paid and the actual value of the painting.

Fraud is a wrong which also generates a right to restitution or recompense as an alternative to damages for loss. Consider the following examples:

---

[7] Damage to property and personal injury can be caused by fraud. For example, A
lets B destroy B's crops because A lied to B that the crops were infected by a pest
or A lies to B that her husband has been killed with the result that B sustains
mental harm. Such cases are very rare.

[8] B could of course elect to rescind the contract and seek repetition of the price.

(a) A tells B that her painting is a copy of a Picasso and worth £50. As a consequence, B sells the painting to A for £50. The painting is a genuine Picasso worth £500k. A has lost approximately £499,950. If A knew that the painting was a genuine Picasso and intended to deceive B, A is guilty of fraud. B could sue A in delict for damages as reparation for his financial loss. Alternatively, B can rescind the contract and obtain restitution of the painting (but he must, of course, return the painting). But if before the contract was rescinded, B had sold the painting for £700k to C, a bona fide purchaser, the right to rescission is lost as *restitutio in integrum* is no longer possible. Although B entered into the contract under an error induced by A's fraudulent misrepresentation, the contract of sale and the conveyance of the ownership of the painting are annullable and not null. Therefore B has a valid, albeit reducible, title to transfer to a third party. The conveyance to C takes place before A has rescinded. As C is a bona fide transferee for value, her title to the painting is no longer vulnerable to reduction. But fraud is a wrong which generates a right to restitution and recompense. Therefore B is entitled to obtain recompense from A not only for the value of the painting but also for the profits he has made on the sale of the painting. As C was in good faith and therefore not a party to the fraud,[9] any rights to restitution or recompense are generated by unjustified enrichment. As C is a bona fide transferee for value, he is not liable to restore the painting to B as C has not been enriched because he paid for the painting.[10]

(b) If A defrauds B of £10k, B is entitled to damages of £10k to compensate him for the loss of his money. However, if B can show that A had used the money to buy assets which are now worth £50k, B is entitled to restitution of the fund and the profits it has earned, i.e. the fraudster is obliged to disgorge the profits. If the fund was transferred to a bona fide transferee, any right to restitution or recompense is generated by unjustified enrichment so that a bona fide transferee for value of the monies, for

---

[9] If C was a party to the fraud, B's rights to restitution and recompense which have been generated by the wrong, i.e. A's fraud, would be enforceable against C.

[10] If C was a bona fide transferee without value, for example a donee, C would be obliged to restore the painting to B in the absence of a change of position defence.

example a person who has provided A with goods and services, will not be liable as he has not been enriched.[11]

Before there is liability for fraud, the pursuer has to establish that the defender did not or could not know or believe that his statement was true. This is extremely difficult to prove. There can be no liability for fraud if the defender, however carelessly or naively in the circumstances, positively believed that his statement was true. In other words, it has to be proved that the fraudster intended to harm his victim. This is the reason that fraud results in criminal as well as civil liability. Because of this, liability for fraud cannot be excluded or limited by an exemption clause.

Negligent Provision of Advice or Services

7–11 Where A and B are parties to a contract, B can owe A a delictual duty to take reasonable care to prevent A sustaining pure economic loss if (i) B has assumed—or it can be objectively inferred from the circumstances that B has assumed—responsibility for A's economic interests and (ii) B knows that A will rely on B's expertise in the provision of advice or other services. The court cannot infer that B assumed responsibility if the terms of the contract expressly stipulate that B has not done so. Where such a disclaimer takes the form of an exemption clause, however, it will only operate to prevent the duty arising if the clause is reasonable in all the circumstances of the case.[12]

However, a duty to prevent pure economic loss can also arise when there is no contractual relationship between the parties. It is enough that B has assumed—or it can be objectively inferred from the circumstances that B has assumed—responsibility for the financial interests of A, knowing that A will rely on B's expertise in the provision of advice or other services. Consider the following example:

A is a surveyor. He enters into a contract with a bank to survey a property. In reliance on the survey, the bank decides that it will lend B the money with which B can purchase the property. The loan will be secured by a standard security over the property. Having obtained the finance, B relies on the survey and purchases the property using the loan to do so. Owing to his carelessness, A failed to notice that the property requires extensive repairs and consequently is only worth half the price B paid for it. If the bank sustains a loss, it can sue A for breach of contract or in delict for

---

[11] If C was a bona transferee without value, for example a donee, C would be obliged to return the money to B in the absence of a change of position defence.
[12] Unfair Contract Terms Act 1977, ss.16(1)(b) and 24(4). The Act only applies when a *business* purports to exclude or limit its liability for negligence.

negligence. What remedy, if any, has B against A? There is no remedy for breach of contract as B is not a party to the contract between A and the bank. B's only remedy lies in delict. This will depend on whether A owes B a duty of care to prevent B sustaining pure economic loss. A duty of care would arise if A assumed—or it could be objectively inferred that A had assumed—responsibility for B's economic interests when he agreed to provide a survey for the bank. This would depend on whether A knew that the survey would be used not only by the bank but also by a potential purchaser of the property. The inference of such an assumption and knowledge of B's concomitant reliance would be enhanced if, for example, A knew that the potential purchaser had paid for the survey instructed by the bank or A knew the identity of B. If A had attempted to avoid delictual liability to a purchaser of the property by a non-contractual notice in the survey disclaiming liability, it will only succeed if it was fair and reasonable to do so.[13] Such a notice might be fair if B was a business purchasing commercial property and able to afford to instruct an independent survey: conversely it might be unfair if B was a first time buyer of a small flat.

The duty to prevent pure economic loss is most likely to arise **7–12** where as a result of information or advice carelessly provided by the defender:

(a) the pursuer is prevented from entering into a prospective contract: for example, where A fails to obtain employment as a consequence of a reference B had agreed to provide but which as a result of B's carelessness was defamatory of A;

(b) the pursuer is induced to enter into an uneconomic contract: for example, where A enters into an uneconomic contract with C because of information provided by B who knew that A was considering to contract with C and would rely on the information provided;

(c) the pursuer is induced to remain in an existing contract which becomes unprofitable: for example where a bank agrees to continue to finance A as a consequence of information given to the bank by B, A's auditor, who knows that the bank will rely on the information in deciding whether or not to continue its support.

These are examples of what is known as relational economic loss, i.e. loss arising as a consequence of negligently interfering with the pursuer's exercise of her power to engage in contractual

---

[13] Unfair Contract Terms Act 1977, ss.16(1)(b) and 24(4). The Act only applies when a *business* purports to exclude as limit its liability for negligence.

relationships. But as a general rule there is no duty of care to prevent non-relational economic loss. So for example, if A buys a car which is defective and has to be repaired, A's remedy is to sue the seller for breach of s.14 of the Sale of Goods Act 1979 (goods not of reasonable quality): A cannot sue the manufacturer in delict for the cost of repair or the difference in price between a defective and non-defective car. Similarly, the builder of a house is not liable in delict to a purchaser for the cost of repair or the difference in value between a defective and non-defective building: the builder would only be liable for pure economic loss if, for example, the builder was also the seller and the purchaser was suing him for breach of contract. This should be contrasted with the potential delictual liability of a surveyor on whose information the purchaser relied when she decided to exercise her power to enter into a contract and purchase the defective property.

7–13   That said, it should always be remembered that cases where there is liability for pure economic loss are comparatively rare. First, there will often be a contract between the parties and it will be simpler to sue in contract than in delict. Secondly, no duty arises unless there has been *both* an assumption of responsibility by the defender *and* knowledge of the pursuer's concomitant reliance. It is not enough that the defender has caused economic loss to the pursuer by increasing the pursuer's costs of performance of a contract or otherwise rendering the pursuer's contracts less profitable. For example, B has a contract with A to lay a pipeline owned by A under the ocean. During the work the pipeline is damaged by a third party, C. As a result, B cannot lay the pipeline within the contractually stipulated time and incurs financial penalties, i.e. pure economic loss. While A the owner of the pipeline might have been able to sue C for physical damage to his property, B cannot sue C for the pure economic loss he has sustained because he could not complete the contract on time. C did not know about the contract between A and B. C did not assume any responsibility for the economic interests of B and B did not rely on C's advice or services. Thus a duty of care to prevent pure economic loss does not arise.

Even where there is such a duty, there is no liability unless the economic loss was sustained as a consequence of the defender's breach of duty, i.e. it must be established that the defender was negligent. What amounts to negligence will be discussed in the next chapter.

Wrongful Interference with Economic Interests

7–14   A and B enter into an onerous contract. Each has a personal right to demand performance from the other. If A fails to perform, that is a breach of contract and B is entitled to seek a decree of specific implement or damages against A. Although B has only a personal right against A to perform the contract, the law treats such a right as a form of incorporeal property which B can assign to a third party, C. To that extent we can say that B owns her contractual rights vis-à-vis A. It is therefore not surprising that the law of delict protects these rights from wrongful interference by a person who is not a party to the contract.

The basic wrong is inducement of breach of contract. A has a contract with B. If C, with the intention of causing economic harm to A, induces B to break his contract with A, A can sue C in delict as an alternative to suing B for breach of contract. Before C is liable, he must know that a contract subsists between A and B: but if such knowledge is established, it will be readily inferred that C acted with the intention of harming A. While C must induce B to break his contract, the means of inducement need not be unlawful; so for example, C will be liable if he gave B a gift if he would break the contract with A. There is a defence if C can prove that the inducement of breach of contract was justified, for example, if it was the only way to stop A engaging in illegal trading practices.

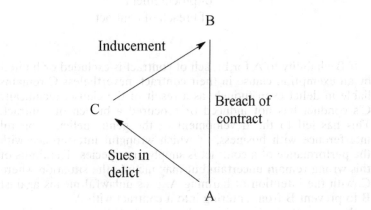

If B is not prepared to break the contract, C may try *to prevent* **7–15** B from performing his obligations thereby *procuring* a breach of B's contract with A. But before there is liability for procurement, the means used by C to prevent B from performing must be unlawful. Thus for example if, with the intention of harming A, C stole B's tools so that he could not fulfil his obligations under a contract with A, C is liable for procuring B's breach of contract with A as the theft constitutes the unlawful means. However, the procurement will usually take place indirectly. Here C with the intention of harming A, induces D to break his contract with B to prevent B performing his contract with A: C's inducement of a breach by D of his contract with B constitutes the unlawful means for the procurement by C of the breach by B of his contract with A. Again there is a defence if C can establish that the procurement was justified.

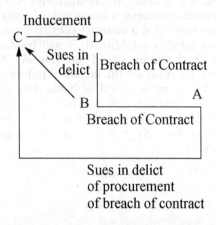

Sues in delict
of procurement
of breach of contract

7–16   If B's liability to A for breach of contract is excluded or limited by an exemption clause in their contract, nevertheless C remains liable in delict even though, as a result of the clause, technically C's conduct has not induced or procured a breach of contract. This has led to the development of the genus delict, wrongful interference with business, of which wrongful interference with the performance of a contract is simply one species. The limits of this wrong remain uncertain but may include the situation where C, with the intention of harming A, uses unlawful means against B to prevent B from entering into a contract with A.

Where, with the intention of harming A, C threatens B with an unlawful act unless B harms A economically, if B yields to the threat and harms A, A can sue C on the grounds of intimidation. The threat must be of unlawful means which will harm B if carried out. B must give into the threats and harm A. But B's actions which harm A need not be unlawful. For example, C threatens to break his existing contract with B if B concludes a contract with C's competitor, A. If B breaks off pre-contractual negotiations, he has committed no wrong against A : B is entitled to do so as no contract has yet been formed with A. But because the reason that B withdrew from the negotiations was to avoid the consequence of C's threatened unlawful act, i.e. C's breach of his contract with B, A is entitled to sue C for intimidation. Intimidation always involves three parties: C, the intimidator, B, the person intimidated and A, the ultimate victim who sustains economic harm as a consequence of B's act which he has carried out to avoid the unlawful means threatened by C. As always C may have the defence of justification.

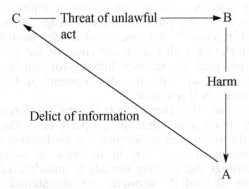

There is no liability in intimidation if C threatens to harm B by **7–17** lawful means. This is because it is a fundamental principle of a capitalist society that one person is entitled to use lawful means to cause economic harm to another. Thus in the interests of competition one retailer is entitled to undercut a rival retailer. But if two or more persons combine together to use lawful means which will cause economic harm to another, then they will be liable if their predominant purpose was to harm that person rather than further their own legitimate ends. This is known as a lawful means conspiracy. There is no liability unless it can be shown that the parties' predominant purpose was to cause harm to the victim. So A and B can agree to lower their prices even if this will cause economic harm to C if their predominant reason was to increase their own profits: but their agreement would be actionable as a lawful means conspiracy if their predominant purpose was to harm C and not advance their own economic interests. Where, however, the parties use unlawful means, they are liable for an unlawful means conspiracy if they had an intention of harming C, even if it was not their predominant intention.[14] The conspirators can rely on the justification defence.

---

[14] Where the unlawful means is itself actionable, for example to induce a third party D to break his contract with C, C will usually sue on the basis of the substantive delict—inducing breach of contract—rather than conspiracy. It is only when the

What all these delicts have in common is that the defender intends to harm the pursuer. Like fraud, they are paradigmatic of intentional wrongdoing. This is important. As we have seen,[15] negligent interference with a party's performance of his contract whereby the performance becomes less profitable (or even unprofitable) is not an actionable wrong. Before there can be delictual liability for causing relational economic loss *unintentionally*, the defender must have breached a pre-existing duty of care arising from his assumption of responsibility for the economic interests of the pursuer and knowledge of the pursuer's concomitant reliance.[16] But once a defender *intends* to cause harm by interfering with the performance of the pursuer's contracts, the prospect of delictual liability for causing pure economic loss opens up with the development of the economic delicts discussed in this section.

We have argued that these delicts involve interference with the pursuer's property albeit that the property takes the form of a personal right to demand performance of contractual obligations. It is interesting to note that in the case of many of these economic wrongs the primary remedy is interdict, i.e. an order stopping the defender's wrongful—or threatened wrongful— conduct. If the pursuer does in fact sustain loss, she is entitled to damages in reparation.

Reputation

7-18   A person's reputation is protected by the law against defamation and verbal injury. A defamatory statement is a statement which tends to lower the pursuer in the estimation of right thinking members of society. These include imputations on moral character, of criminality, professional incompetence and financial unsoundness. When the pursuer establishes that the defender made such a statement then it is presumed to be false and made with the intention of harming the pursuer, i.e. with malice. The defender can rebut the presumption of falsehood by establishing the truth of the statement, *veritas*. There are various defences

---

unlawful means used is not in itself actionable, for example if A and B agree to run their business in breach of statutory regulations which were not designed to give C a right to sue for damages if they were broken, that C would have to sue on the basis of an unlawful means conspiracy.

[15] Above para.7–13.

[16] It has been argued that where parties are connected by a series of contracts, A–B–C, and C knows of the existence of contract A–B and that A will suffer economic loss if C defectively performs his contract with B, then C may have a duty to A not to perform his contract with B negligently. However, this is very controversial.

designed to allow freedom of speech which will exonerate the defender either absolutely or on proof that the statement was made without malice. A statement which is not defamatory may nevertheless be actionable as a verbal injury if it exposes the pursuer to public hatred, ridicule and contempt. But the onus rests on the pursuer to show that it was false and made with malice.

It is again interesting to note that a pursuer will often seek an interdict to prevent publication of an allegedly defamatory statement. If such a statement is published the law presumes that the pursuer was upset and will award damages for the distress (*solatium*): in a case of verbal injury, upset must be established by the pursuer. If the pursuer suffers economic loss, for example loss of profits from her business, as a consequence of defamation or verbal injury, she is entitled to damages in reparation.

Bodily Integrity

Every one is entitled to bodily integrity.[17] Where A intends to **7–19** invade B's physical integrity without B's consent, he is guilty of assault. An assault is an actionable wrong. In many cases of assault the victim suffers physical harm but there is also liability for any mental harm sustained. Indeed, damages can be awarded for the insult of being assaulted (*contumelia*). The victim is also entitled to damages for any pain and suffering (*solatium*) and any derivative economic loss, for example loss of earnings when recovering from her injuries. There is no assault if the victim has consented, for example as when participating in sports which involve bodily contact. There is therefore no assault if a patient has consented to a medical or dental procedure. However, doctors and dentists are under a duty to tell their patients of those risks inherent in the procedure which a responsible body of medical opinion would disclose. Failure to do so is a breach of the doctor or dentist's general duty of care towards her patient and will entitle the patient to damages for professional negligence: but it does not invalidate the patient's consent to the procedure and therefore there is no liability for assault.

Rape is actionable as an assault because the sexual intercourse was obtained without the victim's consent. Where the victim's consent is obtained by deception or abuse of trust, there can be liability for seduction: and if a woman is fraudulently induced to

---

[17] The common law does not recognise a right to privacy outwith the protection of confidential information. Under Art.8 of the European Convention on Human Rights, a person has the right to respect for his private life: breach of this Article could give rise to a claim for damages.

enter marriage which is void, for example because the man is already married, there is liability for entrapment. These are examples of the genus delict, fraud. There is now a statutory delict providing reparation for harassment.[18] A person is also entitled to damages if he has been wrongfully deprived of his liberty.

In practice, few victims of criminal assault seek reparation from their attackers. This is because criminals are usually persons of limited means. Victims can seek compensation from the state under the Criminal Injuries Compensation Scheme.

7–20 In contrast, reparation is often sought for physical and mental harm sustained as a consequence of a defender's careless—as opposed to intentional—conduct.[19] This is because many cases arise from road accidents and accidents at work where the defender is insured and there are funds to pay the damages awarded. For the same reason, claims are increasingly being brought against state agencies such as the police, schools and social services. The need for a "deep pocket" is because claims for reparation for physical and mental harm wrongfully caused by negligence can be very substantial. When a person sustains physical or mental harm, she is entitled to compensation for the pain and suffering she has experienced (*solatium*). This is known as non-patrimonial loss. In addition, she is entitled to compensation for the economic losses which derive from the harm sustained: derivative or parasitic economic loss. This will include the loss of earnings from the date of the accident to the date of the action, future loss of earnings when the pursuer will be unable to return to work (or will only be able to return to work on a lower salary or wage), loss of pension rights and the cost of health care both up to the date of the action and in the future. This is known as patrimonial loss. Where the victim dies, his family can obtain compensation not only for non-patrimonial loss, for example the grief arising from the death but also for patrimonial loss, i.e. the loss of the deceased's financial support.[20] Damages for patrimonial loss, i.e. for derivative or parasitic economic losses, can therefore be very substantial.

Although we do not own our right to physical integrity, the law of delict provides compensation for the economic losses which are sustained when the right is breached as well as *solatium* for the pain and suffering caused. Even in the area of personal

---

[18] Protection from Harassment Act 1997, s.8(1). It is thought that conduct which deliberately caused fear and alarm without causing physical harm was actionable at common law.

[19] Or conduct that is in breach of statutory regulations.

[20] The law has now been put on a statutory basis; in the Damages (Scotland) Act 1976.

injuries, once again we see how private law is primarily concerned with economic interests.

Further reading

Thomson, *Delictual Liability* (3rd ed., 2004)

CHAPTER 8

REPARATION FOR HARM ARISING FROM FAULT OR *CULPA*

Introduction

8–01   In the last chapter, we examined how certain important interests are protected from wrongful interference by the law of delict. In this chapter we are concerned with the general obligation to make reparation, i.e. pay compensation for the harm caused to the pursuer as a consequence of the defender's fault or *culpa*. The essence of the delict is harm *wrongfully* caused to the pursuer: this is encapsulated in the Latin phrase, *damnum injuria datum*. Until the pursuer sustains harm, there is no obligation to make reparation. Harm to the pursuer is a constituent—not merely a consequence—of the general obligation to make reparation for fault or *culpa* based liability. Merely to act carelessly is not a civil wrong unless and until harm is sustained by a person to whom the defender owed a duty of care to prevent such harm.[1]

When is a defender liable under this general obligation to make reparation, i.e. when is a defender at fault for this purpose? There is little difficulty when the defender has caused the harm deliberately. In these circumstances, his conduct is clearly wrongful and he is obliged to make reparation for the harm caused to the pursuer. Depending on the nature of the harm, the pursuer would be able to seek reparation on the basis of fraud, assault or wrongful damage to corporeal moveable property. However, the concept of *culpa* not only includes conduct that is intentionally wrongful but also careless, i.e. unintentionally wrongful conduct. It is now well established that before careless conduct is actionable in delict, it must constitute a breach of a pre-existing duty of care which the defender owed to the pursuer. Put another way, it is only when the defender owes the pursuer a duty of care to prevent her sustaining harm as a consequence of the defender's conduct that carelessness can give rise to a claim for reparation. When carelessness amounts to a breach of a duty of care, it is known as negligence. Delictual liability for negligence is the main subject of this chapter.

---

[1] Accordingly, if no harm has actually been sustained, an interdict will not be granted to prevent careless conduct. It is different if the defender's conduct was intentional or constituted a nuisance.

Duty of Care

When does a duty of care arise? There is no simple answer to **8–02** this question. The reason is that over the years the courts have developed the law of negligence incrementally. The judiciary patrols the frontiers of liability by deciding whether or not to impose a duty of care in a particular, *novel* situation. In doing so, the courts are undoubtedly influenced by matters of policy, i.e. by their conception of what is socially and economically desirable (or, indeed, undesirable). As societal, particularly economic, expectations are always changing, it is not surprising that the *limits* of liability for negligence are in constant flux, though the central core of liability appears stable enough. That said, negligence is one of the areas of private law which is most susceptible to policy driven judicial development.

As a general principle, a duty of care arises when a defender can reasonably foresee that the pursuer would sustain physical harm or physical damage to her property as a consequence of the defender's careless acts or omissions. Thus for example the driver of a motor car owes a duty of care to other road users to prevent them sustaining physical injuries or damage to their vehicles as a result of the defender's careless driving: this is because it is reasonably foreseeable to the driver of a motor car that such people could sustain such harm if he drove carelessly. Similarly, the manufacturer of a product owes a duty of care to the ultimate consumer of the product because it is reasonably foreseeable that she may suffer physical injuries or damage to her property if the product is defective as a consequence of being manufactured carelessly. In short, in many cases of physical injury to the pursuer or physical damage to her property, a duty of care arises simply because such harm was reasonably foreseeable by the defender as a consequence of his careless conduct.

But as we move away from the core cases, the courts have taken **8–03** the view that reasonable foreseeability of harm is not in itself sufficient for the imposition of a duty of care. In addition there must be a degree of proximity between the parities and, most importantly, the court must be satisfied that in the circumstances it would be fair, just and reasonable to impose a duty of care on the defender. Consider the following example:

A enters into a contract with B under which B will carry A's goods aboard B's ship. The ship is damaged in a storm. C advises B that he can continue with the voyage without major repairs. Nevertheless the vessel sinks en route to her port. A's goods are destroyed. Although it was reasonably foreseeable that the ship might sink if C's advice was wrong and that any cargo on board would be destroyed, nevertheless C does not owe a duty of care to A. This is because their relationship is not sufficiently proximate. C does not know the existence let alone the identity of A. Moreover,

A has a remedy against B for breach of contract which is subject to an internationally agreed limitation on the amount which can be recovered as damages. Shippers and ship owners rely on those limitations when insuring the goods and settling the prices of their goods and services. These expectations would be undermined if C was under a delictual obligation to compensate A. It is therefore not fair, just and reasonable to impose a duty of care on C to prevent physical damage to A's property.

Reasonable foreseeability of harm, proximity between the parties and that it is fair, just and reasonable to impose a duty, are known as the tripartite criteria for the imposition of a duty of care.

8-04   An important consideration has been the status of the defender. Where a state agency is involved, a failure to fulfil its statutory obligations does not automatically result in delictual liability, particularly when the agency's statutory duty involves the exercise of discretionary powers. Thus for example, the courts have been reluctant to impose on the police a duty of care to the victims of a criminal whose identity was unknown until late in the criminal investigations: there is a lack of proximity between the victims and the police, and it would not be fair, just and reasonable to do so. On the other hand, the police did owe a duty of care to road users to prevent them sustaining physical harm as a consequence of the collapse of a bridge when the police had taken responsibility for the safety of the road shortly after the bridge had been damaged; here proximity existed between the police and drivers who were approaching the bridge and it was fair, just and reasonable to impose the duty in this case as the police were not involved with a criminal investigation.

Thus even in cases where the pursuer has suffered physical injuries or physical damage to property, a duty of care may not be imposed even if such harm was reasonably foreseeable: the additional criteria of proximity between the parties and "fair, just and reasonable to impose the duty" may have to be satisfied. But it must be emphasised that, particularly when the pursuer has sustained physical harm, resort will only be made to the tripartite criteria if the circumstances constitute a novel situation where delictual liability has hitherto not been established.

8-05   Sometimes a duty of care is imposed by statute. For example, under the Occupiers' Liability (Scotland) Act 1960, the occupiers of property owe a duty to take such care in respect of persons *entering* their property as is reasonable in all the circumstances of the case. This duty of care extends to persons, for example children, who are trespassing on the property. In the event of an overlap, the statutory duty will prevail over the common law. For example, the duty to take reasonable care for the personal safety of a visitor whom I have invited to my house is based on the 1960 Act while the duty to prevent harm to a pedestrian passing by on the street alongside the property is based on the common law, i.e. a duty will only arise if it is reasonably foreseeable that a person in her position could be injured because I have not had the property regularly maintained.

The kind of harm sustained by the pursuer has also been important in determining whether or not a duty of care arises at common law. Two examples must suffice. The first is where the pursuer has suffered mental as opposed to physical harm. A duty of care arises to prevent mental harm if the pursuer was within the area of potential physical harm, i.e. if the defender could reasonably foresee that the pursuer might sustain physical harm. In these circumstances, the pursuer is known as a primary victim. Because physical harm was reasonably foreseeable it does not matter that mental harm was not a reasonably foreseeable consequence of the defender's conduct. Where the pursuer is not a primary victim (and is consequently known as a secondary victim), prima facie no duty of care arises to prevent her suffering mental harm even though mental harm to the pursuer is reasonably foreseeable. Thus, for example, A, a motorist, does not owe a duty of care to B, another road user, to prevent B from sustaining mental harm as a consequence of witnessing C being injured in a road accident caused by A but in which B was not directly involved. If B was directly involved in the road accident, A would owe her a duty of care to prevent her sustaining mental as well as physical harm since in those circumstances B is a primary victim.

Thus as a general rule, no duty is owed to a secondary victim to **8–06** prevent him sustaining mental harm from witnessing the fate of primary victims. The policy reasons for this principle are obvious: the defender would otherwise face indeterminate liability. Nevertheless, a duty of care can arise in the exceptional circumstances where:

- (a) there is a tie of love and affection between the primary and secondary victim;
- (b) the secondary victim was present at the accident or its immediate aftermath; and
- (c) the mental harm was caused by direct perception of the accident or its immediate aftermath.

In the example above, A would owe a duty of care to B if C was B's child whom A had knocked down in an accident which B had witnessed directly. However, no duty of care would be owed if B was simply informed that her child had been knocked down and she did not witness the accident or its immediate aftermath, for example, seeing her injured child in hospital shortly after the accident.

The second is where the pursuer has sustained pure economic **8–07** loss. At one time the courts were reluctant to impose a duty of care to prevent pure economic loss: remedies to recover such losses lay in contract not in delict. However, as we have seen,[2] a duty of care to prevent pure economic loss will arise when:

(a) the defender has voluntarily assumed responsibility for the economic interests of the pursuer;
(b) the defender knows that the pursuer is relying on the defender's professional expertise; and
(c) the terms of any contract (or non-contractual notice) affecting them do not negative delictual liability.

Although we consider that these are now the recognised criteria for the imposition of a general duty of care to prevent pure economic loss, nevertheless in such cases resort is still sometimes made to the tripartite criteria which are used in novel cases.[3] It is thought that the latter criteria should no longer be used in pure economic loss cases.

In practice too much should not be made of the traditional distinctions between pure economic loss and physical damage to property. Consider the following examples:

(a) A is mending a gas main. He accidentally cuts an electric cable owned by B. This causes a power failure at C's factory which is situated nearby. As a consequence, C loses 10 hours production. Can C sue A in delict for that loss? This is a case of pure economic loss. Since A has not assumed responsibility for C's economic interests and there has been no concomitant reliance, A does not owe C a duty of care to prevent C sustaining pure economic loss as a result of A's carelessness.[4] This is a sensible result as C should have insured against loss of production arising from a power cut, howsoever caused.
(b) A is mending a gas main. He accidentally cuts an electric cable owned by B. This causes a power failure at C's factory which is situated nearby. As a consequence the machinery at C's factory is damaged and C loses 10 hours of production while the machines are being repaired. Can C sue A in delict for that loss? This is a case of physical damage to property (i.e. the machinery) and derivative or parasitic economic loss (i.e. the loss of production). The court would

---

[2] Above, paras 7.11–7.13.
[3] This is perhaps not surprising as the tripartite criteria originated in pure economic loss cases where it has subsequently been overtaken by the assumption of responsibility and concomitant reliance test. The tripartite criteria then came to be used in novel cases of physical injury and physical damage to property.
[4] On the other hand, A probably owes a duty of care to B to take reasonable care not to damage B's electric cable.

probably use the tripartite criteria in determining whether or not to impose a duty of care. While the reasonable foreseeability and proximity criteria are probably satisfied, it is thought that it is not fair just or reasonable to do so. As in (a) above, C should have insured against any damage to his machinery arising from a power cut, howsoever caused.

Breach of Duty

Once a duty of care has been established, the defender will be **8–08** liable to make reparation for any harm caused to the pursuer as a result of conduct on the part of the defender which amounts to a breach of that duty. A breach of a duty of care occurs if the following criteria are satisfied:

(a) the relevant act or omission must be voluntary on the part of the defender;

(b) the defender's act or omission must have as its reasonable and probable consequence the harm the pursuer has in fact sustained. In other words, the harm the pursuer has sustained must be within the scope of the defender's duty of care. For example, A is a painter and decorator. He owes a duty of care to the occupants of the house in which he is working to prevent them sustaining physical harm from the way that he works. A accidentally sets the house on fire. An occupant is suffocated by the smoke. A is liable as it is foreseeable as a reasonable and probable consequence of carelessly setting a house on fire that an occupant of the house might be overcome by smoke. But if an occupant died of a heart attack from over exertion when attempting to rescue furniture, A is not liable as it is not reasonably foreseeable as a probable cause of setting the house alight that an occupant would suffer a heart attack as opposed to being burned or suffocated by the smoke. However, provided the kind of harm sustained by the pursuer was reasonably foreseeable as a probable consequence of the defender's conduct it does not matter that the harm in fact sustained was greater than could have been anticipated or that some of the causes of the harm were not foreseeable. Thus for example, if it is reasonably foreseeable that the pursuer might sustain burns from the defender's carelessness it does not matter that the burns in fact sustained by her were worse than could have been reasonably foreseen.

(c) the defender's act or omission must constitute fault or *culpa* on his part, i.e. the defender's acts or omissions must amount to negligence. Even though harm to the pursuer is

reasonably foreseeable as a probable consequence of the
defender's conduct, there is no liability for negligence
unless the defender has failed to meet the standards of the
reasonable person in the position of the defender. While a
defender has to take reasonable care, the law does not
expect him to go beyond that standard. In deciding what
can reasonably be expected of a defender, the court
engages in a balancing process weighing for example the
costs of the precautions and the utility of the defender's
activities against the risk of—and the severity of—harm to
the pursuer. The more likely and serious the degree of
harm, the more reasonable that the defender should take
steps to reduce the risk of the harm materialising. But at
the end of the day the defender has only to take reasonable
care: he is not expected to eliminate the risk if it is too
difficult or expensive to do so. The defender must not be
negligent but he is not obliged to ensure that his acts or
omissions never cause harm to the pursuer. So for example
while school teachers owe children a duty of care to
prevent them suffering from being bullied at school, it is
extremely difficult—if not impossible—to ensure that all
forms of bullying have been eliminated. Failure to have a
policy on controlling bullying or turning a blind eye to
bullying in the class or playground would constitute negligence: but the duty to take reasonable care probably does
not extend to isolated incidents of bullying on public
transport when the children are travelling to and from
school. The crucial issue is to ask what could the defender
reasonably have done to reduce the risk of the pursuer
sustaining foreseeable harm. Only if the defender has failed
to take reasonable care will his conduct constitute negligence. The economic and social costs of eliminating the
risk will be important factors. The only way to ensure that
no one is ever injured in a public park is to exclude the
public: but the loss of the amenity is too great a price and
the occupier of a park is not negligent for failing to do so.
But the occupier would be negligent[5] if he failed to warn
the public that some plants in the park were poisonous or
hadn't repaired the floor of a bandstand whose timbers had
rotted away. Where simple and inexpensive steps can be
taken effectively to reduce the risk, then negligence will
readily be inferred: if not, it can be very difficult to prove

---

[5] The occupier would be liable under the Occupiers' Liability (Scotland) Act 1960
for failing to take such care as is reasonable in all the circumstances to see that
the pursuer will not suffer injury from any dangers on the premises: s.2(1) of the
1960 Act.

that the defender has been negligent and consequently in breach of a duty of care that he owed to the pursuer. In cases of professional negligence, liability will not be established if there is a responsible body of opinion within the profession which regards the defender's conduct to have been reasonable in the circumstances.[6]

Because of the difficulty of proving negligence, in some very important areas the common law has been replaced by statutory regimes which provide for compensation to be paid without proof of fault. This is known as strict liability. For example, where a consumer has been physically harmed by a defective product, the producer of the product is strictly liable to make reparation. The injured consumer does not have to show that the product was defective because the producer was at fault in designing or manufacturing the product.[7] Similarly, if a person is bitten by a dog, the keeper of the dog is strictly liable to make reparation without the pursuer establishing that the keeper was at fault in allowing the dog to bite her.[8]

Causation

Before there is liability to make reparation, the pursuer must **8–09** prove on the balance of probabilities that the defender's breach of duty, i.e. his intentional or negligent wrongdoing, was the cause of the harm she has sustained. The law takes a common sense approach to the concept of causation. As a general rule it must be shown that "but for" the defender's conduct the pursuer would *not* have sustained harm: if the harm would have occurred anyway, for legal purposes, it was not caused by the defender's conduct. For example, a person is suffering a terminal illness and is going to die. An ambulance is delayed when taking him to hospital. But for the delay would the patient have died? The answer is "Yes". Therefore, for legal purposes, the delay was not the cause of the death.

In exceptional circumstances, the courts have been prepared to relax this requirement. Where the defender is responsible for two or more sources of the *same* noxious agent, the causation requirement is satisfied if the negligent source has materially contributed

---

[6] In other words, a defender is not liable merely because his conduct deviated from normal practice; it must be shown that no professional person of ordinary skill would have followed the course taken by the defender. This is to ensure not only that innovative techniques and procedures can be introduced but also recognizes that professional persons often have to exercise judgment and that they are not negligent merely because in retrospect the decision reached was wrong.

[7] Consumer Protection Act 1987, Pt 1.

[8] The Animals (Scotland) Act 1987.

to the harm or materially increased the risk of the harm occurring.[9] It has also been accepted that this principle can apply when more than one person has been responsible for the source of the same noxious agent.[10] On the other hand, in cases like negligent medical diagnosis, it must be shown on the balance of probabilities, i.e. that it was more than 50 per cent likely, that the subsequent deterioration of the pursuer would not have happened: put another way, the pursuer must show that the treatment or medication thereby missed would have had more than a 50 per cent chance of success. The loss of a lower percentage chance will not suffice.

Even where the "but for" test is satisfied, the courts recognise the concept of what can be called causative fade. The causative effects of the defender's negligence may be overtaken by subsequent events for which it is unfair that he should be held responsible. In such circumstances it is said that his negligence is not the legal cause of the harm sustained by the pursuer or that the chain of causation has been broken by the intervention of a new and unforeseen event, a *novus actus interveniens.* For example, A slips on B's carpet and breaks his ankle. On the way to the hospital, A is killed in an accident caused by the negligence of the ambulance driver. B is not legally responsible for A's death as the causative effects of his negligent acts and omissions have been overtaken or faded in the light of the subsequent accident for which the ambulance driver was responsible.

Volenti non fit injuria and Contributory Negligence

8–10   Where the defender has been negligent, the chain of causation will be broken if the pursuer voluntarily undertakes the risk of harm created by the defender's breach of duty, i.e. that the pursuer knowingly and willingly undertook the risk of the danger created by the defender. Such cases are rare. Moreover, where the duty of

---

[9] If the harm sustained by the pursuer could have been caused by more than one noxious agent—as opposed to more than one source of the same noxious agent—the principle does not apply. Thus if the pursuer suffered harm because of breathing dust which came from two sources A and B for which the defender is responsible but only negligent in respect of source B, causation is established if source B materially contributed to—or materially increased the risk of—harm to the pursuer. But if the harm to the pursuer could have been caused by breathing dust or by breathing a chemical to which he had also been exposed whose source was C for which the defender is not responsible, the principle is not applicable.

[10] For example, assume in the example in the footnote immediately above that the pursuer suffered harm by breathing dust from the negligent source B which was the responsibility of his employer X and then his employer Y. It cannot be established scientifically when the harm was incurred. Since Y was responsible for the source of the same noxious substance and through his negligence materially increased the risk of harm to the pursuer while he was working for him, causation is established against Y even though—which *ex hypothesi* cannot be proved—the pursuer might have been harmed by the dust when he was working for X.

care is to prevent the pursuer from acting in a particular way, the duty would be denuded of any content if the defence of *volenti* was available if the pursuer did the act which the defender should have prevented him from doing.[11]

There are also cases where the harm sustained by the pursuer is a consequence of her own fault as well as the fault of the defender. Under the Law Reform (Contributory Negligence) Act 1945, in such cases the court has a discretion to reduce the pursuer's damages to the extent that it considers just and equitable having regard to her share of the responsibility for the harm sustained. For these purposes fault covers the pursuer's deliberate as well as negligent actions.[12] Deductions are common in road accident cases where, for example, an injured car passenger has failed to wear a seat belt or an injured pedestrian was drunk at the time of the accident. The reduction varies between 5 and 80 per cent: it is thought that a deduction of 100 per cent is not possible as the pursuer would then be wholly responsible and therefore would not "share in" the responsibility for the harm sustained. While damages for pure economic loss can be reduced due to contributory negligence, no deduction can be made in a case of a fraudulent—as opposed to negligent—misrepresentation. Once again, this illustrates another important difference between liability for fraud and liability for negligence.

Damages

When the pursuer has established that she has suffered harm as **8–11** a consequence of the defender's breach of a duty of care, she is entitled to damages as reparation for the harm she sustained.[13] The purpose of delict damages is to put the pursuer into the position she would have been if the delict had not taken place. In other words, the pursuer is entitled to compensation for the losses she has incurred from the harm that was constitutive of the delict. For example, A is injured in a car accident which was a result of B's negligence. A is entitled to reparation for the pain and suffering she has incurred (and may incur in the future): this is known as *solatium*. A is also entitled to compensation for the economic losses which derive from or are parasitical upon the physical harm she has sustained. These would include her loss of earnings from the date of the accident to the date of the trial or settlement of the action, loss of future earnings and the cost of nursing and care

---

[11] For example, the police owe prisoners a duty of care to prevent them harming themselves while on remand: if through a breach of the duty a prisoner is able to harm himself, the defence of *volenti* is not available to the police.

[12] To that extent the short title of the Act is inaccurate.

[13] A wrong can also generate a right to restitution and recompense which can compel the defender to disgorge the profits that he has made from the wrong.

which she has incurred and which will be incurred in the future. However, there is no compensation for losses which are too speculative: for example, if as a consequence of her injuries, A was prevented from posting a winning football coupon.

In respect of liability for consequential losses, the general principle is that:

(a) in a case of intentional harm, for example fraud, the pursuer is entitled to compensation for the losses which arise from the harm whether or not they were reasonably foreseeable at the time of the delict ;

(b) in a case of negligence, the pursuer is entitled to compensation for the losses which could reasonably have been foreseen at the time of the delict as arising from the harm. However, there are exceptions to this principle. First, it is well established that in a case of personal injury, the defender takes the victim as he finds him. This means, for example, that if the pursuer sustains a physical injury and as a consequence suffers an unforeseeable mental illness, the defender's liability is based on both the physical and mental harm. Similarly, if the pursuer's death is triggered by a physical injury, the defender is liable for the death even if it was not a reasonably foreseeable consequence of the physical injury. Secondly, sometimes compensation is denied for losses even though they are reasonably foreseeable. For example, A becomes pregnant owing to a failed sterilisation caused by medical negligence. The harm which constitutes the delict is the unplanned conception. A gives birth to a healthy and normal child. A decides to keep the baby. A can recover *solatium* for pain and suffering and damages for loss of earnings relating to the birth. Although the cost of a child's upbringing is a reasonably foreseeable consequence of an unplanned conception, compensation for this loss is not recoverable. Instead, A will receive a non compensatory conventional award (around £15k) in recognition that her right to limit the size of her family has been infringed.

8–12   While *solatium* for pain and suffering is welcome, it will be clear that in personal injury claims the damages for derivative or parasitic economic loss may be very substantial, particularly if the pursuer is unlikely to work again and will need expensive long term care and treatment. These economic losses are known as patrimonial loss. Where the pursuer is a high earner—or a potentially high earner—damages for patrimonial loss will be higher than if she was unemployed and had poor job prospects. Similarly, damages will be less if the victim is a pensioner or approaching pensionable age than if she is at the beginning of a potentially very successful career. The age of the victim will also be important in assessing the cost of future care.

Damages are calculated on the basis of what the pursuer will need to enjoy her lifestyle until death. They are awarded as a lump sum: and it is anticipated that as well as the income generated by the lump sum the pursuer will use up a proportion of the capital each year so that all the damages will have been exhausted by the time she dies. The way in which private law reduces issues to economic interests will again be readily apparent.

When a person dies of personal injuries, members of her family are entitled to sue under the Damages (Scotland) Act 1976 for both patrimonial loss, for example the loss of the deceased's economic support, and non-patrimonial loss (*solatium*), for example grief and sorrow caused by the death. Where the deceased did not support the family economically, the damages will only be for non-patrimonial loss. Thus for example, only damages for solatium will be awarded for the death of a young child. The amounts involved are relatively small compared to the damages for patrimonial loss that would be awarded if the child had not died but required long term medical care: a case where it is cheaper to kill than maim! It should be noted that a claim under the 1976 Act is a dependent action. What this means is that any defence, for example contributory negligence, which the defender could have used if the deceased had pursued a claim for damages for personal injuries, is good against the relatives' actions under the 1976 Act.

Where compensation is claimed for physical damage to property, **8–13** the pursuer is entitled to the cost of repair or replacement. If after repair the property is worth less than before it was damaged, the diminution in value can be recovered. If repairs were delayed owing to the pursuer's impecuniosity, any increased cost of repairs can be obtained. In cases of pure economic loss, sometimes the loss is very simple to calculate. For instance, if the pursuer failed to obtain a legacy from her grandfather because of his solicitor's negligence in drawing up the will, the loss is the value of the lost legacy. Similarly, if a surveyor negligently fails to discover defects in a property, the loss is the cost of repair or the diminution in its value. Where the defender has given the pursuer negligent advice to enter a transaction, he can be liable for all the losses arising from the transaction provided they were reasonably foreseeable. On the other hand, if the defender merely gave negligent information which the pursuer used to decide whether or not to enter the transaction, liability is restricted to the pursuer's loss which was a reasonable consequence of the information being wrong. So any losses arising from the transaction which do not derive from the information being wrong, for example a general fall in the market value of the assets involved, cannot be recovered. But such losses would be recoverable if the information was supplied fraudulently.

Breach of Statutory Duty

8–14   In this chapter we have been primarily concerned with the general *ex lege* obligation to make reparation for harm sustained by the pursuer as a consequence of the defender's fault or *culpa*. This has largely been a product of the common law. No obligation arises unless the defender's fault or *culpa* can be established. But, there are now statutory regimes, for example in relation to defective products and animals, which provide for compensation without proof of fault, i.e. strict liability. Moreover, an act or omission in breach of a statute or statutory regulation can also give rise to a right to damages. The importance of these developments cannot be overstated. For example, it is long settled that an employer is under a common law duty to take reasonable care for the safety of his employees.[14] In order to obtain reparation for physical or mental harm sustained at work, an employee must show that her employer was in breach of that duty, i.e. negligent. But there are hundreds of statutory provisions which regulate in detail health and safety at work. If an employee is injured and can show that this was caused by a breach of such a regulation, then the employer will be liable to make reparation without proof of fault, i.e. there is strict liability for breach of statutory duty.

On the other hand, not every breach of statutory duty gives rise to a right to reparation: indeed, most do not. This is particularly the case when the breach of statute has only caused economic loss. Often the statute will provide its own remedies for breach, ruling out a claim for reparation. But whether or not a breach of statute gives a right to reparation is ultimately a question of construction of the statute. Nor does the existence of a statutory regime automatically rule out the possibility of the imposition of a common law duty of care. So for example, statutory education authorities owe a common law duty of care to ensure that children with special needs receive appropriate education: but, of course, there is no liability for breach of that duty unless fault can be established.

Further reading

Thomson, *Delictual Liability* (3rd ed., 2004)

---

[14] Moreover, where an employee intentionally or negligently injures a fellow employee or a third party, the employer may incur vicarious liability. This arises if the employee's wrongful act or omission fell within the course of his employment, i.e. was a mode—albeit a wrongful mode—of doing what he was employed to do or was so closely connected with his employment that it would be fair, just and reasonable to hold the employer liable. Vicarious liability is a form of strict liability. There is no need to prove that the employer was at fault: indeed, the employer may have instructed the employee to desist from the acts—for example, not to speed—for which he is ultimately vicariously liable should they cause harm to the pursuer.

CHAPTER 9

UNJUSTIFIED ENRICHMENT

Introduction

In Chapter 7 we saw how certain wrongs generate a right in the **9–01** victim to obtain restitution or recompense from the wrongdoer. Thus if corporeal moveable property is stolen, the owner has the right to vindicate it from the thief or any subsequent transferee, including a bona fide transferee for value. This is because ownership of the property remains with the victim of the theft. However, the right to vindicate is lost if the property ceases to exist in its original form. In these circumstances as against the thief (or any other party to the theft) the original owner has the right to recompense for the value of the property and any profit gained from its sale or the sale of its substitute. This right is generated by the wrong, i.e. the theft of the property. Although there is no right to vindicate money, nevertheless a victim of the theft of money has the right to seek recompense from the thief (or any other party to the theft): this right too is generated by the wrong. Similarly, the victim of fraud can seek recompense from the fraudster (or any other party to the fraud) in respect of the value of the property of which he was defrauded and any profits that were made from that property. But the right to restitution or recompenses is not only generated by wrongs. It is now well recognised in Scots law that when one person has been unjustifiedly enriched at the expense of another, these remedies are triggered so that the enrichment can be reversed. In this chapter we shall discuss the principles of unjustified enrichment.

What is an Enrichment?

The concept of enrichment is very wide. The essence is that a **9–02** person's private patrimony, i.e. the totality of his property rights, has been increased by the acquisition of an economic benefit. In other words, the benefit increases his wealth or avoids his wealth decreasing. As a consequence it can be said that the person has been enriched. This could arise in numerous ways:

(a) A transfers property to B: property includes land, corporeal moveables, incorporeal moveables and, of course, money;

117

(b) A performs a service for B, for example giving advice or acting as an agent;

(c) A improves B's property, for example, by carrying out repairs or paying for an extension;

(d) B has unauthorised use of A's property, for example B occupies a house owned by A or uses materials which were owned by A. In these cases, B's private patrimony is increased because he has saved wealth he would otherwise have had to expend if he was to have use of the property;

(e) A performs an obligation which B was obliged to discharge. For example, B owes C £5k. A pays C £5k discharging B's debt to C. B's private patrimony is increased by £5k as B has saved wealth he would otherwise have had to expend if he had to perform his obligation to C and pay C the £5k which he owed him. Put another way, B's private patrimony has increased because B's debt to C has been discharged.

In determining whether the defender has been enriched, we ignore the fact that if the enrichment is unjustified the defender immediately comes under an *ex lege* obligation to make restitution or pay recompense in respect of the benefit received: if we did not, then, since the obligation reduces the private patrimony by the same amount as the benefit received, technically a defender would never be enriched!

Enrichment at the Expense of the Claimant

Before there is liability for unjustified enrichment, it must be established that the enrichment was at the claimant's expense. The paradigmatic case is when A transfers property to B. Here B's gain to his private patrimony, i.e. the property he has received, mirrors A's loss to his private patrimony, i.e. the property he has transferred to B. Where B has used A's property without permission, the benefit has been gained at A's expense because A has been denied the opportunity to bargain with B for the use of the property. B's property is improved at A's expense if A has made or paid for the improvements. Here it is important to notice that the value of the improvement to B may very well differ from the cost to A of making or paying for the improvements.[1] Where A's actions incidentally confer a benefit on B, the benefit will not be treated as at A's expense if A's actions were primarily for his own benefit (*in suo*). Thus, for example, if A decorated his own house, A cannot argue that B, his live in girlfriend, has been enriched *at*

---

[1] It has been argued that A's loss should act as a cap on the recompense that B should pay rather than the value of the improvement to B which could be greater than A's loss. This is a very controversial issue.

A's expense even though B incidentally enjoys the redecoration as she lives in the house with A.

An enrichment may have been conferred at the expense of the claimant even though it has been conferred indirectly. For example, A transfers property to B which B in turn transfers to C. If A can establish that the property C received from B was the property (or its substitute) which A transferred to B, then A can argue that the benefit C has received was indirectly conferred by A. To succeed, it is essential that A can show a causative link between the property he transferred to B and the benefit that C received: in other words, A must be able to trace his property through the various transactions it has undergone and so demonstrate that the benefit that C received was at A's expense. Where the property is money and the money has been mixed with other funds in various bank accounts, this will often be extremely difficult. But it should be noted that where C is a bona fide transferee for value, no claim based on unjustified enrichment can ever lie against her: since she has given value for the property, her private patrimony has not been increased by its acquisition and consequently she has not been enriched.[2]

Where a benefit arises as a result of the claimant's performance of a *valid*[3] contractual obligation, it will not be recognised as indirectly conferring a benefit at his expense for the purposes of unjustified enrichment. For example, A is a jeweller. He sub-contracts repairs to B. Under his contract with A, B repairs C's watch. Although C has received a benefit, i.e. the repair, it has not been at the expense of B. B did the repair in order to perform his contract with A. Accordingly, if A cannot fulfil his contractual obligation to pay B, B has no recourse to C under the law of unjustified enrichment.

When is an Enrichment Unjustified?

An enrichment is unjustified when the defender has no legal **9–03** basis to retain the benefit that he has obtained at the claimant's expense: because he is unjustifiedly enriched, he is under an *ex lege*

---

[2] C may also give value by, for example, accepting the property as discharging an obligation which B owed to her. Again the property has no effect on the overall size of C's private patrimony as it corresponds to the obligation which B owed C and which B has discharged. C is therefore not enriched.

[3] It is different if the contractual obligation was invalid. If A was induced to sell a ring to B as a result of B's innocent misrepresentation, the contract is voidable. B has a valid if vulnerable title to the ring. Before the contract is rescinded, B gifts the ring to C. While C has a valid title, A can claim restitution of the ring or its value from C on the basis that C was indirectly enriched at the expense of A. A similar result would follow if A had been induced to sell the ring as a result of B's fraudulent misrepresentation. Here A's right to restitution of the ring is triggered by the wrong as against B (and C if she was a party to the wrong) and by unjustified enrichment against C if she was a bona fide donee.

obligation to return the benefit or pay recompense to the claimant. There are two situations which should be distinguished. The first is when the defender never had any legal basis for having the benefit. The second is when the defender initially had a legal basis for having the benefit but because of subsequent events this basis is removed and he no longer has any legal basis for the retention of the benefit.

The following are examples of the first situation:

(a) A owes B £100. By error, A transfers £150 to B to discharge the debt. While B is entitled to receive £100 in discharge of the debt, B has no legal basis for retaining the extra £50. B is unjustifiedly enriched and is under an *ex lege* obligation to restore £50 to A. The claim that a transfer of money should be reversed because it was not legally due in the first place is known as the *condictio indebiti*.

(b) A is the executor of a will. Under the will B is to receive a legacy of £10k. Believing that C is B, A pays the legacy to C. C has no legal basis for retaining the legacy which he only received because of A's error as to his identity. C is unjustifiedly enriched and is under an *ex lege* obligation to return the money to A

(c) A enters into a contract with B. The contract is null. A transfers £100k to B in purported performance of the contract. Since the contract is null, B has no legal basis for receiving or retaining the payment. B is unjustifiedly enriched and is under an *ex lege* obligation to return the payment to A.

(d) Without A's knowledge or permission, A rides B's horse every day. A's use of the horse has no legal basis and the benefits he has enjoyed amount to unjustified enrichment. B is under an *ex lege* obligation to pay recompense to A for the benefits he has received: this would generally be the amount A would have charged if he had contracted to hire the horse to B.[4]

9–04 The following are examples of the second situation:

(a) A buys a painting from B for £5k. The contract is annullable because A entered into it under an error induced by B's innocent misrepresentation. A rescinds the contract. Before the contract is rescinded, B has a legal basis for

---

[4] This scenario could also be analysed as a wrongful interference with A's property in which case the obligation to pay recompense arises from the wrong rather than unjustified enrichment. Most cases of taking benefits will involve a wrong: for example, theft and fraud.

having the money: it is the price of the painting he has sold to A. After the contract is rescinded, B no longer has a legal basis for retention of the money. B is unjustifiedly enriched and is under an *ex lege* obligation to return the money to A who is, of course, under a corresponding obligation to transfer the ownership of the painting back to B.

(b) A and B are living together. They agree to marry. A gives B her grandfather's watch. B later breaks off the engagement. Before they broke up, B had a legal basis for having the watch. He was the owner as a result of A's donation of the watch to him. But the gift was conditional, i.e. it is implicit that the watch was only given to B on the expectation they would marry. The gift was therefore subject to an implied resolutive condition that if the couple split up the watch would be returned. Accordingly, when B breaks off the engagement, he no longer has a legal basis for retention of the watch. He is unjustifiedly enriched and is under an *ex lege* obligation to restore the ownership of the ring to A. The claim for the restitution of property which was transferred for a purpose that did not materialise is known as the *condictio causa data causa non secuta*. It is important to note that gifts are usually not conditional. If A and B had never agreed to marry and A had given the watch to B for his birthday, B would have a legal basis for the retention of the watch after the couple split up. The mere fact that the watch had belonged to her grandfather does not make the gift conditional on the parties remaining together when they had never agreed to marry and the gift was for B's birthday. It is of course open to A to ask B to promise to return the watch to her should they separate. If he did so, A would be able to sue B for breach of the promise to return the watch. The claim would lie for a breach of a voluntary obligation rather than being triggered by unjustified enrichment.

(c) B agrees to build a ship for A. The price is to be paid in instalments. A pays the first instalment on the date that the contract is signed. A few weeks later, the contract is frustrated. Before the frustrating event, B had a legal basis for the money: it was the first instalment of the price for building the ship. Once the contract was frustrated, the legal basis for retention of the money is removed. The instalment was paid with the expectation that B would perform his counter-obligation by building the ship. B has been discharged from performing that obligation by the frustrating event. Therefore B is unjustifiedly enriched and is under an *ex lege* obligation to return the payment which was paid for a purpose that failed to materialise. In other words, A is entitled to claim the first instalment under the *condictio causa data causa non secuta.*

(d) A has a contract with B under which A will rewire B's house. After A has completed part of the job, B terminates the contract on the grounds of A's material breach. A provided the benefit to B in anticipation that he would be paid for it. This expectation has failed. B has no legal basis for continuing to enjoy that benefit. Therefore B is unjustifiedly enriched and is under an *ex lege* obligation to pay recompense to A for the value of the work he has done. This will be similar to, but not necessarily the same as, the price that had been agreed for those services.

(e) A sells potatoes to B. A conveys the ownership of the potatoes to B who sells on to C. Before B has paid A, it is discovered that the contract is illegal and B cannot be sued for the price. But the ownership of the potatoes was only conveyed to B on the basis that he would pay the price to A. B therefore has no legal basis for retaining the benefit he has received from the transfer of the ownership of the potatoes. Therefore B is unjustifiedly enriched and is under an *ex lege* obligation to pay A recompense for their value. This will be similar to, but not necessarily the same as, the original price. The claim for restitution or recompense which arises from a transfer made for an illegal or immoral purpose is known as the *condictio ob turpem vel injustam causam.*

It should always be remembered that when there is a contract between the parties they can expressly agree what is to happen in such situations: where there are such contractually stipulated remedies, the principles of unjustified enrichment which would have operated in the absence of such clauses are displaced.

The "inequitable to do so" Defence

9–05   The onus rests on the pursuer to establish that the defender has been unjustifiably enriched at the pursuer's expense. Once this has been done, the defender is under an *ex lege* obligation to reverse the enrichment by restoring the benefit to the pursuer or paying recompense. The liability to do so is strict in the sense that the defender must do so regardless of being at fault. He is being obliged to return, or pay recompense for, a benefit that he has no legal basis to retain and often, indeed, should never have enjoyed at all. It is therefore not unfair to the defender that the benefit should be reversed. But it must be stressed that it is only a prima facie obligation on the defender to make restitution or pay recompense. For it is always open to the defender to argue that in the particular circumstances of the case it would be inequitable to compel him to do so. This is because in Scots law the obligations triggered by unjustified enrichment are ultimately founded in equity.

In cases of the *condictio indebiti*, it has long been accepted that it would be inequitable to order restitution or repetition against a defender if the claimant made the payment knowing that it was not due: in so doing, the pursuer is in effect making a gift to the defender. Where the payment was made in error, the defender can argue that the pursuer's mistake was so inexcusable that it would be inequitable to order restitution or repetition. Where restitution or recompense is sought under the *condictio ob turpem vel injustam causam* if the pursuer also knew about the illegality, then both parties are equally guilty of breaking the law, i.e. they were *in pari delicto*. In these circumstances, it is generally accepted that it would be inequitable not to allow the losses to remain where they fall, i.e. the defender can retain the benefit.

One of the most important situations when it would be inequitable to compel restitution or recompense is when the defender has changed her position in the genuine belief that the benefit conferred was truly hers. For example, A, an executor, pays a legacy of £10k in error to B. B has no legal basis for having the money and is unjustifiedly enriched. When the error is discovered, prima facie B is under an *ex lege* obligation to repay the legacy to A. However, if on receipt of the legacy, B had in good faith spent the legacy on medical treatment for his wife, it would be inequitable to compel him to do so. There has been a change of position. While the law of unjustified enrichment demands that a defender return what was never (or no longer) his due, it will not allow him to become worse off in doing so. Thus the change of position defence. To succeed, however, the defender must show that the expenditure would not have been incurred if he had not received the benefit: and, of course, the expenditure must have been in good faith, i.e. the defender must have believed that the benefit had been due.

It is sometimes said that there is a defence of the bona fide transferee for value. For example, A transfers property to B under error that the transfer is due. B has no legal basis for the retention of the property. B is unjustifiedly enriched and is under an *ex lege* obligation to return the property to A. Instead, he sells the property to C, a bona fide transferee for value. It is thought that the fact that C is a bona fide transferee for value does not provide C with a defence to a claim by A based on unjustified enrichment: instead, because C was in good faith and gave value for the property, her private patrimony has not increased as a result of its acquisition and consequently C has not been enriched.

Where the claim to restitution or recompense is triggered by a wrong rather than unjustified enrichment, the wrongdoer (and anyone who is a party to the wrong) does not have the right to argue that in the circumstances it would be inequitable to compel him to do so.

Nature of the Remedies

9–06　　Where there has been a payment that was not due, the claimant is entitled to the return of the money and interest from the date it should have been returned. There are more difficulties where the defender has used the money profitably by investing wisely in the market or buying or improving heritable property which has increased greatly in value. Although the matter is very controversial, it is thought that the pursuer should be entitled to any increases in value with a deduction to reflect the defender's efforts. Only in that way can an unjustified enrichment be fully reversed. In cases of recompense, the award can take the form of the value of the property or services the defender has enjoyed: for example, the price the pursuer would have charged to allow the defender to use the property.

　　Finally, it should always be remembered that unjustified enrichment only generates a personal right as against the defender to make restitution or pay recompense. The pursuer has no real right in the benefit which is the subject of the claim and forms part of the defender's private patrimony. Moreover, it is also submitted that the defender is not a constructive trustee of that property for the benefit of the claimant. This means that if the defender is insolvent, the pursuer in an unjustified enrichment claim is simply an unsecured creditor and has no priority over other unsecured creditors. In these circumstances, the remedies triggered by unjustified enrichment can be of little or no value. Once again we see the limitations of personal rights as opposed to real rights in property.

Further reading

Evans-Jones, *Unjustified Enrichment* (2004), Vol.1
Hogg, *Obligations* (2003)
MacQueen, *Unjustified Enrichment* (2005)

CHAPTER 10

TRUSTS

Introduction

Scots law has long recognised the concept of a trust. The **10–01** essential feature of a trust is that a person, the trustee, owns property, the trust fund, which he must administer for the benefit of another, the beneficiary. While the trustee is the owner of the property, the trust fund does not enter his private patrimony: instead it is held by him as part of a trust patrimony which is separate from his private patrimony. This means that the trust fund is not vulnerable to the trustee's personal creditors: their claims are limited to the assets in the trustee's private patrimony. The beneficiary is not the owner of the trust fund. Instead she has a personal right against the trustee to compel him to fulfil the purposes of the trust: conversely, the trustee owes the beneficiary an obligation to do so. This obligation is known as a fiduciary obligation because when administering the trust, the trustee must at all times act in the interests of the beneficiary, i.e. put the beneficiary's interests before his own. This is why the trustee's ownership of the trust fund has been described as fiduciary ownership: the trustee owns the trust fund only in order to fulfil the trust purposes and serve the beneficiaries.

The Constitution of a Trust

An express trust involves a tripartite relationship between the **10–02** truster, i.e. the person who wishes to set up the trust, the trustee and the beneficiary. The truster must make a declaration of trust, i.e. declare that he is setting up a trust. In the declaration he will nominate the trustees and the beneficiaries and the property that is to constitute the trust fund. It is also common to stipulate the nature and extent of the trustees' powers to administer the trust fund.

In the vast majority of cases the declaration of trust will be in writing and is known as the trust deed. However, writing is not a requirement for the constitution of a trust: s.1(1) of the Requirements of Writing (Scotland) Act 1995. Thus an oral declaration of trust can be sufficient. There is one exception to this rule.[1] When a person declares himself to be the sole trustee of his own property—or any property which he may acquire in the future—no trust can arise unless the declaration is in writing and signed by the truster: s.1(2)(a)(iii) of the 1995 Act. For example, if A declares that he owns his house as trustee for the benefit of his girl friend, B, a trust cannot be constituted unless the declaration of trust takes the form of a written document signed by A. However, the absence of writing may not prove fatal if ss.1(3) and (4) of the 1985 Act are satisfied. This would occur if B with the knowledge of A had acted in reliance on A's declaration of trust and would be adversely affected if the trust was invalid for lack of formalities. For example, if B with A's knowledge had given up the lease of her flat because she had been told by A that he was holding his house in trust for her, A would not be able to deny the existence of the trust: and the trust would not be regarded as invalid because of the absence of a written declaration of trust. While this appears to be the law, it is perhaps slightly odd. Surely the requirement of writing is to protect the purported trustee's personal creditors. It is to make it more difficult for a debtor to claim that he owns property as a trustee with the result that the property is not available to his personal creditors: it is not to protect the purported trustee from rashly making a declaration of trust of his own property which he might later regret.

The declaration of trust must then be intimated to the trustees whom the truster has nominated. Because of the onerous nature of the obligations, any person nominated as a trustee can refuse to accept the office. When the trustee accepts office, a trust is constituted. Where the truster has declared that he is sole trustee of his own property on trust, the trust is constituted when the declaration is intimated to a beneficiary (or another third party).

10–03   Once a trust has been constituted, the trustees have the right to demand that the truster transfers the ownership of the assets which are to make up the trust fund to them. The beneficiaries have the right to compel the trustees to carry out the trust purposes. This includes the duty on the part of the trustees to demand that the truster transfers of the ownership of the trust fund to them. These rights and duties arise by virtue of the law of trusts and not the general law of obligations.

Since the declaration of trust is a voluntary juristic act, in the vast majority of cases the truster will transfer the ownership of the

---

[1] Writing is also required for the constitution of a *mortis causa* trust because it is a testamentary deed: Requirements of Writing (Scotland) Act 1995, s.1(2)(c). Where the trust fund consists of heritage, writing is not required for the constitution of the declaration of the trust: but the transfer of the ownership of the heritage to the trustees must be in writing: Requirements of Writing (Scotland) Act 1995, s.1(2)(b).

trust fund without the trustee or beneficiary having to demand that he do so. Otherwise the truster's purpose in making the declaration in the first place would be undermined. Thus the intimation of the declaration and the transfer of the assets that make up the trust fund can sometimes appear to take place simultaneously. For example where the trust fund consists of heritable property, the declaration of trust is often to be found in the disposition conveying the land to the nominated trustees. Nevertheless it is important always to remember that the declaration of the trust, the intimation of the declaration to trustees and the conveyance of the ownership of the assets which are to make up the trust fund are all separate juristic acts. And it is the intimation of the declaration, not the transfer of the ownership of the trust fund, that constitutes the trust.

It has been argued that as soon as the trust is constituted, the trustees have the right to compel the truster to convey to them the ownership of the property which is to constitute the trust fund. But this is only a personal right against the truster. Until the ownership of the property is transferred to the trustees, it remains vulnerable to the claims of the truster's personal creditors. In other words, it is only when the ownership of the property has left the private patrimony of the truster and has become part of the trustees' trust patrimony that it is protected from the claims of the truster's personal creditors: this protection therefore does not arise as soon as a trust has been constituted by intimation of the declaration of trust to the nominated trustees. However, where the truster declares that he is holding his own property on trust, intimation of the declaration to a beneficiary (or a co-trustee) appears to be sufficient to transfer the ownership of the trust property from the truster's private patrimony to his trust patrimony.

Inter Vivos and *Mortis Causa* Trusts

There is an important distinction made between *inter vivos* and **10–04** *mortis causa* trusts. An *inter vivos* trust is a trust which is intended to operate during the lifetime of the truster: a *mortis causa* trust (a trust disposition and settlement) is a trust which is intended only to operate when the truster dies. For example:

(a) A sets up a trust under which the income of the trust fund is to be paid to A for the rest of his life (a liferent) and on his death the assets of the fund (the fee) is to be paid to B. This is an *inter vivos* trust as it is intended to take effect as soon as the declaration of trust is intimated to the trustees, i.e. the trust is to be effective during the lifetime of the truster: A receives the income during his life although the trust fund will not be paid out to B until A has died.

(b) A makes a declaration of trust that on his death B will have a liferent of the trust fund and on B's death the fee will be paid to C. This is a *mortis causa* trust as it is not intended to take effect until the death of the truster. Put another way, the declaration of the trust and its intimation to the prospective trustees do not constitute the trust. This is because the trust is intended to have testamentary effect, i.e. it is only to come into effect at the date of the truster's death. In these circumstances, it is only the death of the truster that triggers the declaration whereby the trust is constituted. This means that until he dies, the truster can change his mind and use the property which was intended to be the trust fund as he pleases.[2]

A further point should be noticed about *mortis causa* trusts. Although the trust is not constituted until the truster's death, the truster (or more likely the truster's estate) may incur liability if the truster had promised B or C that he would set up a *mortis causa* trust in their favour. As the promise will usually be a gratuitous unilateral obligation, it will not be constituted unless it is made in writing and subscribed by the granter.[3] However, if the requirements of writing are satisfied, B or C could sue A's estate for A's breach of promise if he failed to do so. Moreover, if A had set up a *mortis causa* trust in favour of D, B or C could seek reduction of the trust if D was a gratuitous beneficiary or was in bad faith, i.e. knew about A's promise to B or C. This is another example of the "off side" goals principle.

Revocation of Trusts

10–05   Although a trust has been constituted, the truster may have retained the right to revoke it. Whether or not he has done so, is ultimately a question of the truster's intention. For example, a truster may set up a trust simply because he wants trustees to administer his property on his behalf. But normally when a trust has been constituted, the truster plays no further part and the trust is regarded as irrevocable.[4]

Where a trust is revocable, the right to do so can be invoked by the truster's creditors who will be entitled to recover the assets which make up the trust fund.

---

[2] This is also the position in relation to wills.

[3] Requirements of Writing (Scotland) Act 1995, s.1(2)(a)(ii). This is, of course, subject to s.1(3) and (4).

[4] However where no beneficiaries exist or none has obtained title to enforce the trust, the trust is treated as for administrative purposes only and remains revocable. A declaration by the truster that the trust is irrevocable cannot in itself render the trust so: but provided the criteria in respect of beneficiaries are satisfied, it is a strong indication that the truster intended that the trust cannot be revoked.

Although the ownership of the property which constitutes the trust fund has been transferred to the trustees, when the trust is revocable, the right to revoke the trust enters into the truster's private patrimony when the property is transferred. The right is therefore available to the truster's personal creditors. It is sometimes said that a trust is revocable until the ownership of the property that is to form the trust fund has been transferred from the truster to the trustees. Where the trust fund has not been transferred, there is no need to classify these trusts as revocable trusts. While a trust is constituted as soon as the declaration of trust has been intimated, the truster's property will remain vulnerable to the claims of his creditors until it has left the truster's private patrimony. Moreover, it is also said that trusts which are intended to have testamentary effect remain revocable until the death of the truster. But in the case of a *mortis causa* trust, the declaration of trust is ineffective until the truster dies and consequently no trust is constituted until his death: there is therefore no trust to revoke during the lifetime of the trustee.

Private and Public Trusts

Scots law makes a distinction between private and public trusts. **10–06** A private trust is set up for the benefit of specific individuals or a specified group of persons. For example, A may set up a trust under which his wife, B, is to have a liferent of the trust fund and on her death the trustees are to distribute the fee to their children. A public trust, on the other hand, is a trust set up for the benefit of the public in general or a specified class of the public in general. For example, A may set up a trust for the relief of poverty or medical research or educational purposes or the benefit of the citizens of Edinburgh or Glasgow. Many public trusts will also qualify as charities when they will enjoy tax benefits.

An important distinction between private and public trust arises if the trust purposes fail before the trust fund is exhausted. In the case of a private trust, the trustees hold the trust fund on what is known as a resulting trust for the benefit of the truster or his representatives: in other words, in the event of failure of the trust purposes, the trust assets revert back to the truster. In the case of a public trust, if the trust was originally effective but its purposes subsequently fail, the court can vary the trust to benefit a similar purpose; for example if the trust was for the benefit of a hospital which was later closed down, the trust can be varied to benefit another local hospital. Moreover, even if the trust purpose fails initially, the fund does not revert back to the truster if it is clear that he had an intention to benefit the public in general rather than a specific institution, i.e. that he had a general charitable intention. If this is so, again the court can vary the trust to benefit a similar purpose. So in our example, if the trust failed because the hospital had closed down before the trust had become effective, the court could vary the trust to benefit another local hospital provided it was satisfied that the truster intended to benefit the work of hospitals generally and not just the particular institution mentioned in the trust deed. This is known as a *cy pres* settlement.

For the remainder of this chapter, we shall consider the law in the context of an express private trust only.

Trustees' Powers and Duties

10–07 Once the trust has been constituted and the trust fund conveyed to them, the trustees are the joint owners of the property that makes up the fund.[5] However, although he is the owner of the trust fund, the trustee holds the property in a patrimony which is separate from his private patrimony. In other words, trustees have a trust patrimony which consists of all the assets and liabilities of the trust. The primary duty of a trustee is to administer the trust fund and fulfil the trust purposes in accordance with the intentions of the truster as expressed in the trust deed. Where—as will usually be the case—the trust is irrevocable, the truster has no right to engage in the administration of the trust unless he has appointed himself as one of the trustees.

It is the beneficiary—as opposed to the truster—who has the right to compel the trustees to administer the trust fund in accordance with the provisions of the trust deed. This is a personal right against the trustees as the beneficiary does not have a real right in the property that constitutes to the trust fund which is owned by the trustees. The fundamental obligation which the trustees owe to the beneficiary is to administer the trust fund in accordance with the provisions of the trust deed. This must be done honestly and in good faith for the furtherance of the purposes for which the trust was set up.

To achieve these ends, the trust deed will usually stipulate the powers which the trustees are to have in order to administer the trust effectively, for example the power to make investments or sell trust property. Moreover, s.4 of the Trusts (Scotland) Act 1921 provides that every trustee shall have the power to do a list of acts, for example sell trust property, as long as such acts are not at variance with the terms or purposes of the trust. Where the trust deed does not give the trustees wide powers of investment, the trustee has the power to make investments as authorised under the 1921 Act.[6]

---

[5] This is one of the rare examples of joint—as opposed to common-ownership in Scots law.

[6] Unless the investment powers under the 1921 Act are inconsistent with the express provisions of the trust deed.

Breach of Trust

The obligation to administer the trust and fulfil its purposes in **10–08**
accordance with the trust deed has—at least—two aspects. The first
is where the trustees dispose of the trust assets in a way that is
contrary to the trust purposes, for example if the trust fund was
conveyed to a person who was not a beneficiary. The second is
where the trustee "administers" the trust by purporting to exercise
a power that he does not have under the trust deed (or statute). In
both cases the trustee has acted in breach of trust *stricto sensu*, i.e.
in breach of the trust deed. The misapplication of the trust fund or
the unauthorised investment of the trust fund are actions which
are, as it were, ultra vires the deed: in other words, beyond the
trustees' powers. The trustee has broken his primary obligation to
fulfil the trust purposes in the way set down by the truster in the
trust deed. Breach of trust in this sense is a wrong and liability is
strict: it is not dependent on proof of fault or *culpa*. It does not
matter that a payment was made to a particular person because the
trustees honestly and reasonably believed that she was a beneficiary
or that an unauthorised investment was made in the reasonable
belief that it was authorised and in the best interests of the trust. In
both cases there is still a breach of trust (although under s.32(1) of
the Trustees (Scotland) Act 1921 a court can relieve a trustee
wholly or partly of his personal liability if it appears to the court
that he acted honestly and reasonably and ought fairly to be
excused for his breach of trust).

An ultra vires breach of trust generates the following remedial
rights in the beneficiaries. Trustees are obliged to account to the
beneficiaries for their intromissions, i.e. how they administer the
trust fund and a beneficiary can obtain such an account in an
action for count, reckoning and payment. Where an intromission
consists of an ultra vires breach of trust, the trustee cannot take
credit for it in the account. If, for example, a trustee made a
payment to someone who was not a beneficiary, he cannot take
credit for that misdisposition and is personally liable to credit the
trust fund with the value of the asset he had wrongfully disposed.
In addition, the trustee must credit the trust fund with the income
the asset would have generated if the misdisposition had not taken
place. Where the trustee has made an unauthorised investment,
again he cannot take credit for it in an account. If the investment
earned less than an authorised investment, the trustee is personally
liable to make up the difference: but if it has earned more than an
authorised investment would have done, the trustee must account
to the beneficiaries for the full value of the investment. In other
words, the trustee must disgorge all the profits that have been
made from the unauthorised investment even where these gains
are greater than what authorised investments would have made. An
ultra vires breach of trust is therefore another example of a wrong

which generates a right of restitution and disgorgement of profits as well as reparation for any losses that have been incurred. Because liability is so strict, in practice trusters use exemption clauses to limit their trustees' liability for all but dishonest conduct.

10–09   The relationship between a trustee and beneficiary is a fiduciary relationship. What this means is that a trustee must exercise his powers in the way that best furthers the interests of the beneficiaries rather than himself. To use traditional terminology, a trustee is under an obligation not to be *auctor in rem suam*, i.e. he must not be actor in his own cause. Accordingly, a trustee cannot profit from his position as a trustee (no profit rule): must avoid any conflict with the interests of the beneficiaries; and not engage in self-dealing with the assets of the trust, for example selling trust assets to other trustees. A breach of the fiduciary relationship is a breach of trust. It constitutes a wrong and liability is strict. It does not matter that a trustee who has profited from his position honestly and reasonably believed that he was entitled to do so: he has been *auctor in rem suam* and is thus liable for breach of trust. It generates remedies which are similar to those arising from an ultra vires breach of trust. In particular, a beneficiary has a right to restitution and disgorgement of all the profits the trustee derived from the breach. Being *auctor in rem suam* is a wrong where the defender trustee is compelled to disgorge any gains he made from the breach even though the pursuer beneficiary has not sustained any corresponding loss. Because liability is so strict, trusters often dilute the obligation by providing in the trust deed that, for example, a trustee is to be entitled to reasonable remuneration for administering the trust.

It is sometimes said that in these situations the trustee holds the misappropriated funds or profits from a breach of trust on what is known as a constructive trust for the benefit of the beneficiaries of the original trust. This is to ensure that the funds so held are protected from the trustee's personal creditors should he become insolvent. This is unnecessarily complicated. Although the trustee has committed a breach of trust, nevertheless his intromissions have been carried out in the course of his office: accordingly, any property misappropriated from the trust fund will be treated as remaining in his trust as opposed to his private patrimony and any profits made in breach of trust will automatically accrue to his trust as opposed to his private patrimony. Thus the property is never at risk from the trustee's private creditors. Moreover, as the beneficiary's rights are generated by a wrong, the defences available in an action for restitution based on non-fault unjustified enrichment, such as change of position, are not available to the trustee.

Liability for breach of trust can also arise when a trustee does badly something that he was entitled to do in order to fulfil the trust purposes in accordance with the truster's directions. Here liability depends on establishing *culpa* or fault. We can call this *intra vires* delictual liability. The trustee must have failed to exercise the degree of diligence which a man of ordinary prudence would exercise in the management of his own affairs: in short, he must have failed to take reasonable care and was therefore negligent. Loss to the beneficiaries is a constituent part of the delict and the trustee is only liable to compensate them for the losses incurred by the trust fund as a consequence of his negligence. If there have been no losses there will be no liability. Once again it is common to find that trusters use exemption clauses in the trust deed to restrict the trustees' liability for all but fraud.

Breach of Trust and Third Parties

We have been considering the remedies available to beneficiaries **10–10** against a trustee who has committed a breach of trust. But what happens when, in breach of trust, a trustee has transferred trust assets to a third party? Does the beneficiary have a remedy against the third party to whom the property has been transferred? Three situations must be considered.

(a) Bona Fide Transferee for Value

The trustee, A, transfers trust assets to a third party, C, who is in **10–11** good faith and provides value for the transfer. C incurs no liability to the beneficiary, B. A is the owner of the property and can therefore transfer a good title to C. Because C has been in good faith and given value, C's title cannot be reduced. Moreover, s.2(1) of the Trusts (Scotland) Act 1961 expressly provides that where there has been an ultra vires breach of trust, neither the transaction or C's title can be impugned if the trustee was purporting to exercise his powers in respect of trust property under s.4 of the Trusts (Scotland) Act 1921.

Moreover as C is in good faith and has given value, C's retention of the property is with cause and therefore B has no claim against C based on unjustified enrichment as C has not been enriched. But because A was acting in the course of his trusteeship when the transfer took place, the value he received for the property automatically becomes part of A's trust patrimony and is therefore subject to the trust obligations which A owes to B (and is, of course, protected from A's private creditors). Thus in a competition between a beneficiary and a bona fide transferee for value of trust assets, Scots law gives preference to the interests of the latter. This result is not unjustified as the beneficiary will always have her remedies against the trustee for breach of trust.

(b) Bona Fide Donee

In breach of trust, the trustee, A, transfers trust assets to a third **10–12** party, C, who is in good faith but does not give value for the transfer. Although A is the owner of the property and can therefore transfer a good title to C, C's title is annullable as she has not given value for the property. Nor does s.2(1) of the Trusts (Scotland) Act 1961 apply, as the transaction is gratuitous and s.4 of the Trust (Scotland) Act 1921 does not give a trustee the power to donate trust property. Accordingly, the conveyance of the property from A to C can be reduced and the property reconveyed to the trustees as trust assets. Thus in a competition between a beneficiary and a bona fide donee of trust assets, Scots law gives preference to the interests of the former. Unlike the case of the bona fide transferee for value where the value automatically enters A's trust patrimony, in the case of a bona fide donee, the trust assets are reduced by the value of the gift: prima facie the beneficiaries should be entitled to have the assets back.

B's right to seek reduction will be lost if *restitutio in integrum* is not possible. However, B may have an alternative remedy based on unjustified enrichment. C has been enriched by A's transfer to C because C has not given value. While the retention of property by a donee is generally with cause as a result of the transferor's intention to donate, a donee's enrichment is treated as unjustified if it was made by the donor in breach of trust. Therefore B is under an obligation generated by the law of unjustified enrichment to return the property or its value to the trustees as trust assets. So for example if, A, a trustee under a *mortis causa* trust, pays by mistake a legacy to C who is not a beneficiary under the trust, C is obliged to return the property. Put another way, the trustees can obtain restitution of the property and distribute the property to the true beneficiary, B.[7] This seems fair. The law of unjustified enrichment is about the reversal of gains enjoyed by the defender at the expense of the pursuer: it is not about reparation of the pursuer's losses caused by the defender's fault. C's obligation to make restitution of the legacy arises from the fact that she received it at the expense of the true recipient, B, an equally innocent party, and for which C gave no value. Although she must return the windfall, C is no worse off than she was before the mis-disposition of the trust assets. Of course, it is open to C to argue that in the particular circumstances of the case it would be inequitable to compel her to return the value of the property. This would arise, for example, if, in good faith, C had changed her position by consuming the benefit, i.e. had spent the legacy.

If C had invested the legacy, it is not thought that she should have to disgorge the profits. This is because she has been in good faith throughout. It is enough that C returns an amount equivalent to the value of the original legacy plus the interest it would have earned if it had remained in the trust fund.

---

[7] And the beneficiaries can demand that the trustee seek restitution.

(c) The Mala Fide *Transferee*

In breach of trust, A, a trustee, transfers trust assets to a third **10–13** party, C, who is in bad faith, i.e. knows that the transfer is in breach of trust (or dishonestly assists A to breach the trust). C may or may not have given value for the transfer.

Although A is the owner of the property and can transfer a good title to C, C's title is annullable as C has been in bad faith. A person cannot benefit from another's wrong unless she is in good faith and given value. Therefore the conveyance of the property from A to C can be reduced and the property reconveyed to the trustees. But the right to reduce the conveyance will be lost if *restitutio in integrum* is not possible. Moreover, where C has given value, s.2(1) of the Trusts (Scotland) Act 1961 may operate to prevent C's title from being challenged as the provision does not expressly stipulate that C has to be unaware that the transaction is in breach of trust. If s.2(1) does apply to a mala fide transaction for value, neither the transaction nor C's title can be impugned: but the value that C has provided will automatically become part of A's trust, as opposed to his private, patrimony and therefore will be subject to the trust obligations which A owes to the beneficiary, B.

Even if the right to reduction is lost, other remedies may be open to B. C is in bad faith because he knows that the transfer is in breach of trust. By entering into the transaction with A in these circumstances, C is knowingly interfering with B's rights against A under the trust. C's knowing interference with B's rights constitutes a wrong.[8] Put another way, C has accessory—art and part—liability for A's breach of trust. This wrong generates remedies in delict. Thus C is liable to make reparation for any losses incurred by the trust fund as a consequence of the breach of trust. In addition, C will be obliged to disgorge any profits that he has made. Because this right to restitution is generated by C's wrong—not unjustified enrichment—C cannot argue that it would be inequitable to compel him to do so. Thus, for example, a change of position defence is not available. Accordingly, because C is in bad faith, B can recover not only any loss from the trust fund but also any gains that C has made as a result of the wrong.[9]

Where a trustee has engaged in dishonest behaviour, he will often need the assistance of a third party in order to invest or otherwise dispose of the property: it is therefore sensible that the law ensures that a beneficiary can have recourse against a *mala fide* third party especially as the dishonest trustee may turn out to be a man of straw.

---

[8] An analogy can be made with the wrongful interference with contracts.

[9] This claim can be brought against C even though the property is no longer part of C's private patrimony and cannot be traced. Again this is because it is generated by C's wrong and not unjustified enrichment.

(d) Breach of Trust—Conclusions

10–14   We have spent a little time exploring the issues raised by breach of trust because it provides a particularly cogent example of how the fundamental principles of private law can interlink and come together to provide principled solutions to difficult problems. It will be noticed that because the beneficiary has no real right in the property of the trust fund, any right she has against a trustee for breach of trust can only be personal. Where the breach of trust involves the transfer of trust assets for value, the value will automatically pass into the trustee's trust patrimony and will therefore be protected from the trustee's private creditors. But this presupposes that there is a trust fund. If the trustee has simply squandered the trust fund, a beneficiary has only her personal right against the trustee to sue for breach of trust and on the trustee's insolvency would rank as an ordinary creditor on the trustee's private patrimony. Similarly, the remedies a beneficiary has against a third party are only personal actions based on either delict or unjustified enrichment. Once again, a beneficiary would rank as an ordinary creditor in the event of the third party's insolvency. In short, Scots law does not accept that the law of obligations can generate in a beneficiary quasi-proprietorial rights in assets which had constituted the trust fund and were misappropriated by the trustee or transferred to a third party in breach of trust. It has been suggested that—at least where he is in bad faith—a third party should be taken as holding the former trust assets on a constructive trust for the benefit of the original beneficiary so long as the property subsists and is traceable. This would protect the beneficiary from the third party's personal creditors in the event that he should become insolvent. Alternatively, the beneficiary's claims in respect of breach of trust could be given priority over the defender's ordinary creditors, at least while the trust property subsists and is traceable. If so, there would be no need to resort to the device of a constructive trust. On the other hand, these solutions might appear unprincipled as they undermine the distinction between real and personal rights which has been a hall mark of Scots law for centuries.

Fulfilling the Trust Purposes

10–15   A trustee's fundamental obligation is to administer the trust in accordance with the provisions of the trust deed and in doing so, to perform his duties honestly and in good faith. In particular he must invest the trust fund in the way that a person of ordinary prudence would manage her own affairs. For example:

A trust is set up under which A is to have a liferent of the trust assets and on A's death the fee is to be divided between B and C.

The trustees are obliged to invest the trust fund[10] as they would their own monies on the basis that they are persons of ordinary prudence. They must then ensure that the income derived from the investments is given to A at regular intervals until she dies. On her death, the trustees must then distribute the capital of the trust fund and transfer the ownership of the property to B and C (or their representatives should either of them have died before the expiry of A's liferent). The trustees are then entitled to a discharge from B or C or the court as the purposes of the trust have been fulfilled and the trust is at an end.[11]

As we have stressed throughout this chapter, the trust fund is held by the trustees as part of their trust, as opposed to their private, patrimony. This means that the trust assets are not vulnerable to the claims of a trustee's private creditors. It is now a statutory rule that if a trustee becomes bankrupt the trust fund does not vest in his, i.e. the trustee's permanent trustee in bankruptcy.[12]

Further reading

Norrie and Scobbie, *Trusts* (1991)
Paisley, *Trusts* (1999)
Wilson and Duncan, *Trusts, Trustees and Executors* (2nd ed., 1995)

---

[10] In many cases the trust assets will consist of the house in which A had lived with the truster. Here A's liferent consists of her right to occupy the house until her death when the trustees must transfer the ownership of the house to B and C. A can "sell" her liferent to a third party, D, but D's right to occupy the house will cease when A dies.

[11] A trust can be terminated prematurely if all the beneficiaries and potential beneficiaries consent. Similarly the purposes of a trust can be varied if all the beneficiaries and potential beneficiaries consent. The court has power under section 1 of the Trusts (Scotland) Act 1961 to consent to a variation on behalf of a beneficiary or potential beneficiary who is unable to consent, for example because she is a child or young person under the age of 18 or is physically unable to consent through illness.

[12] s.33 (1) provides that "The following property of the debtor shall not vest in the permanent trustee—. . . (b) property held on trust by the debtor for any other person."

CHAPTER 11

THE LAW OF SUCCESSION

Introduction

11–01 In this chapter, we shall consider the principles which underlie the law of succession. When a person dies, the law of succession determines how the property which formed her private patrimony at the time of her death is to be distributed. This property is known as the deceased's estate. In many cases a person dies without making a will: in these circumstances we say that the deceased died intestate. The law on intestate succession governs the distribution of the estate. About seventy five per cent of Scots die intestate. On the other hand, during his lifetime a person is free to make a will in which he decides the persons who will inherit his estate on his death. This is known as testate succession. The person who makes the will is called the testator. Under s.1(2)(c) of the Requirements of Writing (Scotland) Act 1995 a will must be in writing and signed by the testator.[1] The persons who are to benefit under the will are known as legatees. As we shall see, in the interests of his surviving spouse, or civil partner or any children, Scots law limits a person's freedom to test, i.e. to make a will. Because a will only takes effect on the testator's death, i.e. it is a testamentary deed, during his lifetime a testator is free to alter the provisions of his will (often done by adding what is known as a codicil) or, indeed, revoke the will and either make a new will or die intestate. If, however, a person promises to give a legacy to another, this would constitute a gratuitous unilateral obligation and under s.1(2)(a)(ii) of the Requirements of Writing (Scotland) Act 1995 has to be constituted in writing unless ss.1(3) and (4) of the 1995 Act apply. If the requirements of writing are met, the promise is enforceable. This means that if the promisor dies without leaving the promised legacy to the promisee, any testamentary deed to the contrary effect can be reduced or the deceased's estate can be sued for the value of the legacy.

---

[1] s.1(2)(c) is not subject to s.1(3) and (4) of the 1995 Act.

Death

The law of succession only comes into operation when a person 11–02
dies. Because of developments in modern medicine, life can be
prolonged for a considerable period before a patient dies: conversely, treatment can lawfully be stopped resulting in premature
death. Persons now attempt to regulate these matters by means of
living wills in which they stipulate that in the event of suffering
certain disabling illnesses they do not consent to certain forms of
treatment designed to prolong their lives. In the vast majority of
cases, however, a death is simply certified by a doctor and an
extract of the registered death certificate is evidence of death.

In certain circumstances it is necessary to presume that a
person who has disappeared is dead. Under the Presumption of
Death (Scotland) Act 1977 any person with sufficient interest can
petition the court for a declarator of death. The Act applies in
two situations. The first is when a person has disappeared in
circumstances which point to her death at a particular time, for
example if a person was travelling on an aeroplane which crashed
into the ocean. A petition can be brought at any time after the
disappearance. The second is when a person simply disappears
and there are no circumstances to suggest that he is dead. Here
no petition can be brought until seven years have elapsed during
which time there has been no evidence that the missing person is
alive. If a declarator is granted, the missing person is presumed to
be dead for all legal purposes including the law of succession.
There are provisions for the variation or discharge of the
declarator if the missing person is discovered to be alive within
five years of the date of the decree.

It may also be important to know whether one person survived
another. For example:

A makes a will under which he leaves a legacy to B. They are
killed in a climbing accident. Before the legacy becomes part of
B's private patrimony, B must have survived A. If the evidence
establishes that B survived A, then the legacy will have vested, i.e.
become part of B's private patrimony. It does not matter that B
only outlived A for a very short time. The result is that A's legacy
to B has become part of B's estate and will be distributed in
accordance with B's will or the law of intestacy as it affects B. For
this reason, it is common for persons in A's position to delay
vesting by including a provision in the will that the legatee must
survive the deceased for a specified period, for example 28 days,
before he is entitled to the legacy. If the evidence establishes that
B predeceased A, then the legacy lapses and the assets which
constituted the legacy fall into the residue of A's estate.

But what if the medical evidence cannot establish who survived 11–03
whom? By s.31(1)(a) of the Succession (Scotland) Act 1964 ("the
1964 Act") if A and B were married or civil partners, it is

presumed that neither survived the other. Accordingly, the legacy would lapse. But where s.31(1)(a) is really important is when A and B die intestate. Because it is presumed that neither survived the other, each estate is not subject to the prior rights and legal rights which a surviving civil partner or spouse enjoys under the law of intestacy. Consequently, the whole estate will be distributed among the deceased's own heirs on intestacy, who invariably will be members of the deceased's family. But it should be emphasised that this presumption only applies when it cannot be established who died first. Assume A and B were civil partners. It is established that A survived B for a very short time: therefore s.31(1)(a) of the 1964 Act does not apply. B dies intestate. Under the law of intestacy, A has substantial prior rights and legal rights in B's estate. These rights vest in A as soon as B dies. When A subsequently dies his rights in relation to B's estate will be part of A's private patrimony and will be distributed according to A's will or to A's heirs on intestacy.

If A and B are not spouses or civil partners then in the absence of evidence of which, if either, of them survived the other, then s.31(1)(b) provides that the younger is presumed to have survived the elder. Accordingly, if in our example B was younger than A, it is presumed that he survived A, and consequently the legacy will become part of B's private patrimony and will be distributed according to B's will or to B's heirs on intestacy.

An important limitation on the scope of this presumption is found in s.31(2) of the 1964 Act. If A has left a legacy to B whom failing to a third party, C, i.e. the legacy is subject to a destination over, then if B dies intestate the presumption in s.31(1)(b) is displaced and it is presumed that A survived B even though B was younger than A. This means that the legacy never entered B's private patrimony. Instead, because B is presumed to have died before A, the legacy will pass to C, as A intended it should do if B did not survive him, rather than be distributed to B's heirs on intestacy. It should be noted that the usual presumption that the younger survived the elder will apply to any legacies that A left to B which are not subject to a destination over. Also, the s.31(1)(b) presumption is only displaced if B dies intestate. For example, A leaves a legacy to B whom failing to a third party C. B has a will in which the local dog and cat home is the only beneficiary. A and B die in a common calamity and it cannot be established who died first. The presumption applies that the younger, B, survived the elder, A. It is not displaced even if B's legacy is subject to a destination over in favour of C because B did not die intestate. The legacy therefore entered B's private patrimony and in turn will become part of B's legacy to the dog and cat home.

These provisions illustrate how in the absence of sufficient evidence the law must proceed by way of presumptions which are in effect rules of law, given the particular circumstances of the case.

Legal Rights

On the death of a spouse or civil partner,[2] a surviving spouse or **11-04** civil partner is entitled to legal rights out of the deceased's net moveable estate. Where the deceased is not survived by issue, i.e. his or her children and their descendants, the surviving spouse or civil partner is entitled to one half of the deceased's net moveable estate: if the deceased is survived by issue, the survivor is entitled to a third of the deceased's net estate. Where a person dies survived by issue, the issue are entitled to what is known as legitim, i.e. legal rights out of the deceased's moveable net estate. Where the deceased is survived by a spouse or civil partner, the issue are entitled to a third of the deceased's net moveable estate: where the deceased is not survived by a spouse or civil partner, the issue are entitled to one half of the net moveable estate.

Representation applies in relation to claims for legitim. This means that if a child has predeceased the deceased, the dead child's issue, for example his children, can represent their deceased parent and claim their parent's right to legitim from their grandfather's estate. Division takes place per capita, i.e. the legitim fund will be divided equally between the claimants if they are all of the same degree of relationship to the deceased. However, where the claimants are not all of the same degree of relationship to the deceased, division of the fund is *per stirpes*. For example:

(a) A dies survived by his children, B and C. He was predeceased by his child, D who is survived by his children, E and F. E and F claim legal rights by representation. As the claimants are not all of the same degree of relationship with the deceased, division of the legitim fund is *per stirpes*. The fund is divided in three, a third to B, a third to C and a third to E and F who are representing their parent, D, and consequently each gets a sixth of the legitim fund.

(b) A dies predeceased by his children, B, C and D. B and C died without issue but D was survived by his children, E and F. E and F claim legal rights by representation. As the claimants are of the same degree of relationship to the deceased, the legitim fund is divided equally between the claimants so that E and F will each receive one half of the legitim fund.

For the purpose of a claim for legitim, it is enough that the claimant was a child of the deceased.[3] No distinction is made

---

[2] Civil Partnership Act 2004, s.131.
[3] Or represents a child of the deceased.

between legitimate and illegitimate children. Adopted children are included but not children whom the deceased had simply accepted as a child of the family, for example a step child. There is no upper age limit so that the deceased's adult children can claim legitim.

During her lifetime a parent may advance a sum to a child which is to be used to set the child up in the world or help him settle down. Put another way, the child is to have the money while the parent is alive rather than have to wait until the parent dies. In such a situation, if the child later claims legitim from the parent's estate, the sum advanced to him must be notionally added to the total legitim fund which is to be distributed among the claimants and then notionally deducted from his share.[4] This is known as collation *inter liberos* and is designed to preserve equality between claimants on the legitim fund. A child is not required to collate if she has discharged her right to claim legitim.

The legal rights may be discharged during the lifetime of the spouses, civil partners or parents. Similarly, legal rights may be renounced after a spouse's, civil partner's or parent's death either expressly or impliedly by acceptance of testamentary provisions which were intended by the deceased to be in satisfaction of legal rights. If a surviving spouse, civil partner or children elect to claim legal rights, they forfeit any testamentary provisions in their favour unless forfeiture has been expressly excluded by the testator.

It will be clear that legal rights are intended to protect the deceased's immediate family from being cut out of succession to at least a portion of the deceased's estate: on the other hand, they can be seen as an anachronistic restriction on a person's freedom to test, for example to leave all their estate to a charity. What is clear is that the current law on legal rights provides very imperfect protection for the deceased's family. First, legal rights are only exigible out of the net moveable property which formed part of the deceased's private patrimony at the date of death. This means that if the deceased had transferred[5] all his moveable property out of his private patrimony when he was alive, there will be no property which will be subject to a claim for legal rights. There is no provision to claw back such *inter vivos* transfers even if the transfer was made to defeat such claims.[6] Second, legal

---

[4] It is in effect a paper transaction. For example, P advances £5k to A. On P's death the legitim fund is £15k to be shared between A and B. The advance is notionally added to the value of the fund *viz.* £5k + £15k = £20k. The fund is then divided between A and B giving £10k each from which the advance of £5k is notionally subtracted from A's share. Thus A receives £5k and B £10k from the actual legitim fund.

[5] One way to do so would be to set up an *inter vivos* trust.

[6] If the transfers took place within seven years before the death, the transferee could be liable to inheritance tax.

rights are not exigible out of heritage. Accordingly the deceased could defeat a claim for legal rights by converting all his property into land, i.e. heritage: he is then free in his will to dispose of the heritage as he pleases, for example leave all the property to a charity.

Although legal rights remain a distinctive feature of the Scots law of succession, their value is limited particularly as they are not exigible from heritable property which will often constitute the deceased's most valuable asset.

Intestate Succession

Prior Rights

When the deceased has died without a will, he has died **11–05** intestate. This is now governed by the Succession (Scotland) Act 1964. If the deceased is survived by a spouse or civil partner, the survivor has substantial statutory prior rights which must be satisfied before the estate can be distributed to the heirs on intestacy. By s.8 of the 1964 Act, a surviving spouse or civil partner is entitled to the deceased's interest in the dwelling house in which the survivor was ordinary resident at the date of the death of the intestate. We are therefore concerned with the house in which the *survivor* was ordinarily resident at the date of the intestate's death. It does not matter that the deceased was not ordinarily resident in the house on the date he died. If more than one house qualifies, the survivor has six months to elect the house which is to be the subject of prior rights. The survivor is entitled to the deceased's interest in the property. If the deceased was the sole owner, the survivor will inherit the ownership of the whole house. If the house was owned in common between the deceased and the survivor, the survivor will inherit the deceased's one half *pro indiviso* share. On the other hand, if the house was owned in common with a destination over to the survivor, the surviving spouse or civil partner obtains the deceased's one half *pro indiviso* share by virtue of the special destination, i.e. under the law of property rather than the statutory prior right. This could be important. If the deceased's interest in the house is worth more than £300k,[7] the surviving spouse or civil partner is no longer entitled to the deceased's interest in the property but a sum of £300k instead. There is no restriction on the value of the property acquired under a special distinction.

In addition, the surviving civil partner or spouse is entitled to the furniture and plenishings of a dwelling house in which she was

---

[7] The current amounts in relation to prior rights were set by the Prior Rights of Surviving Spouse (Scotland) Order 2005.

ordinarily resident at the date of the intestate's death.[8] But, if the value of the furniture and plenishings exceeds £24k, the surviving spouse or civil partner is entitled to such parts of them as he or she may choose to a value not exceeding £24k. It is important here to remember that the monetary limitation on this prior right applies only to the value of the *deceased's* proprietary interest in the furniture and plenishings. Where the furniture and plenishings constitute household goods, there is a presumption that they are owned in common between the spouse and civil partners.[9] If the presumption cannot be rebutted this will substantially reduce the value of the deceased's interest in the furniture and plenishings so that the statutory limit on the prior right can be avoided.

Under s.9 of the 1964 Act, a surviving civil partner or spouse is entitled to financial provision from the intestate's estate. If the deceased is survived by issue, however remote, the surviving spouse or civil partner is entitled to £42k; in other cases, the surviving civil partner or spouse is entitled to £75k. Where the net estate is less than £42k or £75k as the case may be, the surviving civil partner or spouse is entitled to the whole intestate estate. Where it is more, the statutory financial provision is borne by the heritable and moveable parts of the estate in proportion to the respective amounts of those parts.

After satisfaction of these prior rights, the surviving spouse or civil partner is entitled to claim legal rights from the remaining moveable net estate.[10] Only then can the remaining estate be distributed to the deceased's heirs on intestacy.

It will be obvious that these prior rights will exhaust the value of many estates. Consequently a surviving civil partner or spouse may be better off if the deceased died intestate rather than leave a will bequeathing all the estate to him or her. For in the latter case any surviving children will be able to claim legitim: but on an intestacy, children can only succeed to the intestate estate after a surviving spouse or civil partner's prior rights have been satisfied.

A surviving cohabitant has no prior rights in relation to the deceased's intestate estate. However, under s.29 of the Family Law (Scotland) Act 2006 a surviving cohabitant has the right to apply to a court for financial provision from the deceased's net intestate estate. The right will only arise after the prior and legal rights of any surviving spouse or civil partner have been satis-

---

[8] The dwelling house for this purpose need not be the dwelling house which the survivor elected to exercise the prior right to the deceased's interest in the property. The right to furniture and plenishings is not dependent on the deceased having a real right in the dwelling house.

[9] Family (Scotland) Act 1985, s.25.

[10] A surviving cohabitant has no legal rights in respect of the deceased's net moveable estate.

fied.[11] Although the court's discretion is very wide, it cannot award a surviving cohabitant more than that to which she would have been entitled if she had been the deceased's surviving spouse or civil partner.[12]

The Heirs on Intestacy

Once any prior rights have been satisfied, the estate can be **11-06** distributed to the deceased's heirs on intestacy. In the first place, these will be the deceased's children. No distinction is made between legitimate and illegitimate children. Adopted children are included but not children whom the deceased had simply accepted as children of the family, for example step children. As in claims for legal rights, representation operates. For example:

A dies intestate. He is survived by his children B and C. A child, D, predeceased A. D is survived by his children, E and F. As the relatives are not all of an equal degree of relationship to the deceased, the division of the estate is *per stirpes*. B and C will each receive a third and a third will be divided between E and F who represent their parent, D, i.e. E and F will each receive a sixth of the estate. But if B and C had also predeceased their parent, A, and were not survived by issue, then the distribution between E and F would be *per capita* as they are of an equal degree of relationship to the deceased, i.e. each will receive one half of the intestate estate.

Because representation applies, it is only when the deceased is not survived by issue, i.e. descendants however remote, that the estate opens to the next class of heirs. These are the deceased's surviving parent(s) and brothers and sisters,[13] i.e. collaterals. One half the estate goes to the surviving parent(s) and the other half is shared between the brothers and sisters. The issue of a collateral is entitled to the collateral's share by representation. If the deceased is survived only by collaterals, the brothers and sisters are heirs to the whole estate: if the deceased is survived only by parent(s), the parents are the heirs to the whole estate. Only in the absence of any of these heirs does the succession open up to a surviving spouse or civil partner—but not a surviving cohabitant. Failing this, the succession opens out to uncles, aunts, grandparents and remoter ascendants.

---

[11] Family Law (Scotland) Act 2006, s.29(10). The cohabitant's claim therefore takes priority over the legitim claims of the deceased's children, though the court can consider the interests of the children in determining the amount of financial provision to award: ibid, s.29(3)(c).

[12] *ibid.*, s.29(4). The court can consider the length of the cohabitation, the nature of the relationship and the nature and extent of any financial arrangements between the cohabitants: ibid, s.25(2).

[13] Collaterals of the full blood take in preference to collaterals of the half blood.

Because of representation, it is unusual for an estate to be inherited by very remote heirs on intestacy. But where the deceased dies without issue the results can sometimes seem bizarre. Consider the following example:

H and W are married. They have a son C. H deserts W and C. H has a child, D, by a mistress. When he is thirty C is killed in a road accident. He dies intestate without being survived by children. One half of the estate will be divided between H and W. The other half will be inherited by D, his half brother, whom C may never have met.

When there is no heir, the Crown retains the right to take the intestate estate as *ultimus haeres*.

Given the complexity of the rules, it is surprising that so many persons appear happy to die intestate. It is thought that this is a case where ignorance is bliss rather than general satisfaction with the current law.

Testate Succession

11–07   Although a person's freedom to test is limited by the legal rights of a surviving spouse or civil partner or children, nevertheless it is generally thought advisable to make a will and die testate.

Constitution: Formal Validity

11–08   By s.1(2)(c) of the Requirements of Writing (Scotland) Act 1995, a written document is required for "the making of any will, testamentary trust disposition and settlement or codicil." A will is formally valid if it has been subscribed by the testator. Where the signature has been witnessed by at least one witness and each page of the will has been signed by the testator, it will be presumed that the will was subscribed by the testator and is formally valid. But while the document is not self proving unless each page has been subscribed by the testator and the signature witnessed, the will may nevertheless be formally valid if it can be proved that the subscription was in fact made by the testator. For example, if A word processes a will and subscribes the hard copy, it will be formally valid—even in the absence of a witness—if it can be shown that the subscription was in fact that of the testator. The subscription would be self proving, i.e. the subscription would be presumed to be that of the testator if the signature had been witnessed and the testator had subscribed each page of the will. On the other hand, even if the testator has written out a will in her own handwriting, it is not formally valid and therefore ineffective unless and until she has subscribed it.

Constitution: Essential Validity

A will is the expression of the testator's testamentary intent. If **11–09** the testator lacked the capacity to form such an intent, the will is null: if the testator had such capacity but did not exercise it freely when she made the will, then the will can be annulled.

Persons do not have legal capacity to make a will until they reach the age of 12.[14] A person who is of unsound mind is incapable of making a will if as a consequence of a mental illness she did not know what she was doing when she purported to make the will (or changes to an existing will). On the other hand, while she may have capacity, the testator could have been in a facile condition when the will was made: the will can be set aside on this ground on proof of circumvention, usually on the part of a beneficiary under the will. Similarly, a will can be set aside on the grounds of duress or undue influence.

Where the will is null, a declarator of nullity can be obtained. Where the will is annullable, a decree of reduction is necessary. Such actions are usually brought by close relatives of the deceased who stand to benefit if the will is reduced and the estate distributed according to the rules of intestate succession.

Revocation

It is the hall mark of a testamentary deed that it can be revoked **11–10** at any time before the death of the granter. Accordingly, during his lifetime a testator is free to revoke a will or a particular provision in a will. This is usually done when the testator makes a new will in which he expressly revokes all previous wills.[15] A will is also revoked if it is destroyed by the testator.[16] Provisions in a will can be altered by a codicil to the will. In other words, under the law of succession, until she dies a testator is always free to change her mind on how her estate is to be distributed.

---

[14] The Age of Legal Capacity (Scotland) Act 1991, s.2(2).
[15] Any previous will should be destroyed to prevent it reviving should the will which revoked it later be revoked.
[16] A will can be impliedly revoked if the provisions of a later testamentary deed are inconsistent with it. A will is also impliedly revoked by the *conditio si testator sine liberis decesserit*. This is a rebuttable presumption that a testator would not make a will which did not make provision for a child who was born after the will was made. If invoked, the doctrine revokes the will and all previous testamentary writings and the estate is distributed according to the rules of intestate succession. However, the presumption can be rebutted by establishing that the testator did not intend to provide for the child. Moreover the doctrine must be invoked by the child. Since the effect is to render the estate intestate, the child's rights as an heir on intestacy are subject to the satisfaction of the prior rights of the deceased's surviving spouse or civil partner. If so, the child will often be better off claiming legitim rather than invoking the *conditio*: but that would not be the case if, for example, the deceased and the child's mother were unmarried, as a surviving cohabitant does not have prior rights.

What is the position if A promises to give B a legacy but fails to do so? If the promise was made gratuitously, it is a gratuitous unilateral obligation and is not constituted unless in writing and subscribed by A.[17] This is subject to ss.1(3) and (4) of the 1995 Act. For example, the promise may be enforceable in the absence of writing if with the knowledge of A, B had acted to his detriment in reliance of A's promise that A would leave him a substantial legacy. If the requirements of writing can be satisfied, B may be able to obtain reduction of A's will or damages from A's estate for the loss of the legacy.

A person may restrict his capacity to change his will by contracting not to do so. This question has arisen when persons— usually a married couple—enter into a mutual will. This is a deed in which two or more persons give directions as to the disposal of their estates after their deaths. If it is held to be contractual— ultimately a question of construction of the deed—then after one of the parties has died the survivor cannot change the provisions he had agreed with the deceased. For this reason mutual wills should be discouraged.

Legacies

11-11   A legacy is classified according to the nature of its subject. In turn, the legal effect of a legacy in a particular case turns on how it has been classified. The traditional classification is as follows:

Specific or Special Legacies

11-12   This is a legacy of a specified item(s) of property owned by the deceased at the time of his death: for example, "my Wedgwood china", "my grandfather's watch", "my country cottage in Argyll" or "my shares in ICI". If the subject of the specific legacy was not part of the testator's private patrimony at the date of his death, then the legacy is cancelled: this is known as ademption and the legacy is said to have adeemed. This would arise if, for example, the property was destroyed or sold by the testator to a third party before he died. If there are insufficient funds to pay all the legacies, priority is given to specific legacies.[18]

General Legacies

11-13   This is a legacy where the subject matter does not allow it to be distinguished from other things of the same class owned by the testator at the date of his death. The paradigm of a general legacy

---

[17] Requirements of Writing (Scotland) Act 1995, s.1(2)(a)(ii).
[18] A particular kind of specific legacy is known as a demonstrative legacy. This is where the testator not only specifies the amount of the legacy but also stipulates the source of the funds from which the legacy is to be drawn. For example, "£1000 from my account at Coutts": if the testator closed his account at Coutts before he died, the legacy will adeem.

is a legacy of a sum of money where the testator has not stipulated the source of funds from which the legacy is to be drawn: for example, "I leave £5000 to my nephew, James". If there are insufficient funds to pay all the general legacies, special legacies must be paid in full even though there is nothing for the general legatees. Once special legacies have been paid, general legacies abate equally. For example:

A leaves specific legacies of £50k and general legacies of £100k. The estate is worth only £100k. The specific legacies must be paid in full. This leaves £50k for the general legacies. These will be abated equally by fifty per cent so that each general legatee will receive a legacy worth half the amount stipulated in the will.

Residuary Legacies

The residue of an estate is the amount of the estate left after **11–14** the legacies and claims for legal rights have been satisfied. A will should therefore have a clause disposing of the residue to a residuary legatee(s). In the absence of a residuary legatee, the residue will be treated as intestate estate and be distributed according to the rules of intestate succession. If a specific legacy or a general legacy lapses, for example because the legatee predeceased the testator, it falls into the residue and hence to the residuary legatee. If there are insufficient funds to pay the specific and general legacies, there will be no residue and the residual legacy will fail. In practice, however, specific and general legacies often form a very small part of the estate and it is the residuary legatee who is therefore bequeathed the largest portion of the estate. As specific and general legacies are often given free of tax, it is from the residue—and consequently by the residual legatee—that inheritance tax will be paid. Because the residue will fall into intestacy in the absence of a residuary legatee, it is important to nominate a person to be the residuary legatee should the first person nominated predecease the testator, i.e. there should be a destination over: for example, "I nominate A to be my residuary legatee, whom failing B".

Legatum Rei Alienae

As a general rule the subject matter of a specific legacy must be **11–15** part of the testator's private patrimony at the date of his death: otherwise the legacy will adeem. However, Scots law recognises that a testator might wish to make a legacy of something that he did not own at the date of his death but wished his executor to purchase for the legatee: for example, the latest model of a sports car. If the subject cannot be purchased, the legatee is entitled to its value from the estate.

Vesting of Legacies

11–16　　A legacy is said to vest when an *unqualified* right[19] to the legacy becomes part of the legatee's private patrimony. Before vesting, the legatee has only a *spes successionis*, i.e. a chance of acquiring a right to succeed: after vesting, the legatee is clothed with that right. The unqualified right to the legacy means that no one else is entitled to the legacy apart from the legatee. An unqualified right to the legacy does not mean that the legatee has a right to immediate payment or possession of the legacy. For example, a testator might wish to give a child a monetary legacy which is to vest immediately on the testator's death but instruct his executor that the legacy is not to be paid to the legatee until she reaches the age of 18. Similarly, when *mortis causa* trustees are instructed to hold a fund for A in liferent and then to pay the capital to B on A's death, B's right to the fee vests on the date the testator dies even though it will not be paid over until the death of A.

When does a Legacy Vest?

11–17　　To determine when the testator intended a legacy to vest is ultimately a matter of construction of the testamentary provisions. In the event of ambiguity, a court will favour early vesting and attempt to avoid the legacy following into residue or intestacy. As vesting cannot take place until the testator dies, the presumption is in favour of a legacy vesting at the date of the testator's death.

Where a legacy is unconditional, it will vest immediately on the death of the testator.[20] Where a legacy is subject to a condition, for example that the legatee reaches the age of 18, it must be determined whether the testator intended (a) that *vesting* was to be suspended until the legatee reached the age of 18 or (b) that only the *payment* of the legacy was to be suspended until the legatee reached 18 in which case the legacy will vest at the date of the testator's death. Where the legacy states that the legatee must survive for a certain period after the testator's death, for example

---

[19] This is subject to the doctrine of vesting subject to defeasance which is beyond the compass of this book.

[20] A legacy which is payable on an event which must arise in the future is regarded as unconditional. Thus in our example in para.11–16, B's right to the fee vested immediately because A's, the liferenter's, death, must come sooner or later.

28 days, vesting is postponed until the legatee has survived beyond that period.[21]

Where a legacy is subject to a destination over, for example "to A whom failing B", as a general rule the destination over is taken to deal with the contingency that A will not survive the testator: if he does, the destination becomes inoperative and the legacy will vest in A on the date of the testator's death. But if payment is postponed until a later date, vesting is postponed until that date and the legacy will vest in B if A has dies before that date. Similarly, if *mortis causa* trustees are directed to hold a house for A in liferent and the fee for B whom failing C, vesting of the fee is suspended until A's death. If both B and C are alive then the fee vests in B. But if C predeceases A, then the fee vests in B as soon as C dies: similarly, if B predeceases A, then the fee vests in C as soon as B dies.

Where the legacy is a class gift, for example to the children of A, it will vest in those members of the class alive[22] at the date of the testator's death. It therefore does not vest in any child of A who predeceased the testator or any child of A born after the testator has died. But if the legacy is a liferent to A and the fee to A's children, not only will the right to the fee vest in all A's children who are alive at the date of the testator's death but also any child of A who is born before the liferent expires on the death of A: this is because payment of the legacy has been postponed to a date later than the testator's death. As a general rule, the legacy will be divided equally between the members of the group. If one member of the class dies before the date of vesting, his share accresces to the survivors, i.e. his share becomes part of the fund which is to be shared between the members of the class. Similarly, if a legacy is to A and B, if A dies before the legacy has vested, A's share accresces to B: in other words, such a legacy is read as having an implied destination over to the survivor *viz.* to A and B whom failing the survivor. However, if words of severance are used—"equally", "share and share alike"—the doctrine of accretion is displaced. Thus if the legacy is to A and B equally, then if A dies before the legacy has vested,

---

[21] Where the legacy is to A, B and C and the survivor of them, the legacies will vest in those who are alive at the date when the testator intended the subject matter of the bequest to be distributed: in the absence of a direction that, for example, it is to be paid at the expiry of a liferent, the date of distribution is the date of the testator's death. Therefore the legacy will vest in those members of the group, A, B and C who are alive when the testator dies. Of course, the testator could expressly stipulate that the legacy is for the survivor of the group A, B and C: here vesting would be postponed until the survivor could be ascertained, i.e. when the second of the group had died.

[22] A child *in utero* at the date of the testator's death is treated as already born at that date.

the legacy fails and falls to the residuary legatee or in the absence of a residuary legatee into the deceased's intestate estate.

In marked contrast to claims for legitim or a right to a share of an estate on intestacy, there is no claim to a legacy by representation. If a legatee dies before a legacy has vested, the legacy fails and the legacy will fall to the residuary legatee or into intestacy. However, there is an exception to this rule. This is where a testator has left a legacy to his child or grandchild[23] but the grandchild or child dies before the legacy has vested. If the deceased legatee has a child, there is a presumption that the testator would have wished that child to have the legacy rather than have it fail and fall into residue. This presumption can be rebutted by establishing from the other provisions of the will that the testator had a contrary intention.[24] The presumption applies when the legatee predeceases the testator or dies after the testator but before the legacy vests: it does not apply if the legatee was dead when the will was executed. This doctrine is known as the *conditio si institutus sine liberis decesserit.*

Forfeiture

11–18 A legatee will forfeit a legacy if he elects to claim legal rights rather than accept the legacy.

The Importance of Vesting

11–19 A legacy[25] vests when the legatee obtains an unqualified right to the subject matter of the legacy. The right then becomes part of the legatee's private patrimony. It is a right to demand that the executor of the deceased's estate should transfer the subject matter of the legacy to the legatee. As such it is a personal right, a personal right to compel the executor to fulfil the testator's wishes. It is a form of incorporeal property even though it consists of a personal right to have the ownership of the property which constitutes the legacy transferred to the legatee rather than a real right in that property. A vested legacy is therefore a valuable asset and is part of the legatee's private patrimony. As such, the legatee is free to dispose of the legacy *inter vivos*, for example by assigning it to a third party for money. It is subject to the claims of the legatee's personal creditors should he become insolvent, and if the legatee dies before payment, the legacy will form part of his estate for the purposes of the law of succession.

---

[23] Or a nephew or niece in respect of whom the testator has placed himself *in loco parentis*; a step child is not included.

[24] For example, if the testator had made provision for the issue of predeceasing legatees.

[25] It is also true of the vesting of a beneficiary's right under a trust.

Once he has transferred the ownership of the subject matter of the legacy to the legatee, the executor has discharged his obligations and the legacy comes to an end. The property that has been transferred to him then enters the legatee's private patrimony in place of the right to the legacy.

Exclusion from Succession

A person who has murdered the deceased is excluded from **11–20** participation in his victim's testate or intestate estate. When he has committed culpable homicide, the court has a discretion to modify the effect of this rule if it is satisfied that justice requires doing so given, inter alia, the conduct of the perpetrator and the victim.

The Role of the Executor

An executor is the person who administers the deceased's **11–21** estate. He is either appointed by the deceased (an executor-nominate) or by the court (an executor-dative).[26] But the appointment as executor does not in itself confer on him the authority to deal with the deceased's property. Before the executor can do so, an inventory is made of the deceased's property and the executor then applies to court for confirmation, i.e. a decree of the court authorising the executor to "uplift, receive, administer and dispose of" the estate and to act in the office of executor. It is then provided by s.14 of the Succession (Scotland) Act 1964 that "on the death of any person (whether testate or intestate) every part of the estate (whether consisting of moveable or heritable property) falling to be administered under the law of Scotland shall, by virtue of confirmation thereto, vest for the purposes of administration in the executor thereby confirmed and shall be administered and disposed of according to law by such executor".

The executor then ingathers all the deceased's property and pays the deceased's creditors. Where the deceased left a will, he will then satisfy any claims for legal rights, implement the specific and general legacies and transfer the residue to the residuary legatee. Where the deceased died intestate, he will then satisfy any claims for prior rights and legal rights and distribute the estate between the heirs on intestacy.

On confirmation all the property vests in the executor. But it is unlikely that he will register himself as owner of any heritable property in the estate.[27] However, the confirmation acts as a link in title between the deceased owner and the person who is to

---

[26] As will usually be the case when the deceased dies intestate.
[27] Or indeed any other property that requires registration in order to acquire ownership, for example shares.

inherit the property. In so far as the executor is the owner of the estate, for example in relation to moveable property, it is a form of fiduciary ownership as he owns the property solely for the purpose of distributing the estate to the legatees or the heirs on intestacy.[28] To that extent his position resembles that of a trustee.

Further reading

Hiram, *The Scots Law of Succession* (2002)
Macdonald, *Succession* (3rd ed., 2001)
Meston, *Succession (Scotland) Act 1964* (5th ed., 2002)

---

[28] Although the current position appears to give rise to few problems in practice, nevertheless it is unprincipled. In particular, it is not clear who, if anyone, owns the estate during the period between the date of death and the date of confirmation.

CHAPTER 12

FAMILY LAW

Introduction

In this final chapter, we shall look at some of the principles and **12–01**
rules that govern family relationships. We do so for several
reasons. First, in civil law systems the law of persons has traditionally been treated as part of private law: family law can be seen
as the modern equivalent in Scots law. Second, family law consists
largely of statutory rules and illustrates the importance of legislation as a source of contemporary law. Third, because it regulates
persons who live together, family law provides unique rules and
principles to govern the economic consequences of their relationships: these principles result in solutions which are quite different
from those which would arise if the common law rules of property
and obligations were to apply.

ADULT RELATIONSHIPS

The law that governs a couple's relationship depends on several **12–02**
factors. If they are married or civil partners, their status triggers
specific rights and obligations. If they are unmarried or not civil
partners, specific rights and obligations may be triggered from the
nature of their cohabitation, i.e. whether they are in fact living
together as though they were married or civil partners. As we shall
see, while some of the rights and obligations of cohabitants are the
same as those of spouses and civil partners, there are important
differences: as a general rule, cohabitants' rights and obligations
are less extensive than those of civil partners and spouses.

Marriage and Civil Partnership

Entering the Status

In order to achieve the status of marriage or civil partnership, **12–03**
the parties must go through a ceremony of marriage or civil
partnership and have the capacity to do so. For marriage, the
parties can choose between a religious or civil ceremony[1]; for a civil

---

[1] Marriage (Scotland) Act 1977.

partnership, there is only a civil ceremony.[2] After the ceremony, a schedule of the marriage or civil partnership- signed by the celebrant, the parties and two witnesses—must be registered. Scots law recognised that a couple could become married by cohabitation with habit and repute. This means that if a couple who had capacity to marry each other lived together pretending to be married they became validly married after a period of cohabitation, for example a year, without a ceremony or registration of a marriage schedule. The doctrine did not apply if the couple told people they were not married, i.e. if there was no repute that they were married. A civil partnership could not arise by cohabitation with habit and repute. However, as a general rule, marriage by cohabitation with habit and repute has been abolished unless the cohabitation had begun before the Family Law (Scotland) Act 2006 came into force.[3]

In order to have capacity to marry or enter into a civil partnership, both parties must be 16 or over: neither must be married or in a civil partnership nor must they be within the prohibited degrees, i.e. closely related. Consent to the marriage or civil partnership must be freely given and the parties must have sufficient mental capacity to do so. For marriage, the parties must be of the opposite sex: for a civil partnership, the parties must be of the same sex. Persons who undergo sex realignment surgery can register their post-operative sex and marry or enter a civil partnership as a member of that sex. The absence of such capacity renders the marriage or civil partnership null. In addition, in the case of marriage but not civil partnership, the marriage can be annulled if it has not been consummated as a result of the incurable impotency of one or both of the parties.

Consequences of Marriage and Civil Partnership

During the Marriage or Civil Partnership

12–04 As a general rule marriage and civil partnership have few legal consequences for the parties. They will incur legal rights and obligations in the same way as though they were not married or civil partners. Section 24(1) of the Family Law (Scotland) Act 1985 states that marriage or civil partnership shall not of itself affect:

(a) the respective rights of the parties to the marriage or the partners in a civil partnership;
(b) the legal capacity of the parties to the marriage or civil partnership.

---

[2] Civil Partnership Act, ss.85—100. The civil ceremony simply involves the couple signing the schedule of the civil partnership: yet as a matter of law, there is no pre-existing civil partnership to register.

[3] Family Law (Scotland) Act 2006, s.3.

That said, there are some important rights and obligations which arise from the status.

(i) Aliment

Each spouse and civil partner owes an obligation to aliment the other.[4] This is a spouse or civil partner's obligation to provide their partner or spouse with such support as is reasonable in the circumstances, having regard to the matters which a court is required or entitled to consider in determining the amount of aliment to be awarded.[5] The effect of this provision is that a spouse or civil partner always has a prima facie right to aliment from the other partner or spouse but the extent of the defender's duty to aliment will depend on the same factors as govern quantification of an award. The factors which must be considered are set out in s.4(1) of the Family Law (Scotland) Act 1985:

  (a) the needs and resources of the parties;
  (b) the earning capacity of the parties; and
  (c) generally, all the circumstances of the case.

It is expressly enacted in s.4(3)(a) that the court can take into account the fact that the defender is maintaining other persons in his household "whether or not the defender owes an obligation of aliment to that person". This means that if for example the defender is maintaining a lover and her children, these de facto outgoings can be taken into account in determining what, if anything, amounts to reasonable aliment for his wife or civil partner. On the other hand, by s.4(3)(b) the court is not entitled to take into account either party's behaviour unless it would be manifestly inequitable not to do so. Thus as a general rule a right to aliment is not lost merely because the pursuer has behaved badly: if the defender wishes to avoid the obligation, he must divorce or seek dissolution of the civil partnership when the obligation of aliment will cease. There is a general defence under s.2(8) of the 1985 Act if the defender makes an offer to receive the pursuer into the defender's household and to fulfil the obligation of aliment there provided it is reasonable to expect the pursuer to accept such an offer. In considering whether it is reasonable for the pursuer to accept the defender's offer, s.2(9) of the 1985 Act enjoins the court to look at all the relevant circumstances including the defender's conduct, for example that he was violent towards the pursuer: the mere fact that they have agreed to separate does not in itself render the offer unreasonable. The pursuer can claim

12–05

---

[4] Family Law (Scotland) Act 1985, s.1(1)(a), (b) and (bb).
[5] *ibid.*, s.1(2).

aliment even though she is living with the defender; but here it is a defence to show that the defender is fulfilling the obligation to aliment and intends to continue to do so.[6] As a general rule the court can only award periodical payments: it cannot substitute a lump sum for a periodical payment.

(ii) Moveable Property

12–06 **Ownership of household goods and possession and use of furniture and plenishings in the matrimonial or family home.** Section 25(1) of the Family Law (Scotland) Act 1985 provides:

> "If any question arises (whether during or after a marriage or civil partnership) as to the respective rights of ownership of the parties to the marriage or the partners in a civil partnership in any household goods obtained in prospect of or during the marriage or civil partnership other than by gift or succession from a third party, it shall be presumed, unless the contrary is proved, that each has a right to an equal share in the goods in question"

Household goods are defined as "any goods (including decorative or ornamental goods) kept or used at any time for the joint domestic purposes of the parties to the marriage or civil partnership in any family home for the joint domestic purposes of the parties to the marriage or the partners". However, (a) money or securities, (b) any motor car, caravan or other road vehicle and (c) any domestic animal, are expressly excluded.[7]

The effect of the section is a presumption that spouse and civil partners own household goods in common, i.e. each has a one half *pro indiviso* share in the goods. The presumption is rebuttable but it is expressly enacted that the presumption will not be rebutted by the fact that while the parties (a) were married or (b) were in civil partnership and living together, the goods were purchased from a third party by either party alone or by both in unequal shares.[8] In other words the presumption cannot be rebutted by a spouse or civil partner simply saying that she bought the goods.

Before property amounts to household goods, it must be used for joint domestic purposes. So for example a wife's jewellery or a husband's golf clubs would not constitute household goods as they are not usually intended for joint domestic purposes. More difficult to justify is the exclusion of motor cars etc which are often bought as a result of a couple pooling their resources.

---

[6] Family Law (Scotland) Act 1985, s.2(6) and (7).

[7] *ibid.*, s.25(3)(a), (b) and (c).

[8] *ibid.*, s.25(2).

It should be remembered that at common law a presumption of common ownership arises from joint possession of moveable property. But unlike the s.25 presumption, it is thought that this could be rebutted by proof that the property was bought by one of the parties alone or by both parties in unequal shares.

Where the household goods are owned in common, each party has a right to enjoy possession and use of the property as each has a one half *pro indiviso* share in it. Where furniture and plenishings are owned outright by one of the parties, at common law the owner's spouse or civil partner has no right to possess or use the property. However, a spouse[9]who has the right to occupy the matrimonial home or a civil partner[10]who has the right to occupy the family home[11]can apply for an order granting to the applicant the possession or use of furniture and plenishings in the matrimonial or family home. Furniture and plenishings means any article which is situated in the matrimonial or family home which is owned or hired by either spouse and is reasonably necessary to enable the home to be used as a family residence. The court can make such an order as appears to be just and reasonable having regard to all the circumstances of the case including the conduct of the parties, the needs and financial resources of the parties, the needs of any children of the family and the extent to which any item of furniture and plenishings is used in connection with a trade, business or profession of either party. If an order is made its effect is to override the owner's rights to the extent that the applicant is entitled to the possession of the property for the duration of the order.

These provisions have rarely been used in practice. One reason is that they are only applicable when the applicant does not own the furniture or the plenishings. Accordingly, most spouses or civil partners cannot use these provisions as they are presumed under s.25 of the Family Law (Scotland) Act 1985 to own the property in common with the defender. In these circumstances, they must apply for an interdict to stop the defender preventing the applicant from enjoying her right as common owner to possess or use the property.

Savings from Housekeeping. Section 26 of the Family Law (Scotland) Act 1985 provides: **12–07**

"If any question arises (whether during or after a marriage or civil partnership) as to the right of either party to a marriage

---

[9] Matrimonial Homes (Family Protection) (Scotland) Act 1981, s.3(2).

[10] Civil Partnership Act 2004, s.103(2).

[11] The right to occupy can be either because the spouse or civil partner owns or is common owner of the property or has a statutory right of occupation. The statutory right of occupation is discussed in para.12–09.

or as the case may be of a partner in a civil partnership to money derived from any allowance made by either party or partner for their joint household expenses or for similar purposes, or to any property acquired out of such money, the money or property shall, in the absence of any agreement between them to the contrary, be treated as belonging to each party or partner in equal shares".

At common law if one spouse provided the other with an allowance to be used for household expenses, donation could not be inferred (or more accurately, the presumption against donation could not be rebutted). Therefore if the transferee spouse was able to save some of the allowance, the savings belonged to the transferor. Section 26 provides that in the case of spouses and civil partners any savings or property derived from such savings is to be owned in common by the parties. Again, little use appears to have been made of s.26 largely because the concept of a housekeeping allowance—as well as thrifty spouses or civil partners—appear anachronistic in twenty-first century Scotland.

(iii) Heritable Property

12–08   Important inroads have been made into the common law of heritable property when the property is used as a matrimonial or family home. We shall consider two situations *viz.* (a) when the house is owned by one spouse or civil partner and (b) when the house is owned in common between the spouses or civil partners.

12–09   **When the house is owned by one spouse or civil partner.**   At common law, the owner of heritage has the exclusive right to possession of his property. Provided he was prepared to aliment his wife, a husband who owned the matrimonial home could exclude her from the house. However a spouse or civil partner who does not own the property—known as a non-entitled spouse or non-entitled civil partner—has a statutory right to occupy the matrimonial home[12] or family home[13] together with any child of the family. The statutory right arises as soon as the parties marry or register a civil partnership and one of them—known as an entitled spouse or civil partner—acquires a matrimonial or family home. The rights continue even though the couple separate. They cease when the marriage or civil partnership ends in death or divorce or dissolution. Most importantly, the rights of the non-entitled spouse or civil partner are not defeated if, during the marriage or civil partnership, the matrimonial or family home is sold or otherwise

---

[12] Matrimonial Homes (Family Protection) (Scotland) Act 1981, s.1.
[13] Civil Partnership Act 2004, s.101.

disposed of by the entitled spouse or entitled partner to a third party: this is known as a "dealing".

Entitled and non entitled spouses and civil partners can seek orders from the court to regulate the parties' occupancy of the matrimonial or family home. The court is obliged to make such an order as appears to be just and reasonable having regard to all the circumstances of the case including the parties' conduct, their respective needs and financial resources, the needs of any child of the family, the extent to which the property is used in connection with a trade, business or profession of either party and whether the entitled spouse or entitled civil partner offers or has offered to make available to the non-entitled spouse or civil partner any suitable alternative accommodation.[14]

Moreover the court has power to exclude either party from the matrimonial[15]or family home if this is *necessary* for the protection of the applicant or any child of the family from the conduct of the non applicant which is or would be injurious to the physical or mental health of the applicant or child. This necessity test is not easily satisfied: there must be a serious risk of physical or mental harm to the applicant or child emanating from the conduct of the non-applicant party. It is not enough that it would be in the best interests of the applicant and any children that they should have exclusive occupation of the property. Nevertheless, if the necessity criterion is satisfied, an entitled spouse or entitled civil partner can be excluded from a house of which they are owners!

A non-entitled spouse's and a non-entitled civil partner's statutory right of occupation is not to be prejudiced as the result of the entitled party's, i.e. the owner's dealings with the property. Dealings include the sale or lease of the property to a third party or the grant of a standard security over it. Thus for example, if the entitled partner sells the house, the purchaser will take the property subject to the statutory right of occupation and the third party is not entitled to occupy the property or any part of it while the non-entitled spouse[16]or civil partner continues to have the statutory right. This is quite remarkable. A statutory right of occupation cannot be registered in the Land Register. Nevertheless, contrary to the fundamental principles of Scots land law, a bona fide purchaser for value will take the house subject to a property right which does not appear on the Register. Put another way, the bona fide purchaser for value takes subject to the unrecorded statutory right even though he has relied on the faith of the Register.

---

[14] Matrimonial Homes (Family Protection) (Scotland) Act 1981, s.3; Civil Partnership Act 2004, s.103.

[15] *ibid*. 1981 Act, s.4: 2004 Act, s.104.

[16] Matrimonial Homes (Family Protection) (Scotland) Act 1981, s.6; Civil Partnership Act 2004, s.106.

The legislation provides several solutions to this problem. There is no difficulty if the non-entitled spouse or civil partner consents to the dealing. A court also has the power to dispense with the consent on the ground that it was being unreasonably withheld. Moreover, the non-entitled spouse or civil partner can renounce the statutory right. Most importantly, it is provided that the statutory right is not enforceable against a third party where the dealing consists of a transfer for value to a third party who has acted in good faith and there has been produced to the third party by the transferor, a written declaration stating that the subjects of the transfer are not or were not at the time of the dealing a matrimonial or family home in relation to which a spouse or civil partner of the seller has or had occupancy rights.[17] Accordingly, provided the third party transferee is in good faith, then if such a written declaration has been produced, the transferee will take the property free from the statutory right of occupation. If the written declaration is false, the non-entitled spouse or civil partner will have recourse against the entitled partner for compensation for loss of occupancy rights as a result of the entitled party's fraud.[18]

12–10 **When the house is owned in common by both spouses or civil partners.** The statutory rights of occupation are only available to non-entitled spouses and civil partners. Where the matrimonial or family home is owned in common between the spouses or civil partners, at common law each co-owner is entitled to occupy the whole of the property. Therefore there is no need to give co-owners a statutory right of occupation. However, the court has the same power to make regulatory and expulsion orders where both parties are entitled as when one is entitled and the other is not.

It is axiomatic that a co-owner can sell or otherwise dispose of her one half *pro indiviso* share to a third party without the other co-owner's consent. But where the co-owners of the matrimonial or family home are spouses or civil partners, while each is free to dispose of their one half *pro indiviso* share to a third party, the third party is not entitled to occupy the house while the other co-owning spouse or civil partner remains there.[19]

It is also a hallmark of common ownership that either co-owner can demand a division and sale of their property. The court has no discretion to refuse that demand in an action of division and sale. However where a spouse or civil partner brings an action of

---

[17] *ibid.* 1981 Act, s.6(3)(e); 2004 Act, s.103(e) as amended by the Family Law (Scotland) Act 2006, ss.6 and 33 and Sch.1 to the Act.

[18] A similar affidavit is used to protect the rights of a heritable creditor when an entitled party grants a standard security over the property.

[19] Matrimonial Homes (Family Protection) (Scotland) Act 1981, s.9; Civil Partnership Act 2004, s.109.

division and sale of a matrimonial or family home of which the other spouse or civil partner is co-owner, the court has a discretion, after having regard to all the circumstances of the case, to refuse or postpone the granting of decree or only granting decree under conditions.[20] The decree of division and sale is most likely to be refused or delayed when the house is still required as a home for any children of the family.

Where a spouse or civil partner has been violent towards the other spouse or civil partner, the court can grant an interdict to which is attached a power of arrest: this means that he can be arrested immediately should he breach the interdict.[21]

Divorce and Dissolution

A marriage can be brought to an end by a decree of divorce: a **12–11** civil partnership can be brought to an end by a decree of dissolution. In both cases the court can grant decree if and only if, it is established that the marriage or civil partnership has broken down irretrievably (or an interim gender recognition certificate under the Gender Recognition Act 2004 has, after the date of the marriage or the registration of the civil partnership, been issued to either spouse or civil partner).[22] Irretrievable breakdown can only be established by proof of certain facts: but proof of such a fact establishes irretrievable breakdown even though the marriage has not in fact broken down.

The facts which establish irretrievable breakdown of a marriage or civil partnership are:

(a) the defender's unreasonable behaviour towards the pursuer;
(b) the non-cohabitation of the parties for a continuous period of one year and their consents to the divorce or dissolution;
(c) the non-cohabitation of the parties for two years when the consent of the defender is no longer necessary.

In the case of divorce, there is an additional fact *viz.* that since the date of the marriage, the defender has committed adultery.

Once one or more of these facts is proven, the marriage or civil partnership is deemed to have irretrievably broken down and a decree of divorce or dissolution can be granted.

---

[20] *ibid.*1981 Act, s.19: 2004 Act, s.110.
[21] Protection from Abuse (Scotland) Act 2001, s.1 (as amended by the Family Law (Scotland) Act 2006, s.32.
[22] Divorce (Scotland) Act 1976, s.1: Civil Partnership Act 2004, s.117 (as amended by the Family Law (Scotland) Act 2006, ss.11–13, 33 and Sch.1 to the Act).

Financial Provision on Divorce and Dissolution

The Nature of the Orders

12–12   Section 8(1) of the Family Law (Scotland) Act 1985 provides that on divorce or dissolution the court has power to make one or more of the following orders:

- An order for the payment of a capital sum. This order obliges one of the parties to make a payment of a capital sum to the other. It can come into effect at the date of divorce or dissolution or within a period specified by the court. The capital sum can be paid by instalments. While the method of payment can be varied on a material change of circumstances. the total amount of the capital sum cannot be changed after the divorce.
- An order for the transfer of property. This order obliges one of the parties to transfer the ownership of property to the other. Thus for example if H owns the matrimonial home, he can be ordered to transfer the ownership of the house to B.
- An order for the payment of a periodical allowance. Such an order can only be made if a capital sum payment is inappropriate or insufficient and can only be justified by one of the principles in ss.9(1)(c), (d) or (e). The whole thrust of the 1985 Act is to achieve an economic clean break between the parties and therefore capital sum payments and property transfer orders are preferred to orders for periodical payments.
- An order for a capital sum payment in respect of a lump sum which will fall due under a pension scheme.
- A pension sharing order

In addition, the court can make an incidental order under s.14 of the 1985 Act, for example to order interest on a capital sum payment or the sale of the matrimonial or family home. Given this wide range of orders, the court can tailor financial provision to reflect the circumstances of the particular couple.

The Section 9 Principles

12–13   In an application for financial provision on divorce or dissolution, s.8(2) provides that the court shall make such order, if any, as is (a) justified by one or more of the principles in section 9 and (b) reasonable having regard to the resources of the parties. Unless a s.9 principle is appropriate, no financial provision can be awarded. But as is usually the case, where financial provision is justified by the s.9 principles, the award must also be reasonable in the light of the parties' resources at the time of the proceedings. The effect of this provision is that the amount of an award of financial provision which is prima facie justified by the s.9 principles can be reduced as it is no longer reasonable having regard to the payer's resources at the date of the decree of divorce or dissolution.

Principle 9(1)(a): the net value of the matrimonial property or the partnership property should be shared fairly between the parties.

This principle reflects the idea that a marriages and civil **12–14** partnerships are true partnerships in which the parties are committed and provide the necessary emotional support to enable each other to be economically successful. It should therefore follow that the assets acquired by the parties during their partnership should be shared fairly between them. Thus s.9(1)(a) provides that the net value of the couple's matrimonial or partnership property should be shared fairly between them. The net value is ascertained at the relevant date which is the date on which the parties ceased to cohabit.[23]

Matrimonial or partnership property consists of *all* the property belonging to the parties or either of them at the relevant date which was acquired during the marriage or civil partnership but before the relevant date. Therefore property acquired before the marriage or registration of the civil partnership does not amount to matrimonial or partnership property: but an exception is made for property acquired by the parties for use by them as a family home or the furniture and plenishings of such a home. Property acquired after the relevant date is also excluded.

Otherwise everything acquired by the parties during the marriage or civil partnership constitutes matrimonial or partnership property. This will include savings, investments, heritable property, a business, rights or interests under a life policy and any benefits under a pension scheme. The only property expressly excluded is property acquired by way of gift from a third party or by inheritance. But while for example an inheritance of £50k is prima facie excluded and does not constitute matrimonial or partnership property, if the £50k was used to buy a painting, the painting would be such property. It is irrelevant whether as a matter of property law, the property is owned individually or in common. Provided the property was acquired by one or both of the parties during the marriage or civil partnership, it falls into the melting pot of

---

[23] Where the court makes a property transfer order, the net value of the property being transferred is assessed at the date the order is made rather than the relevant date, unless an earlier date is justified by exceptional circumstances: Family Law (Scotland) Act 1985, s.10(3A) (as added by the Family Law (Scotland) Act 2006, s.16).

matrimonial or partnership property and is subject to fair division under s.9(1)(a).[24]

Fair sharing is prima facie equal sharing. Thus for example:

At the relevant date H owns property valued at £400k; at the relevant date W owns property valued at £100k. The matrimonial property therefore amounts to £500k. Fair sharing is equal sharing: therefore both H and W are entitled to £250k. Therefore H must pay W a capital sum payment of £150k.

While fair sharing is prima facie equal sharing, a court can deviate from a 50:50 split in special circumstances. These include the situation where the source of the funds used to acquire the matrimonial or partnership property did not derive from the income or efforts of the parties during the marriage or partnership. Thus in our example of the purchase of a painting from an inheritance, the value of the painting may be shared on the basis of 65% to the spouse or civil partner who was the legatee in order to reflect that the source of the funds used to purchase it was not matrimonial or partnership property. Another important special circumstance is the nature of the matrimonial or partnership property, especially its use for business purposes or as a family home. Where the only substantial asset is the family home, the court may deviate from the 50:50 split in favour of the party with whom the children of the family are to reside giving her, for example 65% of the value of the property so that she will be able to afford to go on living there with the children. Nevertheless, the courts have consistently said that the circumstances must be unusual before they will depart from the norm that fair sharing is equal sharing.

There is little doubt that s.9(1)(a) represents a remarkable inroad into the autonomy of ownership of property. The value of all property acquired by a party during a marriage or civil partnership is subject to fair sharing on divorce or dissolution. Indeed, if the court makes a property transfer order, the party who, for example, owns the family home can be compelled to transfer the ownership of the house to the other party—with or without a counter-balancing capital lump sum payment in return. While each person retains the ownership of his own property during the marriage,[25]that property is pooled on divorce or dissolution so that it can be shared fairly between the parties who had committed themselves to a partnership when they married or registered a civil partnership.

---

[24] The law of property is, of course, used to determine what each party owns at the relevant date.

[25] Of course, under the law of property the parties may already own property in common during the marriage or civil partnership. Common property does not fit easily into the s.9(1)(a) principle as each party already has already has a one half *pro indiviso* share in the property.

Principle 9(1)(b): fair account should be taken of any economic advantage derived by either party from contributions by the other, and of any economic disadvantage suffered by either party in the interests of the other party or of the family.

The purpose of this principle is two-fold. First, it is to provide **12–15** recompense to a party for the benefits she has gratuitously provided for the other party. Secondly, it is to provide compensation for losses incurred by a party in the interests of the other party and the family.

The contribution can occur before as well as during the marriage or civil partnership. Contributions to the economic advantage of the other party would include putting money into the other party's business, working unpaid in the other party's business, working in order to enable the other party to gain a qualification and redecorating the family home. A contribution made by a party in keeping the home and caring for the family is expressly recognised. Economic disadvantage in the interests of the other party or the family would include giving up a well paid career in order to look after children of the family.

These economic advantages and disadvantages are difficult to quantify. Moreover by s.11(2) of the Family Law (Scotland) Act 1985, the court must consider whether the economic advantages or disadvantages sustained by either party have been balanced by the economic advantages or disadvantages sustained by the other: it is only when there is an economic imbalance in the applicant's favour that an award can be made. Thus for example where W has given up a job as a secretary in order to marry, H can set off against W's economic disadvantage, the extravagant life style the couple enjoyed during their marriage.

Where this provision is useful is where there is little matrimonial or partnership property for the purpose of fair sharing under s.9(1)(a). For example:

A owns a farm. He registers a civil partnership with B. As the farm was acquired before the registration, it does not constitute partnership property. B worked the farm along with A for 20 years. As there is no partnership property that is subject to fair sharing, the court would be inclined make a generous award under s.9(1)(a).

Claims under ss.9(1)(a) and (9(1)(b) are cumulative. Having decided that a s.9(1)(b) claim is justified, the court can, for example, decide that the most appropriate form the award should take is an increase in the claimant's share of the family home beyond the 50% to which she is prima facie entitled under s.9(1)(a).

Section 9(1)(b) provides relief which would be difficult to obtain at common law. In most cases a claim for recompense would fail because the benefit received was with cause, i.e. the claimant wanted to donate her money or services to the other party who consequently is not unjustifiably enriched. A claim in delict for the economic disadvantages sustained would fail in the absence of any wrongful conduct on the part of the other party.

Principle 9(1)(c): any economic burden of caring, after divorce or dissolution, for a child of the family under the age of 16 should be shared fairly between the parties.

The purpose of this principle is that the party who looks after the children of the family after divorce or dissolution should not be economically disadvantaged in doing so. In practice this means that the party looking after the children receives additional financial provision: this can take the form of a periodical allowance or can be used to increase the applicant's capital sum payment or her case for an increased share of the value of the family home beyond the 50% to which she is prima facie entitled under s.9(1)(a).

Principle 9(1)(d): a party who has been dependent to a substantial degree on the financial support of the other party should be awarded such financial provision as is reasonable to enable him to adjust over a period of not more than three years from the date of the decree of divorce or dissolution to the loss of that support on divorce or dissolution.

The purpose of this principle is to provide financial support to a party who has been to a substantial degree financially dependent on the other, to enable that party to readjust to life as a single person after the divorce or dissolution. Where a party is not financially dependent, the principle is not triggered or the support might be for far less than three years. Thus sometimes it might not be in a party's financial interests to try to get a job before raising an action for divorce or dissolution. The support runs for a maximum period of three years. The award can take the form of a periodical allowance but the amount can be capitalised and used to increase the capital sum payment or property transfer orders justified under ss.9(1)(a) and (b).

Principle 9(1)(e); a party who at the time of divorce or dissolution seems likely to suffer serious financial hardship as a result of the divorce or dissolution should be awarded such financial provision as is reasonable to relieve him of hardship over a reasonable period.

This is a long stop measure where adequate financial provision cannot be achieved by applying the four previous s.9 principles. It is only triggered when the applicant is suffering serious financial hardship at the time of the divorce: it does not apply even if it is arguable that the applicant may be overtaken by illness or other misfortune after divorce. Moreover the financial hardship must arise as the result of the divorce or dissolution not the fact that the relationship has irretrievably broken down. For all these reasons resort to s.9(1)(e) is rare. The award can take the form of periodical allowance as well as a capital sum payment or a property transfer order.

Conclusion

The Family Law (Scotland) Act 1985 provides a very sophistic- **12–16** ated system of financial provision on divorce. As we have seen, s.9(1)(a) overrides the parties rights of property and section 9(1)(b) provides relief which would usually not be available under the law of obligations. Sections 9(1)(c), (d) and (e) are original principles with no analogy at common law. There is no doubt that the right to claim financial provision on divorce or dissolution is one of the most important consequences of marriage or registration of a civil partnership.

Personal Injury and Death

When a person suffers personal injuries, a member of his family **12–17** may sustain pure economic loss by giving up her work in order to look after him. Under s.8 of the Administration of Justice Act 1982, the injured person can recover as a head of damages a sum which amounts to reasonable remuneration for the necessary services rendered to him by the relative. The injured person then accounts to the relative for the damages recovered by him under this provision. The spouse or civil partner of the injured person is a relative for this purpose. Section 9 of the Administration of Justice Act 1982 provides that an injured person who has been providing gratuitous, i.e. unpaid personal services to a relative can sue for damages if, as a result of the injuries, he or she is unable to continue to do so. Again, a spouse or civil partner is a relative of the injured person for this purpose.

When a person dies in consequence of personal injuries, under s.1(1) of the Damages (Scotland) Act 1976 members of his family can sue for damages if the defender would have been liable to pay damages to the deceased if he had lived. The relative's right to sue is a dependent action in the sense that it is conditional on the defender being liable if an action had been brought by the deceased in respect of the personal injuries he had sustained. Accordingly, the relative's claim can be defeated if the deceased's claim would have failed because, for example the defender did not owe a duty of care to the deceased or had not been negligent or the deceased was *volens*. The relative's damages will also be reduced on the grounds of the deceased's contributory negligence.

Where the relative is a member of the deceased's immediate family, he can recover damages for the following:

(a) Loss of the financial support he would have received from the deceased if he had not died from the injuries. This covers both loss of support up until the date of death and loss of support in the future. These claims can be substantial.

(b) Such sum, if any, as the court thinks just by way of compensation for all or any of the following:

    (i) distress and anxiety endured by the relative in contemplation of the suffering of the deceased before he or she died;

    (ii) the grief and sorrow of the relative caused by the deceased's death;

    (iii) the loss of such non-patrimonial benefit as the relative might be expected to derive from the deceased's society and guidance if the deceased had not died.[26]

(c) Reasonable funeral expenses

A wider class of relatives—the specified relatives—have no title to sue for non-patrimonial loss, i.e. their claim is restricted to the loss of the deceased's support and reasonable funeral expenses.

The deceased's spouse or civil partner is a member of the deceased's immediate family for the purposes of the 1976 Act. The legal and prior rights enjoyed by a surviving spouse or civil partner under the law of succession were discussed at length in the previous chapter.

Conclusion

12–18 Marriage and civil partnership creates a status for the parties. This gives rise to legal rights and obligations. During the marriage or civil partnership, the most important is probably the mutual obligation to aliment. Ironically, however, the status becomes profoundly significant when it comes to an end either (i) by divorce or dissolution; or (ii) the death of one of the parties. In the former case, the courts have powers to re-allocate the couple's capital and—to a lesser extent—their income with a view to distributing the parties' wealth fairly between them. In the latter, legal rights and prior rights attempt to ensure that a surviving spouse or civil partner has a guaranteed share of the deceased's estate.

Cohabitation

Introduction

12–19 Unlike marriage and civil partnership, cohabitation is not a legal institution which creates a status. Instead, it is a factual situation where the law is prepared to give parties rights and impose

---

[26] Damages (Scotland) Act 1976, s.1.

obligations. Given that the parties have not voluntarily undertaken any obligations, imposing obligations merely because the parties have cohabited together must be recognised as an important restriction on their freedom to choose a lifestyle that does not involve emotional or financial commitment. The development of the law has been piecemeal. For many years only opposite sex cohabitation was recognised. However, in order to avoid violations of the European Convention on Human Rights, many statutory provisions must now be read as applying to same sex cohabitation. In addition, statutes are being amended to include provisions for same sex cohabitants. This section therefore proceeds on the basis that the current law applies to both opposite sex and same sex cohabitation.

The nature of the cohabitation

Legal rights and obligations do not arise merely from the fact **12–20** that a couple have sex or engage in a sexual relationship. Before cohabitation is recognised as a source of rights and obligations, there has to be some degree of stability and emotional commitment. The law attempts to encapsulate such a relationship by utilising the paradigm of marriage and civil partnership. Legally relevant cohabitation thus becomes a relationship where persons not being spouses or civil partners live with each other *as if* they were husband and wife or civil partners. In determining whether such a conclusion can be drawn from a particular relationship, the court will consider all the circumstances including the length of time the parties have lived together, whether they socialised as a couple, the degree of financial dependence and whether there are any children. There is no minimum period of cohabitation before rights and obligations arise.[27]

Property Issues

Unlike spouses or civil partners,[28] cohabitants do not owe a mutual obligation to aliment each other. However, there is a rebuttable statutory presumption of common ownership in household goods acquired by cohabitants during their cohabitation.[29] This is similar to the presumption that arises when the couple are spouses or civil partners.[30] The only difference is that in the case of cohabitants the presumption can be rebutted by evidence that the goods were bought by one cohabitant alone or by both in unequal shares.[31] There is also a presumption of equal ownership of savings

---

[27] See for example, Family Law (Scotland) Act 2006, s.25.
[28] Above para.12—05.
[29] Family Law (Scotland) Act 2006, s.26.
[30] Family Law (Scotland) Act 1985, s.25 discussed above para. 12—06.
[31] Cf. *ibid.*, s.25(2).

from housekeeping.[32] Although the presumption also applies to any property derived from such savings, it is expressly provided that property does not include the house in which the couple live.[33] Financial provision on termination of cohabitation other than death.

When the cohabitation breaks down, by s.28 of the Family Law (Scotland) Act 2006 a cohabitant can seek financial provision from her former partner. The court's discretion is guided by two principles[34] analogous to s.9(1)(b) and (c) of the 1985 Act.[35] But there is no equivalent of s.9(1)(a).[36] Accordingly, unlike spouses and civil partners, the property acquired by each of the cohabitants during the relationship is not subject to fair sharing when it comes to an end. A cohabitant's claim is restricted to recompense for economic contributions made to and economic disadvantages sustained from the relationship as well as compensation for the economic burden of caring for the couple's child(ren) after the relationship has terminated. In exercising this discretion, however, the court can take into account the length of the cohabitation, the nature of the relationship and the nature and extent of the financial arrangements between the parties[37]

Occupancy Rights

12–21 Under s.18(1) of the Matrimonial Homes (Family Protection) (Scotland) Act 1981,[38] where a couple are cohabiting and one partner is entitled to occupy the house and the other partner is not entitled, the non-entitled partner may apply to a court for the grant of occupancy rights in relation to the house in which they are living. Occupancy rights can be granted for a period of up to six months, although the initial period can be extended for further periods of not more than six months. The non-entitled partner's statutory right of occupation is the same as that of a non-entitled spouse or civil partner. While the statutory right is in force, regulatory and exclusion orders are available but there is no protection from dealings with third parties. Where both cohabitants are entitled to occupy the house, for example because they are common owners, there is no need for an application under

---

[32] Family Law (Scotland) Act 2006, s.27: cf Family Law (Scotland) Act 1985, s.26 discussed above para.12—07.

[33] There is no express restriction in s.26 of the 1985 Act but it is thought that as a matter of principle the presumption is automatically rebutted by evidence of the title in which the property is registered.

[34] Family Law (Scotland) Act 2006, ss.28(2)(b) and (3)–(6).

[35] Discussed above para. 12—15.

[36] Discussed above para. 12—14.

[37] Family Law (Scotland) Act 2006, s.25(2).

[38] As amended by the Family Law (Scotland) Act 2006, ss.31 and 34.

s.18(1) before regulatory and exclusion orders are available. However, a court has no discretion to refuse or delay an application for division and sale.

In both situations the court can grant an interdict with a power of arrest.

Personal Injury and Death

A cohabitant is a relative for the purpose of ss.8 and 9 of the **12–22** Administration of Justice Act 1982 and a member of the deceased's immediate family for the purposes of the Damages (Scotland) Act 1976. The right of a surviving cohabitant to seek financial provision from her deceased cohabitant's net intestate estate was discussed in the previous chapter.

PARENT AND CHILD

Establishing Parentage

Children's rights are prima facie exigible against their birth **12–23** parents. A child's mother is the woman who carried and gave birth to the child.[39]

The child's father is the man who fertilised the ovum from which the child developed. As in other areas,[40] the law proceeds on the basis of a series of presumptions which can be rebutted by evidence, for example DNA profiling,[41] that the man is not the child's father. Thus by s.5(1)(a) of the Law Reform (Parent and Child) (Scotland) Act 1986, a man is presumed to be the father of a child if he was married to the mother of the child at any time during the period beginning with the conception and ending with the birth of the child. A man who marries a woman after the birth of her child is not presumed to be the child's father. Secondly, by s.5(1)(b) of the 1986 Act, a man is presumed to be the father of a child if both he and the child's mother have acknowledged that he is the father and the child has been registered as such.

Where a child has been adopted, he is treated in law as the child of his adoptive parents and not as the child of his birth parents. Where a child lives with a step-parent, he remains the child of his birth parent. However, the step parent will incur an obligation to aliment the child if he accepts the child as a child of family.

---

[39] Human Fertilisation and Embryology Act 1990, s.27(1). It is irrelevant that the woman is not genetically related to the child she is carrying or has borne.

[40] For example, the presumptions in relation to the occurrence of death in the case of a common calamity.

[41] Where the child was conceived by AID, the presumptive father is treated in law as the father and the donor is not treated as the father unless the presumptive father has not agreed to the AID.

The obligation of aliment

12-24   By s.1(1)(c) of the Family Law (Scotland) Act 1985, an obligation of aliment is owed by a mother and father or his or her child,
i.e. both parents are under an obligation to aliment their children.
It is irrelevant that the parents never married. Section 1(1)(d) of
the 1985 Act places an obligation to aliment a child on a person
who has accepted the child as a child of his family, for example a
step parent or a grand parent who brings up a grandchild. A child
is a person under the age of 18. But the obligation to aliment can
continue until the child reaches the age of 25 if he is undergoing
instruction at an educational institution, for example a university,
or training for employment. As in the case of aliment between
spouses and civil partners, the obligation of aliment is to provide
such support as is reasonable having regard to the factors which
are used to determine the amount of aliment, i.e. the needs and
resources of the parties, their earning capacities and generally all
the circumstances of the case. Where two or more persons owe a
child an obligation of aliment, there is no order of liability but the
court in determining how much, if any, aliment to award must take
into account that other persons are also under an obligation to
aliment the child. Where a child is under the age of 16, it is no
defence that the obligor offered to receive the child into his
household and thereby fulfil the obligation there.

The child's right to aliment is an independent right. Accordingly,
a child can sue his parents for aliment. Children's claim for aliment
must be satisfied before a spouse's or civil partner's claim for
financial provision on divorce or dissolution. In practice, in an
action for divorce or dissolution, the pursuer will bring claims on
behalf of the children of the family: these will include not only the
parties' biological children but any child accepted by either of them
as a child of the family.

Where a child is below the age of 16 and is not living with his
natural father, his right to seek aliment from his natural father is
suspended: instead a maintenance calculation must be sought from
the natural father under the Child Support Act 1991.[42] Because of
the expansion of higher education, the right to sue for aliment
between the ages of 16 and 25 is becoming increasingly important.

Parental Responsibilities and Rights

12-25   Under s.1(1) of the Children (Scotland) Act 1995, aparent has
the following responsibilities towards a child:

   (a) to safeguard and promote the child's health, development
   and welfare;

---

[42] A maintenance calculation can be obtained from the natural mother if the child
does not live with her.

(b) to provide direction and guidance in a manner appropriate to the stage of the child's development;

(c) to maintain personal relations and direct contact with the child if the child is not living with the parent; and

(d) to act as the child's legal representative.

These responsibilities have to be carried out to the extent that it is practicable and in the interests of the child to do so. In order to fulfil these responsibilities, under s.2(1) of the 1995 Act a parent has the following rights:

(a) to have the child reside with him;

(b) to control, direct or guide the child's upbringing in a manner appropriate to the child's stage of development;

(c) to have contact on a regular basis

(d) to act as the child's legal representative.

These rights can only be exercised in so far as it is practicable and in the interests of the child to do so. When reaching any major decision in fulfilling parental responsibilities or exercising parental rights, the parent must have regard so far as practicable to the views of the child: a child aged 12 or more is presumed to be of sufficient age and maturity to form a view. Parental rights end when the child reaches 16: responsibilities also end at that age except the duty to give a child guidance which lasts until the child is 18.

A child's mother automatically has parental responsibilities and rights in relation to her child. A child's father automatically obtains parental responsibilities and rights if (a) he is or was married to the child's mother at the date of the child's conception or any time thereafter; or (b)[43] he is presumed to be the child's father under s.5(1)(b) of the Law Reform (Parent and Child) (Scotland) Act 1986.[44] The latter does not apply if the child was born before the Family Law (Scotland) Act 2006 came into force. In these circumstances, the father does not automatically have parental responsibilities and rights. However by virtue of s.4 of the 1995 Act, a mother can give him parental responsibilities and rights by agreeing with him to do so. Otherwise he must apply for them in proceedings under s.11 of the 1995 Act when they will not be granted unless it is in the child's welfare to do so. Similarly, any other person with an interest, for example a step parent or grandparent, must use s.11 in order to obtain parental responsibilities and rights.

---

[43] Children (Scotland) Act 1995, s.3 as amended by the Family Law (Scotland) Act 2006, s.23.

[44] Discussed above, para.12–23.

If, as is usual, two or more persons have parental responsibilities and rights, each can exercise a right without the consent of the other: but a child cannot be removed from the UK without the agreement of each person who has a right to the child's residence or contact with the child.[45] A dispute about parental responsibilities and rights will be heard in s.11 proceedings and will be determined on the basis that the welfare of the child is the paramount consideration and that an order should not be made unless it is better for the child to do so. In reaching this decision, the court is under a duty to consult the child.[46] In this way, the court will try to resolve such issues as where a child should reside and with whom, contact with the child and specific issues such as the child's education or religious upbringing.

Physical injury and Death

12–26   A child is a relative for the purposes of s.8 and 9 of the Administration of Justice Act 1982. She is also a member of the deceased's immediate family for the purpose of the Damages (Scotland) Act 1976. This means that he has title to sue when his parent dies as a consequence of personal injuries caused by the fault of the defender. Conversely a parent is a member of the deceased's immediate family so that a parent has title to sue under the 1976 Act on the death of a child.

A child's right to legitim and her rights as an heir on intestacy were discussed at length in the previous chapter.

Active and Passive Legal Capacity

12–27   When a child is born alive, the child enjoys the full panoply of private law rights. The child has full passive capacity, i.e. his rights will form part of his own private patrimony. In particular a child can be the owner of moveable and heritable property. A child is also entitled to reparation for any wrongs that he has sustained. These include injuries suffered when she was *in utero*. Such injuries become actionable wrongs if the child is born alive when he is deemed to have sustained the physical harm which is a constituent part of liability for fault or *culpa*.

Although a child has full passive capacity at birth, he lacks the mental capacity to pursue his legal rights. Put another way, a child does not have active legal capacity. That is why a child's parent has the parental responsibility and right to act as the child's legal representative. When a child has active legal capacity to enter a particular transaction, a parent ceases to have a right to act as his

---

[45] Children (Scotland) Act 1995, s.2(2), (3) and (6).
[46] *ibid.*, s.11(7).

legal representative in relation to such a transaction.[47] A parent, acting as a child's representative, administers the child's property and must act as a reasonable and prudent person would act on her own behalf. The parent is liable to account to the child for her intromissions with the child's property when the child reaches the age of 16.[48] To that extent, a parent's obligations as the child's legal representative resemble that of a trustee. As well as administering the child's property, a parent as the child's legal representative can enter into a wide range of transactions on behalf of a child below the age of 16: these would include, for example, selling the child's property or making investments on behalf of the child. If the transaction is prejudicial to the interests of the child, it cannot be set aside but the parent will later have to account to the child. As legal representative, a parent can give consent on behalf of a child: this includes consent to medical treatment.

When will a child obtain active legal capacity? This is governed by the Age of Legal Capacity (Scotland) Act 1991. As a general principle, a child and young person has no active legal capacity until the age of 16.[49] If a child under that age purports to engage in a juristic act, for example make a contract, the transaction is null. The child's parent, as her legal representative, must enter into legal transactions on her behalf. But there are important exceptions to the general rule. A child under the age of 16 has legal capacity to enter into a transaction of a kind commonly entered into by persons of the child's age and circumstances provided the terms of the transaction are not unreasonable. So for example, a child of 8 has the capacity to purchase a bus ticket to take her to school but not a first class air ticket to Sydney. A child has legal capacity to make a will on reaching the age of 12.[50]

A child under the age of 16 can have capacity to consent to **12–28** medical treatment if, in the opinion of the doctor or dentist attending the child, the child understands the nature and possible consequences of the procedure or treatment.[51] It should be noticed that the question whether the child has active *legal* capacity is determined by a *medical* practitioner. If the child is considered to have capacity to consent, the child's parent ceases to be the child's legal representative in respect of consent to the medical procedure or treatment in issue. Thus for example, in Scots law there should not be a conflict between a parent and child over whether the child should or should not have her pregnancy terminated: either the

---

[47] *ibid.*, 1995 Act, s.15(5).
[48] *ibid.*, 1995 Act, s.10.
[49] Age of Legal Capacity (Scotland) Act 1991, s.1.
[50] At 12 a child's consent is required before she can be adopted: therefore she must have capacity to consent at that age.
[51] Age of Legal Capacity (Scotland) Act 1991, s.2(4).

child does not have capacity to consent when the issue is one for the parents or the child does have capacity to consent when the issue is one for the child. If a girl under the age of 16 has a baby she is deemed to have legal capacity to exercise her parental responsibilities and rights.[52]

A child under 16 has legal capacity to instruct a solicitor in connection with any civil, i.e. private law, matter provided the child has a general understanding of what it means to do so.[53] A child aged 12 or more is presumed to be of sufficient age and understanding but a child below 12 will have such capacity if in fact she has.

While a young person has active legal capacity on reaching the age of 16, any transactions made by him between the ages of 16 and 18 can be set aside by a court as a prejudicial transaction.[54] The court has power to do so until the young person reaches the age of 21. Certain transactions cannot be set aside however prejudicial to the young persons. Significantly, these include transactions which the young person has made in the course of her trade, business or profession.[55] Because of the possibility that a transaction can be set aside, s.4 of the 1991 Act provides that all the parties to a proposed transaction can apply to the court to have the transaction ratified: if a transaction is ratified, it can no longer be set aside as a prejudicial transaction. The court will ratify a transaction unless it is satisfied that an adult exercising reasonable prudence would not have entered into the proposed transaction. Thus for example, a person who intends to purchase heritable property from a young person aged 17, should have the transaction ratified before buying the property: otherwise the sale and the subsequent conveyance remain liable to be reduced as prejudicial transactions until the young person reaches the age of 21.

Little, if any, use appears to have been made of these complex provisions designed to protect young persons between 16 and 18. There is much to be said for a simple rule that—apart from those situations where it is obtained earlier—the age of active legal capacity is 16. Then the young person would have legal capacity to enter into the juristic acts which give rise to the rights and obligations which we have discussed in earlier chapters.

---

[52] *ibid.*, s.1(3)(g).

[53] *ibid.*, s.2(4A).

[54] *ibid.*, s.3(1). A prejudicial transaction is a transaction which an adult, exercising reasonable prudence, would not have entered into in the circumstances of the young person at the time of entering into the transaction and has caused or is likely to cause substantial prejudice to the child: *ibid.*, 1991 Act, s.3(2).

[55] Age of Legal Capacity (Scotland) Act 1991, s.3(3). Other transactions which cannot be set aside are consent to adoption orders, consent to medical treatment or procedures, transactions induced by the fraudulent misrepresentation of the young person as to her age and transactions ratified by the young person after the age of 18 which he knew could be set aside.

Further reading

Clive, *Husband and Wife* (4th ed., 1997)
Inness, Gavin and Malcolm, *Cohabitation* (2005)
Norrie, *Children (Scotland) Act 1995* (2nd ed., 2004)
Norrie, *Parent and Child* (2nd ed., 1999)
Sutherland, *Child and Family Law* (2nd ed., 2006)
Thomson, *Family Law Reform* (2006)
Thomson, *Family Law in Scotland* (5th ed., 2006)

INDEX